DISPATCHES FROM FARM COUNTRY

A journalist's decadeslong search for the soul of rural America in a changing world

Print ISBN: 979-8-35097-161-3
eBook ISBN: 979-8-35097-162-0

Printed in the United States of America

To Gretchen: I love coming home to you.

To Ryan and Kathleen: This is what I was doing while you were growing up.

TABLE CONTENTS

INTRODUCTION

I grew up in the suburbs of St. Louis. Although I had country cousins, gravel roads ran through territory foreign to me, and those who lived in small towns or in farmhouses were aliens whose lives and culture were of only minor interest. My knowledge of rural life was limited to novels, movies and TV shows. For all I knew, "Green Acres" and "The Beverly Hillbillies" were documentaries.

I never intended to focus my journalism career on farm country, but a series of fortunate accidents guided me in that direction. The subject matter was so fascinating, I transplanted my family from Philadelphia to a farm town in northwest Missouri where I became imbedded in rural culture. I traded my city clothes and an Oldsmobile Cutlass for blue jeans and a Ford F150.

From a journalist's perspective, my timing was impeccable. Farming and the culture around it were about to undergo the most sweeping period of change since humans first learned to plant seeds into the ground. I experienced up close the 1980s farm depression, which decimated thousands of family farms. I saw the rise of megafarms and watched livestock farms morph from farmyard ventures to meat factories. I witnessed a technological revolution that enhanced farming productivity while at the same time accelerating the decline of farm towns.

My life became richer as I explored two-lanes and county roads. In the last four decades, I've ridden horseback in cattle drives, piloted ATVs through forests and used my 4-wheel-drive truck to plow through muddy pastures. More importantly, I have gotten to know farmers, ranchers, equipment manufacturers, agricultural economists, soil scientists, large animal veterinarians, Extension personnel and all manner of rural folk. My overseas assignments taught me that farmers and villagers in Central America and New Zealand have much in common with farmers and villagers in Kentucky and New Jersey. I flatter myself to think I've learned what it means to farm and what it means to live beyond the glow of city lights. I've learned to love much of rural life.

It's been a glorious ride filled with discovery and surprises. But it also came with a few, "Oh, wells."

For instance, I've learned that--having been born and raised "in the city"--I will always be an outsider in rural America. That fact was made clear to me after I'd lived for more than a decade in a wonderful old house in rural Plattsburg, Missouri. Toward the end of my time there, a native Plattsburger, who I'd never met, asked me where I lived. When I described the house, the native said, "Oh, you mean the Halferty house?" The Halferty family had not lived in that house for two generations. But in Plattsburg's collective mind, it would always be the Halferty house. Things never change in rural communities, which is why after all these years of exploring and living in rural America, I'm still an outsider.

Even as an outsider, I've learned to respect rural America's timeless nature and its sometimes brutal realities. I've come to know that rural culture can be insular, suspicious and paranoid. It can be dark and violent. Its self-image of nostalgic innocence is stained by oppressive poverty, drug use and bigotry. It is a culture whose complexities rival those found in cities.

I've come to understand that Red America and Blue America have much in common but little understanding of one another. The two

Americas speak different languages and have wildly divergent visions of the country's past, present and future.

With feet in both worlds, I wrote this book of stories for an urban audience. It is aimed at people who want to bridge the gap between the two Americas and a learn little about rural lives.

Someone else will have to try to explain urban dwellers to rural folks.

"Dispatches From Farm Country" is my attempt to explain an altered farming landscape to folks who see it only from the windows of airliners. –July 2024, Plattsburg, Missouri

CHAPTER 1

ROOTS

My grandfather Luigi Patrico was a farmer of sorts. He emigrated from Sicily to St. Louis, Missouri, in 1901. According to family lore, in Sicily he was either a cavalryman or a jeweler. Maybe both. Depends on which of my relatives is telling the story. In any case, we agree that he eventually became a truck farmer on the outskirts of St. Louis. That made sense for an Italian immigrant. Many newly minted Americans from Italy settled in cities but were in the fruit and vegetable business across the country. It was a niche to which they gravitated in the same way many Irish immigrants became cops: They had family ties to the business.

I don't know how long Luigi farmed or what he did after that. I only remember him as a feeble old man sitting in a wheelchair in my Aunt Mary's tiny brick house in north St. Louis. In my memory, he has wispy white hair and a drooping white mustache. He smells of old cigar smoke and beckons me with his cupped hand. I sit on his lap, and his hoarse voice utters Italian words I never understood.

Now I like to imagine him as a young farmer and see him bent over a row of cabbages somewhere outside the city. It's a flat field with rich black dirt, and the sky above is a blue sea with floating white clouds. At the end of the row is a "stake truck," an ancestor of the pickup with an open flatbed and removable wooden slats that hold cargo in place. My grandfather loads a wooden wheelbarrow with crates of cabbages and pushes them slowly toward the truck. Where he goes after that I only imagine. Maybe he heads to Soulard Market, a bustling, chaotic mass of people and produce stands near downtown.

In Luigi's day, Soulard was essential to its times. Luigi and his comrades unloaded their stake trucks into dew-damp stalls every morning (except Sunday) before the sun rose over the nearby Mississippi River. Wholesalers and retailers were waiting to buy produce in bulk to take to grocery stores. Housewives arrived soon after and squeezed tomatoes and haggled with individual vendors over prices. Space in the icebox at home was limited, so it was important for the women to choose wisely. By early afternoon, piles of fruits and vegetables had dwindled to scraps and picked-overs.

Today Soulard has a forgotten-world feel. It's still there on the edge of downtown. But its nature has subtly changed. It still serves as a place for wholesalers to meet retailers. But it's not a neighborhood place anymore. It has a touristy feel and thrives mainly on Saturdays. Young locals come to soak up atmosphere they can't find in a supermarket and to select—perhaps without the expertise of their great-grandmothers—fruits and vegetables that come in crates from both far-flung fields. It's a hip place where young adults push fancy strollers and sip lattes from recyclable paper cups while chatting with other couples out for a lark. To me, Soulard still has a lingering scent of history. When I visit, I think of Luigi.

My other grandfather, Joseph Malcolm Navin, was German/Irish and grew up in the wooded hills and rolling fields of Marion County, Missouri, 100 miles up the Mississippi River from St. Louis. Grampa's hometown of New London is just south of Mark Twain's Hannibal, and whenever we Patricos visited during family reunions, I thought of Tom Sawyer and Huck Finn. I could almost see them darting through the rough countryside on some boyhood adventure.

Our cousins who lived in that neighborhood were country folk and farmers. They dressed differently and lived differently than we urbanites/ suburbanites. I remember one of our older female cousins lived in a house that still had a hand pump in the kitchen sink and an outhouse out back. The yard consisted of mostly packed dirt with chicken feathers drifting lazily in the dust and multiple dogs moseying around looking for a shady spot in which to nap. A dilapidated henhouse sat in front of a line of trees and emitted a dried manure odor. In the distance were tall cornfields and the gravel drive that had funneled us to the house.

I don't know for a fact that Grampa ever farmed. Our family lore isn't clear on that point. I only assume he did because his relatives did, and he wore bib overalls around the house. I do know for certain that he was a doughboy in World War I. He drove a locomotive for the Army and helped the Navy scuttle a ship from which he liberated a brass ship's clock that now sits on my shelf. More importantly, he brought home a French bride, my Gramma, Marianne Nerrienet.

Gramma told me many years later that her German mother-in-law in Marion County was unkind to her and mocked her lack of English and her foreign way of dress. Not surprisingly, Gramma didn't develop a love for many of her country in-laws, especially the German ones. With her French heritage, she still bore a grudge against "Les Boches" for the War to End All Wars. Soon after she arrived in Missouri, she and Grampa moved to St. Louis, where he began work as a teamster and later as a construction laborer.

Many new government buildings were going up in the 1930s because of federal spending designed to defeat the Great Depression. If you look at downtown St. Louis today, you see numerous white stone courthouses, government buildings and banks built during the period. Grampa told us once that a stone fell from one of the buildings where he was working, and it hit him in the noggin. "Good thing I had a hard head," he joked.

I didn't arrive until after he retired, and he and Gramma had moved from north St. Louis to a house in Black Jack, Missouri, a village northwest of downtown. Black Jack was only an intersection of three roads in those days and contained a saloon, a grocery store and a hardware store. It was as country as country could be only 20 miles from a major city. The Navins had an acre and a third of land in Black Jack, and I thought they were farmers.

Gramma, a tiny woman who wore print dresses and possessed an indomitable spirit, had a lush flower garden behind the brown brick, two-bedroom house. She tended it diligently despite a pronounced limp, which she acquired when a surgeon years previously fused the bones in her left knee—maybe by accident, maybe because that's the way they treated knee problems back then. That impediment left her more dependent on Grampa than she'd like to be. Out in her garden, she would call him from whatever chore he was doing to pull water from the well house, which he did using a metal bucket and a chain on a wheel. He'd pour the cold water into a metal watering can for her, and she'd judiciously sprinkle it around the base of her roses and peonies.

Flowers were her joy. But they were a minor part of Gramma's "farm" work. To the east of the house was a half-acre vegetable garden. Potatoes. Tomatoes. String beans. Cucumbers. Peppers. A small patch of asparagus grew at the edge in soil mounded with chicken manure for fertilizer. Out of this garden came mountains of food. Grampa oversaw the planting and the harvesting. But it was Gramma's duty to make sure we could eat it at harvest time and all through the winter ahead. Canned tomato juice and string beans were her specialties, and she made ketchup, which she kept in old 7UP bottles. Gramma also put up dozens of jars of pickles from home-grown cucumbers: dill, sweet and bread-and-butter.

As harvest began on hot summer days, she and Mom would set up a canning assembly line in the brick house's spacious kitchen. They washed tomatoes in the big porcelain sink, then parboiled them in a large pot on the gas stove. When the red-yellow skins began to crack, out the toma-toes would come to be plunged into a cold water bath. The two women in their stained aprons would then peel the skins and squeeze the juice out of the meaty tomatoes using a conical sieve and a wooden pestle. The sieve would strain the seeds and any remaining skin as Gramma and Mom mashed and twisted that wooden pin against the softened tomatoes. The juice would flow into a bowl, which they emptied through a metal funnel into mason jars.

When they had enough jars to make a batch, the women aligned them on a rack in an enormous steel pressure cooker and turned the T-clamps to seal the lid tight. They put the pressure cooker on the stove and turned on the gas burner. We kids would watch the gauge on the top of the cooker as its finger climbed the dial. "Tell us when it gets to the green zone," Gramma instructed us. "We don't want it to get into the red."

"Why? What happens if it gets into the red?"

"The whole thing could explode," she said.

That got our attention. We watched the gauge intently as tiny spirits of steam leaked from a pressure valve. Please don't explode!

String beans came on at about the same time as tomatoes, and the kitchen hummed with activity again as Grampa dumped onto the kitchen table a bushel basket of beans we had helped picked earlier. He headed to his basement kingdom for a beer break while the rest of us sat around the round oak table and began snapping beans. It was fun at first. But we were kids and easily bored. Soon the grab-snap-grab routine got old. To keep our attention, Gramma and Mom would talk to us and to each other about anything that came to mind. Gramma was skilled at asking about what we had learned in school that year and what library books we were reading now. She'd also tell stories about Grampa and the trouble he'd gotten into before she tamed him.

Before we knew it, the mountain of beans had been snapped, cut into 2-inch-long segments and scraped into a large bowl for washing. About then, Gramma would walk to the head of the basement steps and yell: "Joe, we need another bushel." Sometimes Grampa responded, and sometimes he didn't.

"Oh, that man. He's pretending he can't hear me. Jim, go down there and tell him we need more beans."

I descended the stairs into Grampa's kingdom and saw him standing at his bar looking peacefully out the window, a bottle of Falstaff to his lips.

"Grampa, we need more beans."

He had a twinkle in his eye when he said, "No, really? I didn't hear."

The beans went through a similar process as the tomatoes. Wash. Pour into mason jars. Add water and spices. Put in the pressure cooker.

When there was a pause in the action, Gramma would pour big glasses of iced tea served with graham crackers and butter. It was probably the best snack the world has ever seen. We sat at the kitchen table, enjoyed the treat and soaked in the bittersweet canning smells still hanging in the air.

Tomato and string bean canning happened in waves as the summer progressed and the garden kept pumping out food. As more raw material came in, the kitchen factory worked apace. Soon, full mason jars lined windowsills and sat on temporary wooden tables in the basement that Grampa had made from sawhorses and rough-hewn planks. When the jars were cool, we would help transfer them to the fruit cellar, which we accessed through a creaky wooden door at the far end of the basement near the coal bin.

I didn't like the fruit cellar. It was damp and dark, and lit with a weak, bare lightbulb that hung from the ceiling and was turned on with a pull chain. Spiderwebs and cobwebs also hung from the ceiling and were sticky on my face and my eyes. I hated going into that small room as we took turns placing jars on crude wooden planks Grampa had fashioned into shelves. I was relieved when the last of the jars were stored away. But I knew that sometime in the autumn or winter, Mom or Gramma would say, "I need a jar of tomato juice, Jim. Go get one from the fruit cellar."

Just beyond the flower garden on the north, Grampa had planted a half-dozen fruit trees—apples, cherries and peaches. Gramma and Mom made the world's best pies from those trees' fruit. My favorites were the cherry pies. They had a tartness that makes sweet cherry pie filling from cans seem like the work of amateurs. The green apples also were tart, and we grandkids were warned that eating too many of them would give us a stomachache. I don't know whether that warning was given as health advice or as a strategy to keep us from eating all the harvest. Whichever, I do not remember ever getting sick on green apples. But I do remember the guilty pleasure of pulling a green one from a tree, taking one bite and flinging it as far as I could over the fence. Then I picked another, probably in the childish hope that the second wouldn't be as tart as the first.

Grampa never had much luck with the peaches, which are tricky to grow that far north. One late frost, and blossoms don't develop into peaches. None of us dared steal one of the survivors; they were too rare.

Grampa was a tough, gruff son of a bitch whose favorite adjective was "goddamned," as in, "That goddammed dog couldn't strike a goddammed rabbit if his goddammed life depended on it." But we loved him. His hugs were sometimes so tight they were a test of endurance, and he laughed devilishly as he bestowed them. His kisses came with chewing tobacco saliva that made us squirm, much to his delight.

One winter morning after I had spent the night in Black Jack, I followed Grampa as he did his chores, which amounted to gathering eggs from the henhouse and feeding the hunting dogs in their pens at the back of the property. He was dressed in a checked overcoat and a hat with earflaps. From behind, I probably looked like his miniature self at about 5 or 6 years old. It had snowed a bit overnight, just enough to cover most of the grass so that only the brown tips showed, and we wore rubber boots—his pullons, mine held tight with metal buckles that were almost impossible for me to snap on my own.

"We'll feed the dogs first," Grampa said, "and gather the eggs on the way back to the house."

He always kept three or four beagle bitches, invariably named Queeny, Lady, Bell or Duchess. When one ran away or got hung up in a barbed wire fence and died while hunting rabbits, he'd replace it with a pup he'd name Queeny, Lady, Bell or Duchess. He also had an old black-and-tan hound named Parker that wasn't expected to earn his keep as a hunter anymore. Parker was a retired friend that happened to live with the beagles but spent much of his time out of the pen and roaming the yard at his leisure. He was the closest thing to an actual pet that Grampa had, and the old man loved the old dog.

This morning, the beagles were eager for their food and howled that beagle howl that marks them as hunting dogs. "I've spotted a rabbit over here!" it says when in the field. "I'm hungry! Let's eat!" it says when you approach with food. Grampa bought dry food by the barrelful, which he kept in a shed outside the pens and scooped into large stainless steel bowls to carry to the dogs. He had me hold one of the bowls while he unlocked the gate to the 6-foot-tall hog wire pens. The pens were that tall because some of the beagles could climb. I think it was one of the Bells who got so proficient at climbing that Grampa had to attach a separate strip of wire netting horizontally at the inside top so Bell couldn't climb out.

I tried to pet the dogs as we entered the pens, but they were interested only in the food and ignored me, heads in the bowls and white-tipped tails tagging like crazy.

"Where's Parker?" I asked.

"It's not like him to not come and eat," Grampa said. "Let's go find him."

Parker and the beagles slept under a tar paper shed inside the pen, which was raised a foot or two off the ground, and served as a refuge from the cold winds in the winter and as a shady cool spot in the summer. Grampa got down slowly on his hands and knees to look under the shed, and as he went down, I could tell he was anxious about what he might find. The top half of him disappeared under the shed, and I heard him groan once, then go silent. Finally, he began edging his way out. I saw with a shock that he was dragging Parker along the ground. The poor dog was dead and stiff, and it was all Grampa could do to get the big body from under the shed. When he finally had Parker out, Grampa lay the dog's head on his knees and gave the gray muzzle a gentle stroke. Then he looked at me and said, "Jim, he's gone." Grampa looked as close to crying as I had ever seen. "One day you'll find me just like this, dead and cold," he whispered.

I started crying and ran to the house at full speed while Grampa found a burlap sack in which to bury Parker.

Grampa spent most of the warm months in his vegetable garden, which was to my eyes enormous. Every spring, he would get out the walk-behind tractor (which he called an iron horse) and deep-till the soil. The black dirt smelled sweet and sour simultaneously as it came out from under its winter blanket of dead stalks and grass. I remember Grampa fighting that tractor, gripping its handles and using his strong shoulders and widespread legs to guide it as straight as possible, which was a struggle because the polished steel plow blade had to penetrate 6 inches of thick soil. The tractor's engine popped and blew smoke as the plow created a 90-degree black ribbon of dirt, which lay open to the air and shiny from rubbing against the plow. I'd follow behind and grab a handful of the soil. It was damp and clumpy and full of life. It meant spring, and I loved it.

Around St. Patrick's Day, Grampa would plant potatoes. He was part Irish, after all, and believed that it was good luck to put potatoes in the ground under the patron saint's gaze. We grandkids got to help. That meant reaching into an old burlap bag and pulling out seed potatoes, which were last year's potatoes that had been stored in a cool, dark place and then sliced into quarters to expose the inner flesh. Every 6 inches or so, we'd press that flesh into the side of the furrow with the potato's eyes showing. When we'd worked our way to the end of the row, Grampa would turn that stubborn tractor around to plow the seed potatoes under the soil where they would sprout and reproduce. I can still see Grampa cursing and sweating, even in the early-spring cool.

There were lots of grandkids to help in the garden. I had four siblings. In order of birth, we were: Pat, me, Jeanne, Sue and Joe. We had cousins from the Navin side: Mike and Joan from my Uncle Joe and Aunt Marie Navin, and Jackie, Tommy and Patty from Uncle Jack and Aunt Ruth Navin. We Patricos were more often at the house in Black Jack because our Mom (Jeannette) loved to spend time with her mother. Daughters-in-law Marie and Ruth had less attachment for the place and their in-laws. Hence, our cousins tended to be infrequent weekend visitors to Black Jack, while we Patricos were there whenever Mom wanted to visit her parents. She would also drop us off at Grampa and Gramma's after school or in the summer if she wanted us out from underfoot for a few hours. On rare occasions, we kids spent the night so Mom and Dad could have a date night.

Our family lived in suburban Florissant, Missouri, only four miles from Black Jack and a short drive from St. Louis. Our patient, loving Dad (Joe) worked as an electrician at the Naval Air Station base at nearby Lambert Airport. In summer, he would come rushing home from school, bolt down dinner and drive Pat or me to baseball practice. This was four or five days a week, because Pat and I, of course, played on separate teams, which meant our practice and game schedules consumed most evenings. Dad would alternate years. One year he would be manager for Pat's team and assistant coach for mine. The next year he would be assistant coach for Pat and manager for me. I don't know where he got the energy.

Somehow, he found the time over 20 years to convert our tiny tract home from a two-bedroom to a four-bedroom. To keep up with our family's growth, he first added a bedroom in place of the porch off the back of the house. At the time, four of us—two brothers and two sisters—were living in a bedroom so small, Pat and I had to walk across Jeanne and Sue's fold-out bed just to get out of the room. By the time baby brother, Joe, came along, Dad had finished the basement, converting it into a fourth bedroom, family room and second bathroom.

While Dad was gone to work and school was out, we kids spent long summer days in the "country." As we got older, Mom would allow us to go on an adventure and walk unescorted those four miles through subdivision streets and country lanes until we got to Grampa and Gramma's. Mom would pick us up later in the car because, honestly, four miles is enough for kids to walk in one day.

But the trip was worth it to be able to play at the Black Jack house. Tree climbing. "House ball" (throwing a rubber ball off the steps and wall of the house). Wagon races on the sidewalk. Grampa let us play until the summer crops matured. Then he'd put us to work. Picking string beans is only fun for a while. It doesn't take long before stooping over bushy plants in the hot summer sun becomes drudgery. But Grampa was a taskmaster and was not shy about using the word "lazy" while he let loose a spit of chewing tobacco.

Once when I was helping him fix a fence in the dog pens, Cousin Mike arrived for a visit. Soon, he and I drifted off and played at some game or other. When Mike departed an hour later, I went back to help Grampa. "You know," he said to me, his hands busy with pliers and baling wire, "you're a pretty good little worker when you're here by yourself. But when Mike comes over, you ain't worth a shit." And he spat some tobacco.

I was stung, but I kept working. If I'd stopped, I'd not only have been lazy, I'd have been a crybaby.

If verbal scorn was his punishment stick, Grampa also offered lots of carrots as incentives to reward our work. The refrigerator in his basement was always nearly full of beer (he bought two cases a week from the Rexall Drug store in Florissant), but there always was room for a few cold sodas. And his shaded backyard offered refuge from both summer heat and labor. We drank cold water from the well house in a metal cup and swung slowly in a homemade and patched canvas hammock strung between two sycamores. We found plenty of time to play catch and create make-believe baseball games. Summer nights we sat in the backyard listening to Harry Caray and Jack Buck broadcast St. Louis Cardinal baseball games on KMOX through an ancient radio. The mating calls of cicadas still buzz in my memory as I think about those days and the magic of baseball and Grampa's backyard in the country.

Looking back, I understand that the place in Black Jack was a far cry from a farm, especially the real working farms I later visited in my career. But for a kid who grew up in the suburbs, it sure seemed country.

Years later, when I'd introduce myself to farmers and ranchers, they'd invariably ask: "Did you grow up on a farm?" That was a test of sorts. Was I able to relate to their lives as farmers?

I'd lend myself credibility by saying "No, I grew up in town. But both of my grandfathers farmed at one time or another, and I spent most summers helping out on the farm."

It wasn't so much a fib as a fantasy that I was somehow a farm boy.

CHAPTER 2

THE GREAT SOYBEAN RAID

I was new to the world of ag journalism when the farm crisis of the 1980s began wrecking rural America. I was naive to the factors that affect the farm economy. I had no idea that a Soviet invasion of Afghanistan could lead to a wheat embargo by the United States, which in turn could lead to the collapse of commodity prices across America. I did not know that a change in federal bank lending policies (at a time when interest rates skyrocketed to 20% and beyond) could push families off land they had owned for generations and lead to bank foreclosures on American farms at a pace not seen since the Great Depression. When Ronald Reagan's ag secretary told farmers to "Get big or get out," he was unwittingly uttering a prophecy that was about to be fulfilled.

The '80s were a disastrous decade for farmers. They killed the farming dreams of a new generation and caused such despair that farmer suicides became routine items in rural newspapers.

The '80s farm crisis taught me a lot about the farm economy. More, it taught me about the nature of rural America. I learned it is fragile while at the same time being resilient. I learned that it can be angry, violent and ugly. It can also be unperturbed, peaceful and beautiful. The farm crisis was a crucible that mixed and melted social hot metals of the time and poured out a changed rural America.

Every crisis creates a hero, and for this one, Wayne Cryts—a grain farmer from Puxico, Missouri, in the state's Bootheel region—fit the hero role as well as anyone. He was the prototypical "everyman" who heroically fought the system and somehow won. His singular and very public acts of defiance resonated with farmers and the public at large, and cast a spotlight on agriculture's plight. His defiance had the practical effect of changing bankruptcy laws in a way more favorable to farmers. And it gave Cryts legend status overnight.

This momentary hero earned his fame and his infamy by audaciously stealing more than 32,000 bushels of soybeans from a bankrupt grain elevator near the unincorporated village of Ristine, Missouri. He claimed that those beans were rightfully his and that a bankruptcy court that counted them as part of the elevator's assets had overstepped its authority. In those days, farmers were the last creditors to be paid when a grain elevator declared bankruptcy. And if they got paid at all, it was pennies on the dollar.

Citing righteousness over legality, Cryts took back his beans, and he did it in broad daylight in front of federal marshals, sheriff's deputies and highway patrolmen.

Watching him was a tense crowd of supporters, some of whom had traveled hundreds of miles to see the theft. Cryts' brazen crime was a statement that thousands of farmers were right: the economy, the government and the courts were against them. Cryts gave voice to their anger and fear.

The farming community lionized him as a kind of modern-day Robin Hood. The national press wrote adoringly about him. Governors, congressmen and senators elbowed their way into his spotlight to get attention. Songs and books were written about him; a movie was rumored in the works.

Like all heroes, of course, Cryts had his detractors. They called him a common criminal, a selfish poseur. He was more like Jesse James than Robin Hood, they said.

The first time I saw Wayne Cryts was the day of the Great Soybean Raid, February 16, 1981. He was standing on a grain truck in the middle of the muddy yard of the bankrupt Ristine Grain Elevator. It was lightly raining, and he was giving a speech to more than 1,000 farmers and farm activists about law, justice and the sometimes-critical difference between them. The 35-year-old wore a new denim jacket, open to a plaid shirt even in the chilly air. Threaded through his new-looking jeans was a beaded leather belt. Other than scuffed farmer boots, he seemed to have dressed carefully for his audience, not the weather.

Cryts had thick black eyebrows and dark hair that spilled from under his American Agriculture Movement cap. He was not a natural public speaker, but he was earnest, and the crowd was with him.

He told them he had come to liberate soybeans valued at about $210,000. He claimed the beans belonged to him and were merely stored at the elevator. He made the case that if bankruptcy courts could take his beans, they could take anybody's beans, including those belonging to every farmer in the crowd.

Law enforcement officers interspersed in the gathering were not so sure about the ownership issue. Some may have sympathized with Cryts. But their superiors had told them that Cryts' beans, along with mountains of other beans stored at the Ristine elevator, were under the jurisdiction of a bankruptcy court. If Cryts took the beans, it would be theft, plain and simple.

The crowd milled around nervously as Cryts finished talking. Foreboding filled the amphitheater created by the grain bins. Finally, I saw three men with crowbars and a power saw step forward and begin to peel back the corrugated metal sides of one of the bins. Beans spilled out. Someone inserted a large vacuum hose and began to suck beans into Cryts' grain truck. The crowd watched, unsure at first whether to cheer or to step away from the crime scene. For a moment, the only sounds were the put-put-put of the vacuum's gas engine and the rattle of beans flowing through the plastic hose. Gradually, a human noise built; it morphed from individual yells to a rolling roar of approval. This wasn't a riot so much as a planned action, yet it was fueled by a wave of emotion.

I looked at the lawmen. They, too, had come the Ristine with a plan. Wordlessly they stepped aside and let Wayne Cryts steal his beans.

Federal marshal Howard Safir later said, "We didn't want to see innocent people get hurt."

Across the Midwest, the farm crisis had roiled farming communities. Panic and anger rose like floodwaters for farm families and leaked onto Main Streets as broke businesses boarded up their windows and doors. Public protests became everyday headlines and sound bites on news rural media. Even city folks took notice of the turmoil they saw on the nightly news. Amidst the flashy tractorcades and organized rallies that rolled into Washington D.C. and state capitals, Cryts' soybean raid was somehow different. Although it was well-planned, it seemed spontaneous and real. The movement needed a hero, and Cryts had volunteered his services.

A day earlier my boss, Larry Harper, editor of Missouri Ruralist magazine, had gotten word that Cryts and some of his friends with the activist group American Agriculture Movement (AAM) were planning a public political statement about the bankruptcy of the James Brothers Farm Centers Inc., which owned grain-storage facilities in Arkansas and Missouri, including the Ristine elevator.

Larry typically didn't get excited about much. He'd been around Missouri agriculture a long time and had seen its storylines rapidly change. But this one seemed to have his full attention. "Jim," he said over the phone that night, "how'd you like to go the Bootheel for me first thing tomorrow morning?" He gave me the outline of the story and told me he had arranged for a plane to fly me to Sikeston, Missouri.

A chartered flight? Must be important.

While I was flying early the next morning, Cryts was meeting with farmers and AAM members at a motel in Sikeston. They had arranged a convoy of grain trucks to the Ristine elevator near New Madrid to publicize the injustice of Missouri's bankruptcy laws. Key to the plan was Cryts, who already had a personal stake in the issue. He'd missed loan payments the previous fall because he could not sell the beans he had harvested in 1979 and had stored in the Ristine elevator. Worse, his 1980 bean crop had burned up in a drought. With two consecutive crops gone, Cryts and his family were desperate. Any bankruptcy settlement was likely to take two years at least. In the meantime, his lender had called his loan and Cryts was broke. As he told me later, "I had nothing to lose."

Cryts offered himself to AAM as a figurehead for its demonstration.

As they gather at the motel, Cryts and his co-conspirators waited anxiously—half hoping a call would come from the governor or one of his deputies with a last-minute settlement offer, half hoping they could go through with their plan to publicize their cause. The call never came, and the convoy left the Sikeston motel at about 10 a.m.

Later, Cryts told me, he had waivered that morning at the motel. He had never been in trouble with the law, and this seemed like an irreversible and dangerous step. Was it worth it? How would it affect his wife, Sandy, and his teenaged kids, Paula and Terry? He hadn't slept in two days and was exhausted with worry. He almost backed out. But by then, pressure from AAM was building, and TV crews were hanging out in the parking lot. It was too late to do anything but drive to the Ristine elevator.

Rain was falling when the grain trucks and hundreds of supporters got to the private road leading to the elevator. Supporters had to park their pickups on the shoulder of the nearby state highway in a line of vehicles that stretched a half-mile north and a half-mile south of the elevator. When I got there in a rented car, I saw that one pickup had pulled too far off the road and had slid sideways on the slick grass into a ditch. The driver scrambled up the embankment and joined a parade of farmers who walked the last few hundred yards to the elevator. He figured he'd get help later with his truck. He didn't want to miss this show.

I walked with the others up the gravel and through the mud. All around were farmers in muck boots and canvas jackets, hooded sweatshirts and rain gear. Some carried grain shovels to help with the crime. Others carried signs: "These beans are Wayne's beans." A large, wet American flag hung from a pole hoisted onto a farmer's shoulder. A light breezed caused it to wave weakly.

The cause was different, and the clothes were different, but the scene reminded me of the antiwar events I'd attended a few years earlier. It had that same thrilling sense of group action and uncertainty. The crowd felt energized for and united in a symbolic purpose. But would some idiot in the crowd do something violent? What would the cops do? Would there be arrests?

A hint of danger floated in the air.

From a professional perspective, I knew this would be a challenge to my ability to do two things simultaneously. The photographer in me saw some memorable images: rough-looking farmers standing side by side leaning on shovels; stone-faced deputies positioned next to animated members of the crowd; two worried women watching from under an umbrella. How to capture those images and still take notes? I'd have to choose between photos and interviews. As always, I couldn't do as much of either as I wanted.

Along with the logistics of words-and-pictures storytelling, there also was the classic conundrum for a journalist: How do you stay neutral when you naturally sympathize with a cause or a character? Here was a lone farmer—part of the culture in which I was immersed—standing up to dozens of lawmen who seemed to be doing the work of evil forces. I knew how I felt but hoped I could see both sides of the issues clearly and later portray both without prejudice. An impossible task?

All of this was on my mind as I moved toward the elevator. I was wet from the rain, soaked in adrenaline and struggling to contain my emotions. It was a great day to be a journalist.

I arrived at the bin site just as Cryts began to give his speech. He told the farmers the fact they were at the elevator was a victory for a cause, his and theirs. He said, "I decided that the court order is without the weight of law, and it doesn't have jurisdiction over me. Before we made this decision, we had to decide if we were willing to lose everything we own and go to jail."

Cryts did go to jail—but it took a while.

SLOW-MOTION JUSTICE

This was one of the slowest thefts ever. It took hours to load all those beans into 77 trucks. In fact, the slow motion raid carried over into the next afternoon. Cryts and his cohorts took the beans to another elevator with the idea that he would sell them to pay off his loans. Of course, it wasn't that easy. Accepting grain of questionable provenance has its own set of problems for buyers or even storage facilities. Out of caution, one after another of the local elevators refused to store the beans.

So some of Cryts' neighbors took beans to their farms, eventually sold them and gave Cryts the proceeds.

In the months that followed, Cryts and law enforcement played a game of legal chicken. A few weeks after the Ristine raid, he was arrested for conspiracy to commit a crime. But a grand jury in St. Louis refused to indict him. That summer he was charged with contempt of court—not for his original raid but for a second trip to the Ristine elevator during which he and others pulled trucks to barricade the entrance and block the court-ordered sale of the remaining beans. Cryts believed money from the sale should go to the farmers who had grown and stored those beans, not to creditors. The contempt charges were quickly dropped.

Finally, on April 28, 1982, more than a year after the original Ristine raid, bankruptcy judge Charles Baker called Cryts into a courtroom in Little Rock, Arkansas, and asked for the names of the men who had helped him move the grain that day. Cryts refused to comply. The judge asked him again, and again, Cryts refused. Judge Baker had him arrested for contempt of court and thrown in jail.

WE MEET AGAIN

The second time I saw Wayne Cryts, it was the spring of 1982 in the Pope County Detention Center in Russellville, Arkansas. He was sitting at a table in a common room outside the cell area while finishing a plate of fried chicken and fixings his mother and father had brought to him. Some friends and relatives were sharing the lunch, as were a couple of uniformed guards.

The scene reminded me of episodes from the quintessential rural comedy "The Andy Griffith Show," in which the town drunk, Otis, had the run of the jail. He only went into his cell when he wanted to take a nap; otherwise, he mingled with his jailers, just one of the guys.

Likewise, Wayne Cryts seemed free to roam. His jailers took phone messages for him and let in visitors—everyone from family members to supporters to former Arkansas Governor Bill Clinton.

As Cryts' celebrity grew, Sen. Charles Grassley of Iowa offered to take his place in jail or to help on the farm. A local high school class came to the jail to get a civics lesson from Cryts. Headline-sucking attorney F. Lee Bailey joined his legal team. Congressmen took to the floor at the U.S. Capitol to praise Cryts. He was even flown from his jail cell in Arkansas to Washington D.C. to testify before a Congressional committee that was discussing a revision in bankruptcy laws. Ron Russell, the mayor of Russellville, stopped by to give Cryts a ceremonial key to the city.

Wayne Cryts was a star.

I had called him a few weeks before my visit to the Russellville jail. It was my first real conversation with him, and I was impressed by his steady voice and thoughtful answers. He opened up more than many interviewees do over the phone.

He painted a picture of himself as an unlikely hero: "I was always backward and shy," he told me. "Sandy and I didn't associate with people that much. I was a workaholic. If I took off a Sunday from the farm, I felt guilty. We just would not do anything because there was always farmwork to do."

If Cryts had any social outlets, they were farming organizations. Years earlier, he went to an AAM meeting—considered radical by many mainstream farm organization—but was unimpressed at first. Then, he attended one of AAM's tractorcades and was hooked. "I could talk for hours about that," he told me. He was drawn by the commitment he saw from "everyday farmers in blue jeans and work shirts." The sight of them driving tractors through town to address the problems caused by the farm crisis touched his soul. While meetings weren't Cryts' thing, demonstrations were.

He also found urgency and truth in the populist AAM message that American farmers were in trouble because of outside forces, not their own shortcomings. Just like Cryts, farmers across America were working their butts off and getting deeper in debt, because the game was rigged against them. Before long, he joined AAM wholeheartedly, and by the time of the Great Soybean Raid, he was president of its Missouri chapter.

When I visited the Pope County Detention Center, the building was only 3 months old, modern and clean in a metal, glass and concrete block sort of way. Cryts had the run of the place. His jailers gave him use

24

of a conference room with a multiline phone. One of the uniformed officers would answer an incoming call and tell the caller to hang on because Wayne was on another line. Cryts would work his way down the flashing lights on the telephone until he had answered each call—then he would start again.

When I walked into the conference room, Cryts greeted me and asked his lunch visitors to excuse him for a few minutes. We went into another room and, as we shook hands, he said with a smile, "If you have to be in jail, this is a good place to do it."

He was wearing a blue prisoner uniform, which was the only hint he wasn't a visitor here. But the longer we talked about his incarceration, the less he seemed comfortable. His fingers twirled knots in his hair. He pulled a cigarette out of a pack but forgot to light it. His voice was that of a man under pressure. Even with the visitor-friendly common room, the unrestricted use of a phone and the fried chicken lunches, Cryts was in jail and did not know when or if he would be released.

All it would take would be a phone call to Judge Baker, a quick apology, a few names, and he would be free. But Cryts was a stubborn and a principled man. He knew the judge already had the names of his accomplices in the soybean raid, because a multitude of lawmen at the elevator had taken photos and made notes. They even had made sure that every man who drove a truck of those beans out of Ristine had given his full name and address.

But Judge Baker had a mission of his own. In his mind, no one should be allowed to openly flout the law as Cryts had done. The judge was determined to make this farmer publicly betray his friends. He would make the soybean raider look less like a hero and more like a common criminal. Except, Cryts refused to cooperate.

Judge Baker acknowledged Cryts' courage. He told a reporter, "I'll say this for Mr. Cryts: He's a stout man."

Cryts got no such compliment from Robert Lindsey, the bankruptcy trustee appointed to handle the James Brothers mess. Lindsey took a lot of flak from farmers and the general public. In the media, he came across as a bully and a villain, and that didn't sit right with him. During a phone interview, he told me, Cryts "was taking grain that belonged to his neighbors." It galled Lindsey that Cryts somehow became the hero in this story. "I can talk until I'm blue in the face giving my side of the story, and nobody listens to me. Wayne Cryts opens his mouth, and people lay down and piss on themselves."

Cryts told me he didn't feel like a hero. The truth is that desperation drove him to do what he had done. "They have hung a title of 'hero' on me, 'one man with courage' and all that. Well, that's not true. I had my farming operation on the line … At Ristine, I was as scared as I have ever been in my life. I am not a hero. I am just somebody who took something back that was mine in the first place."

If there were heroes, Cryts said, it was the men and women who came to the elevator that day to help him get his grain back and make a point. They had everything to lose and nothing to gain if they got arrested. He was not going to betray them.

That's why Cryts wouldn't answer the judge's questions.

When our interview ended, and it came time to take photos, I asked Cryts if we could leave the featureless conference room and go to the cell-block. He led me down a hallway, made a turn, and we came to another hallway with a barred entry door that was wide open. "This OK?" he asked.

"Sure, can we swing that door closed?"

He stepped inside, then rested his arm on the door and looked at me through the bars, every bit a prisoner. That was the picture.

ONE LAST VISIT

Cryts stayed in the Russellville jail for more than a month until Judge Baker relented. He kicked Cryts free but imposed a $287,000 judgment against the farmer. That judgment was later vacated, but Cryts' legal troubles did not end.

His tussle with Judge Baker had been a civil—not a criminal—matter. Criminal charges still lurked.

That fall, Cryts was arrested again. This time it came on a day when he was to serve as grand marshal for a town parade in Gravette, Arkansas. Federal marshals approached him on the sidewalk before the parade and announced they were there to arrest him. He asked if they could wait until after the parade. They agreed, and when the parade ended, they handcuffed him and drove him away.

Soon Cryts was in a jail in Fayetteville, Arkansas, charged with obstruction of justice. He was acquitted by a sympathetic jury but soon faced criminal contempt of court charges. Another sympathetic jury acquitted him. Next up was a civil contempt of court charge for a different set of circumstances. For this, a judge—not a jury—found him guilty and fined him $341,000.

Cryts, ever stubborn, told me later that he never did pay that fine.

In the meantime, the political storm he had helped spawn picked up strength. Cryts made national television appearances and gave interviews to The Wall Street Journal, Time magazine and People magazine. Some city folks finally understood—at least partially because of Cryts—that there was a farm crisis and that bankruptcy laws treated farmers unfairly. Ever so slowly, wheels in Washington and in state houses across the country managed to grind out changes to bankruptcy laws to make them less onerous for farmers. By mid-decade, farmers had protection on both federal and state levels.

Cryts—against all odds—had won. He and Sandy celebrated the legal victories and tried to pick up their interrupted lives.

I saw Wayne Cryts again in 2006, this time at his home in Puxico. It had been 25 years since the Great Soybean Raid, and to commemorate that event, family friend Jerry Hobbs had coauthored with Cryts a memoir: "One Man With Courage. The Wayne Cryts Story."

When I heard about the book, I called Cryts and was pleased that he invited me to come to talk to him about it. He said he would tell me what he had been doing since I saw him in the Russellville jail.

A few days later, I drove from Puxico down a country road and up to his modest ranch-style house. It had an impressively large American flag waving from a freestanding flagpole in the front yard. Cryts greeted me at the door with a strong handshake and smile. He'd gotten heavier, and his once-black hair was mostly gray. But he was dressed almost identically to the first time I first saw him standing on a truck at the bankrupt grain elevator all those years ago: an open denim jacket, plain shirt and blue jeans. Gone was his AAM cap.

The years immediately after the Ristine raid had not been kind to Cryts. His mountain of legal fees and other costs stemming from that day at Ristine had taken a toll. His finances were in shambles, and he lost the farm in 1987.

"When you lose a family farm," Cryts told me, "it's like losing a family member."

He took on carpentry work, roofing and remodeling jobs, which he enjoyed almost as much as farming. After a few years, he and Sandy needed the security and benefits of full-time work. So he took a position as maintenance supervisor for the Puxico school district. Sandy became a cook at the school. He ran for Congress in 1986 and barely lost. He ran again in 1988 and, with his fame fading, did not come close to winning. Now, he told me, he was finished with politics.

Cryts showed me to a dining room with bare walls, a large window that poured in light and a small round wooden table. In the corner was a carton of his new books with red, white and blue dust jackets. A photo on the cover showed a determined Cryts staring with furrowed brow into the lens.

The book is a relentlessly positive narrative, told with Cryts' voice. He comes across as a common man, but one who is stubborn, proud and unwavering in his convictions. The last words in the book are: "Finally, I thank God above that I live in a country as fine as the good ol' USA."

I'd brought along a large, matted print of the photo I had taken in the Russellville jail 25 years earlier and presented it to Cryts. I intended it both as a gift and as a prop for a portrait I wanted to take: Wayne Cryts then and now. He seemed touched and posed for my photo with a faint smile.

As we shook hands and I prepared to leave, he gave me a copy of his book, which he signed: "Thank you for being at the elevator and Russellville. Your friend, Wayne Cryts."

CHAPTER 3

THE LONG HOLLOWING OUT

I'd left a farm one spring evening in the early 2000s and was headed to a hotel room in Fort Dodge, Iowa. It had been a good interview and photo session, and I was feeling rather satisfied with myself. I also felt an urgent need to pee.

Suppressing the need to pee probably is not a knack you would expect to be a job requirement for an agricultural journalist. But it can be. Depending on where you practice the craft, it's sometimes impossible to find a good spot to go. Iowa is a place that tests the bladder. I'd been in this situation often because I frequented Iowa all my career, and its wide-open spaces sometimes offer neither towns, convenience stores or rest stops. Beer or farmhouse coffee have a way of asserting themselves on long Iowa drives, especially as I've grown into middle age and acquired a bladder that was more insistent than it had been in my youth.

That day, the farmer and I had ended my visit with a friendly beer and, even though he'd offered me use of his shop's restroom before I left, I'd not felt the need and foolishly had declined his invitation. Now I was on a two-lane back road with a burning desire to find a secluded place to pull off and relieve myself of the beer.

I suppose I could have just pulled onto the shoulder and aimed into the ditch. After all, rural two-lanes in this part of the country are sparsely traveled. Chances were slim that someone would see me peeing. But I've always had this almost irrational concern that as soon as I unzipped, a random vehicle would come along—probably occupied with a mother and her gawking young children—and I'd be embarrassed to think they had seen me standing by the side of the road urinating.

On this evening, I eventually spotted an opportunity and turned into the driveway of an abandoned farmhouse sheltered by a thick windbreak of trees. It was ideal for my purposes. I exited my truck and gratefully used one of the trees as a urinal.

Zipping my fly, I looked more closely at the farmhouse. I'd seen many such discarded dwellings, of course. The rural areas I traveled were dotted with them, sitting forlorn and forgotten on the edges of farm fields. I'd seen so many that they had become part of the landscape and were no longer remarkable. But today, this abandoned home called to me.

It had once been white but now had turned grey with age and sad with memories. It was a small, two-story clapboard house with partially collapsed wooden front stairs leading to a porch with broken rail spindles and a sagging floor. The aluminum storm door hung open because the spring that served as its closer dangled uselessly from the door frame. The lower half of the main door had lost most of its paint. But the glass in the upper half was still intact. Above the porch, a gable decorated with scrolled woodwork were like eyebrows framing a pair of windows that looked for all the world as if they were keeping watch in case the farm family that had once lived here decided to come home.

It had been a fine little farmhouse when it was built, which I guessed was during the 1930s or 1940s. It was solid and had sheltered a family from many Iowa winter winds and hot summer suns. But it had not been able to shelter the family from economic ruin. Now it was merely a reminder of the past and of a family that had moved on. I had no idea how long it'd been empty, but from the sad look of its exterior, at least a couple of decades.

On a whim, I decided to investigate and gingerly walked onto the porch to try the doorknob. It turned freely and, with a little pressure, I pushed the door open and walked into a front hallway clothed in yellowed and peeling wallpaper. On one side of the hallway was a bedroom, on the other a parlor. In the parlor was a fireplace littered with feathers, bird droppings and an andiron that still cradled a charred log. Beneath one window lay the skeletal remains of a bird who probably had flown down the chimney, got lost in the room and beat against the window until exhausted.

In the bedroom, decaying newspapers were strewn on the floor beside a stack of curled magazines. I looked at them and saw, to my surprise, that one was a 1980s issue of a farm magazine I had once worked for. Had the family abandoned the place during the farm depression of the 1980s?

There was a stairway to the second floor that had a dark, stained wood banister and treads that were scratched and indented by generations of feet. At the top of the stairs was a window that seeped light from a dusk sky. I imagined that up there were a couple of small bedrooms where children had slept under sloping dormer ceilings.

Down the hall was the kitchen. An old propane gas stove sat with its oven door agape. When the owners moved, they had left behind a small wooden table whose white enamel paint now was alligatored and chipped. The room itself smelled of ancient grease and recent mice. A large dusty window over the cast-iron and porcelain-coated sink looked out on what was once a family's backyard but now was an overgrown and weedy mess.

I stood for a moment in the twilight kitchen and felt the presence of the family who had moved away. They hadn't left in a hurry. They'd left after much deliberation and heartache. They'd left a house and land they loved because they couldn't afford to farm anymore.

As I drove away, I reflected on the thousands of families that had to abandon their farms and their dreams over the last few decades. These empty houses were monuments to a long hollowing out of large sections of America's farm country, a slow but relentless process that continues today.

A CONTINUATION

In 1880, rural Americans made up 94% of the nation's population. From there, the percentage of Americans who live in the countryside has been in steady decline. The second industrial revolution that spanned the end of the 19th century into the early 20th century pulled young men and their families away from farms and into cities, where factories jobs and commerce beckoned. The cities swelled, and urban sprawl swallowed up farmland that had been owned by the same families for generations.

There are many reasons for population loss in rural America. Droughts, economic swings and evolutionary forces weed out the weakest farmers. The altered nature of agriculture is also a major factor. Farming went from horse and mule in the 1930s and 1940s to 400-horsepower tractors in the 1980s. Such technology brought efficiencies and economies of scale. But it meant that fewer farm families were necessary to plant the same acres. Small farms were absorbed by larger ones, and the families who had farmed the smaller operations fled to find work in the cities.

This American out-migration wasn't just farm families. Residents of rural communities also chased city jobs, and small towns struggled to survive as both farming customers and town customers disappeared. By 1990, only 25% of Americans were rural dwellers. At more than 61 million, that was still a lot of people. But since about 2010, those numbers have shrunk as depopulation sped up. By the 2020 census, only 17% of Americans lived in rural areas.

It's important to understand that such census numbers for rural communities include all sorts of folks not involved in agriculture. Townspeople, resort owners, retirees and commuters are counted as rural residents.

Meanwhile, the number of actual farmers inexorably has declined for more than a century. In 1920, there were about 32 million men and women, about 30% of the entire population, who made their living growing crops and raising livestock. By 2020, the number of full-time American farmers had fallen to a mere 2 million, less than 1 percent of the total population.

When I first started writing about agriculture in the late 1970s, a 1,000-acre Midwestern farm was almost inconceivably large. It was too expansive to manage, too complex to be profitable. Today, 10,000-acre farms are commonplace; 20,000-acre farms are barely remarkable. What has become rare are 40- and 240-acre farms, which were once abundant and of sufficient size and income potential for a family to prosper. Maybe the abandoned farmhouse I had explored was one of those families.

As farm size grew larger, farm families had to make wrenching decisions. Could they afford to buy more land? Could they survive if they didn't farm larger? These were questions not just for the present generation; they were crucial for the next generation. As farm kids become adults, they have families of their own. Could the original family afford to buy or rent enough land to support son, Johnny, and his new family? How about a third family as daughter, Jenny, gets married?

Also, there is a sort of natural selection that sends some farm kids packing. A farming lifestyle might not suit their personalities. Instead of staying, they move to a city to pursue entirely different careers.

It is inevitable that farm families will fragment and that much of the next generation will move away. That leaves Dad and Mom to farm, and they grow older. The average age of a farmer in a 2022 USDA survey was 57.5 years.

Over the years, I've been witness to much of rural America's depopulation. I've written about it and photographed it. As a kid from the suburbs, I originally didn't appreciate what out-migration meant to those who inhabit rural America. Now that I have lived in a small town for almost half my life, I've begun to understand the loss to the community when friends and relatives move away, never to return. It is a diminished culture. Or at least it is a culture transformed into something less recognizable, less like home. Rural America has become more fragile, and farming Americans and their rural neighbors have become fearful about what the future holds.

WORTH COUNTY

In the late 1970s, I was new to ag journalism and just becoming aware that the countryside was leaking population like a rusty well bucket. Perhaps the emptying out first struck me in the winter of 1979, when Larry Harper, who was my boss at The Missouri Ruralist magazine, assigned me to investigate what was happening in Worth County, Missouri's smallest county.

Dangling from the Iowa border, tiny Worth County was shedding people at a rate that would reduce its population to zero in 30 years if trends continued. Zero. Latest evidence of that depopulation recently had made news in The New York Times, which reported to the nation that the county was so broke, it had closed its courthouse and, by some definitions, gone out of business.

"Seriously?" I asked Larry.

"That's what I read. Go check it out."

A few weeks and a dozen phone calls later, I was on the road from Columbia to Grant City, county seat of Worth County.

The counties across my state's mid-section are blessed with good farmland. The Missouri River and the Grand River valleys are some of the best farmlands you'll find. But as you drive north, the topsoils became thinner, and the cropland is hillier and less productive. Consequently, most farmers in the northern counties always have relied on livestock, especially beef cattle, to help pay the mortgage. That's the case in Worth

County, where out my windshield scrubby hills rolled into more scrubby hills speckled with beef cattle grazing the sparse winter vegetation.

I had read that in 1900, Worth County was home to almost 10,000 souls, mostly farmers or businessmen who traded with farmers. By 1950, the population had fallen to about 5,100, in part because those thin soils couldn't compete with soils in other areas of the state. With poor production and consequent meager income, many farmers had fled in search of city work. Bigger machinery also spurred the out-migration. It had made larger farms possible and had made small farms—and the families that worked them—expendable. To compound its woes, Worth County did not offer many alternate ways to earn a living: no manufacturing, no mining, no tourist attractions. By the time I drove across the county line in January 1980, Worth County's 267 square miles was home to only 3,000 residents. The county seat, Grant City, had a population of about 1,100.

Under a steel gray sky, Grant City's town square looks especially bleak to me. Many of the storefronts are vacant. Some are boarded up. Others have stunned looks on their facades, as if they can't believe they have been abandoned. A few cars and pickups are parked on the square in front of a café, a bank and a florist. I don't see a single person walking the sidewalks.

The courthouse itself looks like a movie set gone to seed. It is two-and-a-half stories of nearly century-old reddish brick with incongruous flourishes of Classical and Renaissance Revival architecture. It has rounded arched-stone entryways and dirty windows sitting on grimy limestone sills. It is topped by a bell tower, a faded ornate clock that is stuck at quarter after five, and a flagpole—without a flag. The courthouse feels haunted.

The building is closed because the county can't afford the heating bills. Pending a spring warm-up, the sheriff's department has moved to Sheriff Jack Baker's house. Circuit Clerk/Recorder of Deeds Bill Maxwell has set up shop in a vacant space that was once a doctor's office. Circuit Judge W.T. Osborne is holding court in his basement. And County Clerk

Larry Thompson has moved his office and the county administrative judges' (county commissioners) meeting place to his garage.

That's where I am supposed to meet Thompson, who has invited me to attend the judges' weekly session. Thompson answers my knock at his plain ranch-style house and leads me across a driveway to a detached two-car garage. Inside, under a fluorescent shop light suspended by chains from the ceiling, is an 8-foot folding table and some mismatched chairs. A small row of filing cabinets sits against a wall, and a wood stove offers the comfort of heat and atmosphere. This is Worth County's seat of government.

The county's three judges are seated at the table: Presiding Judge Bill Cottrell, Judge Roy Clay Poole and Judge Ken Clayton. Clerk Thompson, in a grey felt cowboy hat and flowered shirt, takes a seat at the end of the judges' table and lights a cigarette while he patiently explains to me how things got this bad for his county.

First, there are too few people in Worth County to shoulder the burden. Tax revenues might once have been enough to pay for services. But inflation and other factors make those services more expensive each year. The county needs more money and twice in 1979 asked voters to pay more taxes.

To make the county's case to the voters, Thompson compiled a list of expenditures that are required by state or federal laws. They include salaries, mileage, Social Security payments, insurance and other routine items. The bottom line for mandated expenses read: $117,960.84. On the other side of the ledger are the county's expected revenues from taxes and other sources. Its total was $111,082.16. Before the year got underway, Worth County was $6,874.68 in the hole.

Thompson tells me: "By the time we take care of our unpaid obligations for this year, we won't have enough funds for next year's statutory requirements, let alone supplies for the assessor and the collector. As far as

I'm concerned, if the assessor can't make a tax book, and the collector can't send out tax bills and collect funds, we're out of business."

For months, he and the judges warned county residents that a tax hike was the only way to keep the government functioning. In August, they submitted to the voters a 35-cent tax hike on every $100 of assessed property value. It failed to get the two-thirds majority necessary for passage under Missouri law. Although 60% of Worth Countians heeded the judges' warnings, 40% did not. In November, the judges gave it one more shot—and lost by almost exactly the same margin.

So the judges closed the courthouse; they simply didn't have the funds to pay even basics, such as utility bills. They laid off the county's road and bridge crews. Same with two courthouse secretaries and the janitor. The clerk, circuit clerk and recorder, treasurer, collector, associate circuit judge, prosecuting attorney and the three administrative judges now work sporadically and for free. They won't get paid until the beginning of the new fiscal year in July.

You might call what happened in Worth County a one-off tax revolt. But the truth is Worth County is like every rural county I've visited. It contains a block of voters who oppose anything government does. They have axes to grind and old grievances to nurture; that's just who they are. They are a definite "no" vote, especially when it comes to raising taxes. Logic and Thompson's numbers had no chance of convincing them otherwise.

Salary increases the state legislature recently had mandated made matters worse. The mandate galled even those who voted "yes" because it felt like the legislature used too broad a brush when crafting the mandate. In Worth County's case, the salary increases totaled about $8,000.

Presiding Judge Bill Cottrell sympathizes with "no" voters on this score: "I don't begrudge anybody a raise. But damn it, the state needs to think a minute about what they're doing to small counties like ours."

I wanted to understand the mindset of Worth Countians. So even before making my trip, I made a phone call to George Young, the owner of a local livestock sales barn and organizer of a group that supported the tax increase. "I'll tell you part of the problem," Young said. "There are people in this county who have some sort of a grudge against Grant City and everything Grant City does. They've been mad so long they don't remember what they are mad about."

I ask Cottrell about this, and he agrees. "Some of them, they don't care what the issue is, they will vote 'no' just to be safe."

A vocal opponent of the tax increase is businessman Berkley Carr. He told me during a phone call that there was more to the naysayers' position than a stubborn unwillingness to tax themselves. He railed against government waste. For instance, he said, employing two secretaries in the courthouse was an extravagance. "Ask Larry Thompson if he needs a secretary. Can't he handle that job by himself?"

It sounded to me like Carr was looking for excuses to vote 'no,' and I asked him why else he thought the taxpayers weren't getting their money's worth. He circled back to those secretaries' salaries and their cost to the county's budget: "Last winter, if a farmer wanted his road cleared of snow, he went out and hired a bulldozer. He didn't even ask the county because the county didn't have any money. It was all consumed in salaries. That farmer could not find one shred of evidence his tax money was benefitting him."

Then Carr let fly a libertarian rant about the state's mandates for counties. "To hell with the statutes. The statues are what got us where we are today. So why don't we operate without the statues like we had some sense? Let the attorney general come up here and tell us we have to follow the statutes. I haven't seen him up here yet, and I don't expect I ever will."

I ask Cottrell if Carr was typical of those who voted "no." He won't speak about Carr's motivations but says I should be aware that a consolidation of county schools a few years ago had caused bad blood. In fact, the county bore the rank smell of an old-fashioned feud.

It started when a decline in student populations made it impossible for some of the towns' school districts to afford the teachers, buses and supplies needed to keep their classrooms open. Much of the operating funds for local school districts comes from the state, which uses the number of students enrolled in a district to determine how much money it receives. The fewer students, the fewer the dollars. That leaves some rural districts in a bind. Over the fierce objections of many parents, most of Worth County's local school districts decided they must consolidate into one district and close most of the other school buildings. Kids from towns like Allendale, Denver and Sheridan now rode buses to Grant City.

You must understand that in rural America, towns derive much of their identity from their schools. Townsfolk share memories of childhoods spent in their town's school, of rooting for its sports team, of attending fundraisers and prom dances. A school is the soul of a small town. Without it, the town is unanchored. A truism I've heard over and over says: "Once a town's school closes, the town is doomed."

"That school consolidation thing caused quite a bit of bitterness," Cottrell tells me. "Some of them will take that to their graves."

Maybe some of that bitterness was reflected in Carr's voice over the phone. "They say, 'Vote for this increase or we will close the courthouse.' I don't care if they close the goddamned courthouse. They can just keep it closed. The only time I go there is to pay my taxes, and I guarantee they'll find some other way for me to pay my taxes."

For his part, George Young told me, "I am ashamed this county had to close its courthouse just because people would not vote enough money to keep it open."

I've checked back with Worth County a few times over the years. There was talk of merging with neighboring counties. But nothing came of it. Maybe the other counties didn't see an advantage to absorbing a county that couldn't or wouldn't support itself; maybe Worth County didn't want to give up its identity. It eventually did manage to pass a tax increase sufficient to reopen the courthouse doors. But as of 2014, it still had to close off some rooms in the old brick structure to conserve heat in the winter. And its population continued to shrink. By the 2020 census, Worth County could claim only 1,973 residents. Grant City was reduced to fewer than 800 people.

TAKEAWAY

As I reflect on Worth County, I see what a powerful force depopulation has been in the county's life. And I wonder if the rigid and bitter attitudes caused by that depopulation aren't emblematic of the disenfranchisement and alienation felt in many areas of rural America.

Worth County couldn't pay its bills because not enough citizens were willing or able to share the load. That engendered a sense of justifiable paranoia that the county's very existence as an entity was threatened. When groups of people are threatened, they look for someone or something to blame. State government is an easy target, but it is often a misplaced bugaboo. The man who complained that Worth County didn't plow farm roads after a snow seemed to forget that most of the roads in the county were plowed by the state. They are state-maintained highways and the state-paid crews to drive the plows. He also didn't make the connection that if he and others had voted to approve a tax increase, the county would have had the finances needed to plow those farm roads.

School consolidation? Enrollment in Sheridan's schools shrank so much, the district was forced to either consolidate with the larger Grant City school district or allow its children to go uneducated. Rather than identify the problem as one of depopulation, many Sheridan parents blamed Grant City for what they perceived as a power grab.

A tax increase to pay government employees' salaries? Forget that salary increases would benefit the local economy by circulating more dollars to be spent locally. Instead, blame state politicians who chose to mandate living wages for workers statewide.

Farm families moving out? Blame corporate farms and a perceived lack of government support.

The blame game is the same whether it's in Worth County, Missouri, Miner County, South Dakota, or Colquitt County, Georgia. It's insidious and consistent. It is self-defeating and self-perpetuating. Worse, it makes rural Americans susceptible to the siren call of demagogues who pound the podium and yell that the establishment, big government and even Hollywood is at fault. These same demagogues and their acolytes use AM radio and cable television to incessantly tell rural Americans that they are the victims of plots by liberals in league with illegal immigrants, minorities and coastal elites. Parts of hollowed out America eat up such propaganda with a spoon and a smile. They are eager to have someone—anyone—to blame for their problems. That's one reason why Donald Trump—who wouldn't know a corn plant from a foxtail weed but is an expert at casting blame—won the rural vote in 2016. He got 62% of rural America's votes in 2016 and 65% in 2020, even though the farm economy was diminished after four years of Trump trade wars and confused farm policies.

The blame game has no winners.

TECHNOLOGY AND MEGA LIVESTOCK FARMS

Bill Macklin, the esteemed editor of The New Ulm Journal, where I worked my first newspaper job in the mid-1970s, told me once that there was a simple answer to a question I posed to him one day in the newsroom: "Why are all the towns along Highway 14 in southern Minnesota seven miles apart?"

"Railroads," Bill said.

When the Winona & St. Peter Railroad first laid tracks westward in the Minnesota River Valley in 1872, the steam locomotives it used had to stop frequently to take on more water. To meet that need, the railroad installed a water tower every seven miles and hired a man to keep it filled. Quickly, the water tower became the basis of a farm town. While the locomotives stopped to quench their thirst, the other cars in the train delivered mail, picked up passengers, took onboard farm goods destined for city markets and dropped off supplies to farm families spread across the prairie.

Transportation technology in the form of railroads helped build agrarian communities the entire width of southern Minnesota.

But an improvement on that technology later helped dismantle some of those same farm villages. Not long after the railroad helped birth towns like Essig and Cobden, it began to kill them because the next generation of locomotives could go twice as far—14 miles—before stopping for a drink of water. That meant that some farm towns prospered, while others shriveled. For instance, it's 14 miles as the train chugs from New Ulm (population about 13,000) west to Sleepy Eye (population about 3,500). Halfway between is the almost vanished village of Essig (population 49). Likewise, it's 14 miles between Sleepy Eye westward to Springfield (population about 2,100). Seven miles between them is wide-spot-in-the-road Cobden (population 36). When the trains no longer stopped in Essig and Cobden, farmers traveled the extra seven miles to New Ulm, Sleepy Eye or Springfield to buy and sell goods.

Improved highways also were a key factor in population shifts because better roads meant swifter trips, which meant Cobden's merchants had to compete with Springfield's. With a larger population in Springfield, it won and Cobden lost.

Bill's train story stuck with me because it provided a structure for my thinking about how population patterns of rural America change over time and how changes in technology play a pivotal role in those patterns. In general, as farming technology improves, farm populations dwindle because fewer people are needed to farm the land. Speedy tractors replaced slow plow horses, for instance, which meant that fewer people were needed to farm the same number of acres. Rural populations dwindled.

Technology changes also affected the livestock industry, especially poultry and hog production. Farmyard operations that utilized chicken coops and pigpens changed dramatically as farmers and outside investors sought innovative ways to increase production to match increasing meat demand in expanding urban populations. A major step toward what some call factory farming was the advent of confinement buildings. These facilities can house hundreds of chickens in one space but required new technologies to ensure the birds survived in close quarters. That meant air-moving systems to help prevent the spread of disease. It meant watering systems and feeding systems. It meant crates and cages. It meant antibiotics and beak trimming.

By the 1950s, intensive poultry production was going strong. In the beginning, independent farmers used the technology to increase the number of eggs or birds they could market, just as crop farmers used technology to increase the number of acres they farmed. But soon the transformed poultry industry became dominated by vertical integrators who owned the birds, paid farmers to care for them, supplied the feed and trucked eggs and mature birds to processing plants that they, themselves, owned. It was a closed loop with no room for independent farmers.

While the business model was, and is, controversial among farmers and animal-welfare activists, poultry farming based on a factory model became the profitable norm. In the 1960s, 1970s and 1980s, the same model began to take hold in hog production. Large, galvanized steel hog buildings began to dot the countryside from the Carolinas to the Corn Belt. Technology made possible industrialized pork production, which eventually concentrated ownership in the hands of a few corporations. Megafarms replaced independent farms and pushed many families off the land.

Despite their tendency to displace farmers, mega livestock farms can be a tempting proposition for some rural counties. When they move to an area, megafarms create instant economic development—new jobs, increased tax bases, an infusion of fresh faces and neighbors. The downsides: When a megafarm begins production, it immediately brings water- and air-quality concerns; it puts pressure on existing farms to compete or to change business models; it transforms the social fabric of small towns. So when a megafarm—especially a hog farm consisting of several units producing 10,000 or more animals and spread throughout a compact area—announces its arrival, it causes divisions in the community. It divides towns and counties into pro camps and con camps. It pits neighbor against neighbor.

In 1989, when Doug Fairley and I rode in his pickup through what was left of northern Missouri's Sullivan County, it was like touring an economic disaster zone. The remains of several generations of failed farms lay rotting in groves of trees. Rolling land that once produced cattle and crops was now covered in weeds. And small ghost towns squatted at the roadside, their empty storefronts and broken windows scolding at a world that did not need them anymore.

Sullivan County's troubles were long in the making. Its population steadily declined from a peak of 20,000 in 1900 to about 6,000 in 1989. The exodus occurred largely because the area's topsoils gave out. From the beginning, they were thin and unproductive. But now they could no longer compete with better soils in other regions, and farm families—having exhausted their Sullivan County dreams—moved on. The Great Depression quickened the process. And as American agriculture grew less diversified, mixed operations of livestock and crops became the exception. There was even less reason to stay in Sullivan County, whose redeeming quality had been that a combination of cattle, hogs and crops could sustain a family. By the killing years of the 1980s, stubbornness and family ties were the only reasons for residents to stay.

Into this cheerless scene in 1989 came Premium Standard Farms (PSF), a new company with grandiose ideas for vertically integrating the pork industry. It planned to control meat-making from farrow to finish and feed mills to packing plants. It would own the means of production and hire people by the hour to replace farmers as livestock herders.

PSF earlier had tried its business model in Iowa but left under pressure from neighbors, environmentalists and even the governor, who didn't take kindly to such a huge operation changing the landscape. The wide-open spaces and sparce population of northern Missouri offered a second chance for PSF. And while few warmed to the idea of a hog conglomerate in the neighborhood, some Missourians saw PSF as a second chance.

"We had nothing on the horizon," Fairley told me as we drove neglected blacktops and rutted gravel roads. "There was no light at the end of our tunnel. If PSF coming here could buy us a little time—five, 10 years—well, we are better off with them than without them."

County administrative judges concurred with Fairley's point of view and granted PSF permission to locate in Sullivan County. Construction began on the county's new identity.

As Fairley and I continued our tour, I took a photo of him leaning on a dilapidated fence in front of an abandoned farmhouse. He didn't object to the negative connotation of the image. "It's what we live with," he said. I wrote a small story about PSF and promised myself I would come back to Sullivan County to see how the company's plans had worked.

Six years later, Fairley and I are riding the same roller-coaster roads of Sullivan County. Things have changed. On the crest of a hill, Fairley pulls over to show me the new vista. Dotting the hills are gleaming silver hog houses where, six years ago, there was nothing but weeds or scattered grazing cattle. PSF now fed 80,000 hogs in three Missouri counties. It had taken an act of the legislature and the good will of Governor John Ashcroft to exempt Sullivan, Putnam and Mercer from the state's anticorporate farming laws. But PSF was thriving in northern Missouri. It breeds, farrows and finishes hogs in those three counties, and ships them to Milan, Sullivan's county seat, to a processing plant it owns and operates. The company claims it provides more than 1,000 direct jobs and more than 1,000 spin-off jobs.

As we scan the hills and feel the breeze, Fairley tells me he used to worry about the odor potential of huge hog houses. He's less concerned now. Even though his own house is surrounded by hog houses—at a distance—he says the smell is not as bad as he feared.

Fairley manages the Fowler Elevator, in Newtown (population 100). He could foresee from the beginning that PSF would hurt his business. And it has. PSF bought about 40,000 acres as a buffer from its neighbors and as cropland on which to spread manure waste. Previously, Fairley's elevator sold fertilizer for use on some of that same land. PSF, of course, does not buy much fertilizer for land because it spreads its own manure to add nitrogen to the soil. That has cut the elevator's total revenues by 10%. "And I'm not going to be able to sell them any feed either," Fairley tells me with a grimace.

Nonetheless, Fairley is a PSF supporter. As president of a district school board, he credits PSF with saving the local school. "Three years ago, we were talking about consolidating our school with others," he says. "But our student numbers grew from 69 to 99 because of PSF families. That means more money from the state. Also, assessed valuations [the basis for local school property taxes] have more than doubled because of PSF. Now it looks like the school is here to stay. That's important to a town. I've seen lots of towns around here lose their schools. Three to five years later, the town itself is dead."

Newtown seems far from dead as we drive into it. Its homey café is elbow-to-elbow at noon, mostly men in coveralls and boots. We wedge ourselves into the only empty booth, and Fairley covertly points out diners who work for PSF or have relatives working there. After a tasty hamburger served with french fries and iced tea, we walk across the street, and grocery store manager Stacey Lair tells me she sees new customers almost every week. Business is good.

Across the line in Mercer County, Princeton bank president Jack Tucker can't say enough good things about PSF's economic impact on the area. He rhapsodizes about higher property values, new home construction for the first time in a decade, business startups and positive attitudes among locals.

As we sit in his small-town bank office, he tells me: "Six years ago, if a company had come here wanting to create 10 new jobs, we would have been thrilled. But to have a company come here and create 2,000 new jobs is beyond our wildest dreams."

Not everyone in the area shares Tucker's enthusiasm. Forty-five miles away in Green City, I'm seated in Rolf and Ilse Christen's farmhouse listening to opponents of corporate hog farms vent. Around the kitchen table are farmers Gary Godfrey, Ron Kelley and banker-farmer Bob Whitacre. They are in the process of forming an organization—one of several in north Missouri—to oppose new mega hog farms. To these people, PSF is a dirty word.

Their first complaint is the odor thousands of pigs generate when concentrated in one place. "It stinks," says Rolf Christen, who lives two miles south of a grower unit. "There's no other word for it. You don't want to fish in your pond or sit outdoors or leave your windows open. It's awful."

Some might dismiss odor as unimportant, Godfrey tells me. But it is not a trivial matter if you are forced to live with it. "PSF has taken away part of what we loved about our lives. They have invaded our property without setting foot in it. And we are helpless to change that."

Smell isn't the only thing about the megafarms that rankles. Like most rural areas, Sullivan County and its neighboring counties are insular. People who live in these rolling hills grew up here; they share histories and backgrounds. Strangers might be welcome to visit, but they draw suspicious stares when they walk into the coffee shop. To have a new family move into the area would create a disturbance in the hive. And many of the people PSF hires and brings to town are not like the natives—they are immigrants, some are brown.

The talk around the Christen kitchen table isn't overtly racist. But the group is leery about the unknown backgrounds of people PSF is importing into their backyards. They didn't grow up here. They haven't been vetted by years lived in the county. They are outsiders.

"Why have people like us wanted to live here?" Whitacre asks the group. "Because you can leave the keys in your pickup or leave the front door unlocked. You can't do that now. The welfare rolls in Sullivan County have gone up since this 'progress' arrived. Our social structure has been changed, and a lot of us didn't think it needed changing."

Whitacre tells me that he also worries about the future of the land itself. "When all this land is in corporate hands, it's never going to be sold again in 100- or 500-acre units so that a young family could get started farming. It's going to be sold in huge blocks to another corporation. Essentially, it's lost forever."

Some fear the community will become totally dependent on PSF, that the whole area will become a kind of company town. For evidence, they point to neighboring Putnam County, which once was home to Missouri Mining Co. When the coal pits shut down many years ago, "It just about killed the county," Kelley says, his face working into an angry mask. "We don't want that to happen to us when PSF goes under."

Godfrey worries what megafarms portend, not only for Sullivan County but also for distant rural communities and for thousands of small farmers across the country. "What PSF is doing is transferring economies from other areas to here. In these three counties in Missouri, they are going to produce 1.7 to 2 million hogs a year, which is roughly 2% of national production. If you had 50 areas like this, you could produce all the hogs in the country. If you do that, what happens in small towns in Iowa and Nebraska? What about those communities' economies? What happens to 100,000 small hog producers and their families?"

Godfrey's questions are not unique. Economists and sociologists who study rural America have the same concerns. One of the more vocal opponents of megafarms at the time is Marty Strange, co-founder of the Center for Rural Affairs in Walthill, Nebraska. He tells me in a phone call, "By planting its feet in a desperate community, PSF may bring hope. But it can wreck 15 other communities."

The sheer volume of pork produced by megafarms also can create an oversupply, which will drive down prices, which will put financial pressure on independent hog farmers elsewhere and perhaps force them out of business, Strange tells me. And that could be disastrous for rural towns and villages that depend on local farmers. "It does make a difference to a community what kind of pork-production system we have. Large operations produce more hogs per worker, and that sounds efficient. But another way to look at it is that megafarms produce fewer jobs per hog. That means less money for the community."

What's more, Strange says, independent producers reinvest their profits in the community. But a corporation or capital investment firm takes its profits and distributes them to far-flung investors, leaving locals to wonder what became of the profits they helped earn.

Strange's position is not shared by all researchers in the mega-farm field.

North Carolina was the epicenter of mega hog farms in the 1990s. A contemporary North Carolina State University (NCSU) study concluded that individual rural communities and the state as a whole benefit from the boom in megafarms. NCSU ag economist Kelly Zering co-wrote the report. "It would be awfully difficult to argue that North Carolina is worse off now than before the big hog units," he tells me in a phone conversation. "Tax bases, property values and job opportunities have all increased in the major hog-producing counties. Can there be healthy rural communities based on large livestock operations? Yes. But we are also going to see lots of rural communities die with or without those operations? That has been going on for decades."

Closer to home, a University of Missouri study of PSF's impact predicted that a five-county area in north Missouri would benefit by $24 million annually in payroll, local purchases and taxes from PSF. "The long-term effects may be even greater," one of the study's authors tells me. Agricultural economist Dennis DiPietre says: "In a few years, as people gain confidence that PSF is here to stay, there will be more investment in the area, collateral businesses will develop, niche markets will appear."

DiPietre tells me that critics of PSF don't know local history. "What did this area have before PSF? Its businesses were in decline, and investors had moved away. People talk as if PSF came in and replaced a viable economy. It didn't. It filled a void."

That's not to imply that DiPietre thinks megafarms assure rural communities a bright future. "Not all large corporations are as conscientious or as community-minded as PSF," he says. "And not all of them will have a positive net effect on a community."

Back in Sullivan County, I'm riding in Doug Fairley's pickup again. This time, we're going to visit Jerry Brown, whose family farms 1,500 acres and runs hogs and cattle. The day before our visit, Jerry, 58, and his son Dave, 36, finally had decided to quit the hog business. It was a difficult and emotional decision. "We've had hogs on this farm since I was a kid," Jerry tells me outside the barns were he and Dave feed hogs. "Truthfully," he says with a quick grin, "I've never much liked hogs. But they paid the mortgage."

The Browns' decision to quit hogs was not directly related to PSF. Current low hog prices mean the Browns take a loss on every animal they sell. And their production facilities are old and outdated. "I can't see spending $250,000 on buildings and on lagoons for the manure," Jerry says. "I don't think it would pencil out for us."

When the Browns stop feeding hogs in a few months, Dave plans to look for work with PSF. When I ask if he is looking forward to working for someone else, Dave just shrugs and says, "Don't know. Never done it before. I've always worked with Dad."

Jerry looks from Dave to me. "I didn't much like seeing PSF come here," he says. "But I guess I'm glad they are here now. At least Dave can work and stay close to home."

Over the years since that visit, I've occasionally checked in with Sullivan, Putnam and Mercer counties to see how the PSF experiment has played out. I learned that PSF itself has had a wild ride. In 1990, it sold 51% of its ownership to Wall Street investment giant Morgan Stanley. With new financial backing, PSF expanded its operations in Missouri, built farms in Texas and acquired another processing plant to seal the last hole in its production loop. But by 1996, hog prices had tanked, and PSF had run afoul of lawsuits by local landowners and the state resulting from allegations of pollution from leaking waste lagoons. To shelter its assets, it declared Chapter 11 bankruptcy. In 1998, Continental Grain Co. replaced Morgan Stanley as majority owner. In 2006, Smithfield Foods, the largest pork producer in the country, acquired PSF. Smithfield itself was bought by a Chinese company in 2013.

Meanwhile, population numbers in the three Missouri counties where PSF got its start have slipped backwards. When I first visited Sullivan County in 1989, its population was 6,326. It rose to 7,219 in 2000 and then began falling. The 2020 census counted only 5,999 souls. Putnam County went from 5,079 in the 1990 census to 4,681 in 2020. And Mercer County went from 3,757 in 1990 to 3,538 in 2020.

Obviously, PSF was not the magic wand that could reverse the hollowing out of rural north Missouri counties. I've come to doubt there is a magic wand. Perhaps rural America is destined to slide further and further into irrelevance until one day, historical cycles somehow restore it to prominence. Personally, I think America needs its agrarian traditions; it needs to nurture small-town culture. America is somehow not America without independent families working the land, providing the food and backbone our nation needs.

BUFFALO COMMONS

At the end of the 19th century, Native American tribes on the Great Plains had been pushed almost entirely off their traditional migratory range by white settlers, transcontinental railroads and the U.S. Cavalry. In response, some tribes adopted a ritualistic ceremony—the Ghost Dance— in the belief that if they danced long enough and were sincere enough, white farmers and ranchers would disappear from the Great Plains, and buffalo would return to reestablish the world as it had been from the beginning of time.

In the late 1980s, one school of academic thought speculated that the Ghost Dancers might have been right: The end of white domination of the Great Plains was indeed at hand.

"We believe that over the next generation, the Plains will, as a result of the largest, longest-running agricultural and environmental miscalculation in American history, become almost totally depopulated." Those words appeared in a December 1987 scholarly paper with the ominous title of "Great Plains: Dust to Dust" by the husband-and-wife team of Frank and Deborah Popper, of Rutgers University.

The Poppers wrote that this massive depopulation is already underway and will pick up momentum. The white man will finally understand what he should have known all along: The Great Plains are too tough to tame. Harsh climate, fickle economic conditions, limited rain and an irreversible draining of the Ogallala Aquifer will send farmers and ranchers packing. There will be no choice but to let large segments of the Great Plains revert to the buffalo paradise it was before their slaughter began.

The Poppers dubbed the recreated landscape "Buffalo Commons."

As you can imagine, farmers and ranchers whose ancestors had plowed the Great Plains and whose families now lived on its hills and in its valleys were not pleased with the Poppers. Folks in parts of Colorado, the Dakotas, Kansas, Montana, Nebraska, Oklahoma, Texas and Wyoming were convinced Buffalo Commons was just another wild ass idea by East Coast ivory tower dwellers. And they said so—loudly.

"There was a hell of a lot of interest in our ideas, mainly from the press, academia and pissed-off people," Frank Popper told me when I called his office in Brunswick, New Jersey, to inquire about Buffalo Commons. "The people of North Dakota took special offence. I'm completely puzzled by their reaction."

I might have accepted his puzzlement if I hadn't detected an ironic chuckle on the other end of the phone line. This was going to be an entertaining interview.

As background, I know something about the Great Plains. I live on its eastern edge and have traveled the length and breadth of its U.S. component. (It extends from the Prairie Provinces of Canada deep into Texas and from Kansas through Wyoming.) My visits to the Great Plains had special emphasis on Kansas and Nebraska. But I have extensively explored the Dakotas, Montana, New Mexico, Oklahoma and Texas. It's an unforgiving land with temperature extremes, a quirky environment and constant winds that require farmers and ranchers to be adaptive if they are to survive, much less prosper. John Russnogle, a Nebraska-born friend, shared with me local lore about a homemade device for measuring the cruel winds that torment Plains people. The device, John said, is a log chain attached to a stake in the backyard. If the chain stands out straight in the wind and starts waving, and you see some links start to snap off, you know that a strong wind is coming.

I learned in my travels that plainsmen and plainswomen are not delicate creatures. They have taken Nature's best punches and stuck out their chins for more. I couldn't imagine the ones I've met abandoning their farms and ranches, many of which are generations old and date to the Homestead Act of 1862. That legislation was created in part to "settle" the Great Plains and gave 160 acres to anyone brave enough and stout enough to survive on the land for five years. Of course, the land had been home to native tribesmen for millennia. But the Act didn't mention that.

Pioneers built sod huts before they were able to build farm towns, and they gradually created a farming ecoculture. The fact that the Great Plains is a semiarid region didn't deter them, because they believed what promoters of their midcontinent migration preached: "Rain follows the plow." They believed that if they busted open the ancient sod, Nature would reward them with plentiful rains.

Except that's not remotely true.

While the pioneers had some good years—even some good decades—the true nature of the Great Plains over time has asserted itself. It is a boom-and-bust environment that is bound to break farmers' hearts.

In the 1890s, blizzards, droughts and a national economic panic drove many farmers and ranchers off the Great Plains, sending them back east or farther west. That was followed by an agricultural boom created by the First World War's imperative to feed both Americans and their European allies, whose farm fields had become battlefields. Seeking to capitalize on what appeared to be a bright future, a new influx of farmers seeped into the Great Plains.

The 1920s and 1930s saw droughts of horrific malevolence. Dust storms born of soil that should never have been plowed swept across the Great Plains and darkened the skies as far east as Washington D.C. The

Great Depression was an even blacker cloud that cast its shadow on the entire economy. Those years saw massive out-migration. But the majority of Great Plains folk stuck it out and waited for better times to return.

This boom-and-bust pattern continued well into the second half of the 20th century. Great Plains farmers prospered during and after the Second World War. In the 1950s, irrigation wells tapped into the Ogallala Aquifer, crop yields spiked and the future seemed limitless. But soon, the farm crisis of the 1980s gave modern meaning to the term "bust." Thousands of farms disappeared, their owners departing for parts unknown. This was the economic environment in which the Poppers began studying the Great Plains.

Frank Popper told me he and Deborah were convinced that the 1980s were a harbinger of worse and worse times for farmers and ranchers on the Great Plains. "Many will fight to keep their things going. But they won't succeed."

As he and Deborah wrote: "It will be up to the federal government to ease the social transition of the economic refugees who are being forced off the land. For they will feel aggrieved and impoverished, penalized for staying too long in a place they loved and pursuing occupations the nation supposedly respected but evidently did not."

And when the "refugees" are gone, what will remain? The Buffalo Commons. It will be a vast depopulated region where the federal government and private agencies try to "recreate the 19th century."

Buffalo Commons will be a land of buffalo, jackrabbits and tourists. A few towns will remain to service visitors who come equipped with cameras and guns to take safari-like trips into the wild interior. Tellingly, the concept makes no mention of farmers and ranchers who buck the trend and somehow sustain themselves. No mention of families that persist in the face of monumental adversity.

"The Buffalo Commons will become the world's largest historic preservation project, the ultimate national park," the Poppers wrote in 1987.

"Most of the Great Plains will become what all of the United States once was—a vast landmass, largely empty and unexploited."

On the phone, I ask Frank if he is serious. He chuckles and admits that part of what he and Deborah want to do is to start a conversation about the fate of the Great Plains. They are, he says, agitators for change. He later wrote that the Buffalo Commons concept is, "part proposal, part metaphor for a long-term series of land-use changes, and an appeal for rethinking Plains possibilities. We want to offer something to the people of the Plains, not take something away."

"From Dust to Dust" didn't explain it quite that way. It was an outsider's proposal for the disposition of a way of life forged over generations.

I asked Bernie Hunhoff, who at the time edited South Dakota magazine, what his readers thought. Based on letters to the editor about a piece he did on Buffalo Commons, Hunhoff told me, "Most said the Poppers didn't understand that the people here are survivors. What the Poppers really didn't understand is that people live here because they love the lifestyle. They don't want to live in New Jersey."

I also asked Fran Kaye, editor of the Great Plains Quarterly, a publication of the Center for Great Plains Studies at the University of Nebraska-Lincoln, what she thought of "From Dust to Dust." "The Poppers' history is OK, even if their ideas are old as the hills. What is new is the scope of the approach of Buffalo Commons."

When she first read the paper, Kaye told me, she called Frank to ask how much of it was straight and how much was for effect. "He told me it was 50-50. The secret is you can't take everything he says seriously. You have to treat it as a game. If you do that, it's great fun to talk about something like Buffalo Commons. Otherwise, all you are going to do is make people mad."

I'll admit that by the time I finished my interview with Frank, I was convinced he was something of an academic charlatan. He was more interested in publishing and getting notoriety than in the fate of the Great Plains and its people. Over the years, however, Frank and Deborah surprised me. They displayed a steadfast interest in the region and have been active in organizations created to serve it. For instance, Frank was a long-time board member of The Great Plains Restoration Council, which calls itself an "Ecological health organization that helps people take care of their own health through restoring and protecting native ecosystems, particularly damaged prairies, plains and waters."

The Poppers also have been involved in projects aimed at restoring buffalo to the region as economic drivers to enhance—not replace—existing agricultural enterprises. Some of those projects included Native American tribes, which the Poppers had barely mentioned in "From Dust to Dust."

So I give the Poppers credit for being sincere, even though they wrote half in jest and intentionally pissed off so many plainsmen.

It is gratifying to note that not of the all the Great Plains is emptying out as the Poppers predicted. On the agricultural front, conservation techniques begun in the Dust Bowl have helped rebuild soils across the region. Farmers have adopted digital mapping and application technologies for maximizing production in the Great Plains' demanding environment. The Interstate 80 corridor in Nebraska is home to some of the most innovative and prosperous farmers in America. New irrigation rigs employ satellites and real-time moisture sensors to make irrigation more efficient and to help prolong the life of the precious Ogalala Aquifer. And the meatpacking industry has attracted tens of thousands of workers to southwest Kansas.

In the energy sector, wind farms now appear on many horizons on the Great Plains. Population in North Dakota's northwest corner has exploded because of the shale oil boom built on the Permian Basin deposits, and oil drilling also has brought new residents to parts of the Texas Panhandle and Oklahoma.

Although the Poppers certainly had solid evidence of the depopulation of the Great Plains, they may have overstated their case. They did not calculate how persistent Plains people are or how circumstances and outside forces might intervene. Populations might dwindle, but Plains folk continue to assert their will against Nature's vagaries. Or, better, they learn to understand Nature's ways and find sustainable methods to survive and, perhaps, prosper.

All is not gloom and doom on the Great Plains.

CHAPTER 4

BEER AND MILK

If a dairy farmer hadn't fallen off a barn roof, his family would never have started a brewery, and I'd never have come to Barre, Massachusetts. More importantly, I would not have met a group of people who took extraordinary measures to keep a family farm alive.

It was 2018, and I was freelancing again, having retired from Progressive Farmer magazine after 20 years on staff. I was 67 and wanted time to work on personal projects and to have more freedom to visit my kids and grandkids. Since my son Ryan and his family lived near Boston, I did what any freelance journalist would do—I hunted for story ideas that could pay my way to Massachusetts.

My research led me to a New York Times article about a few struggling dairy farms that had begun brewing craft beer to diversify and expand their income. One of those farms was about 70 miles west of Boston in rocky and forested western Massachusetts. The Carter & Stevens Farm milks about 200 cows there, and its family makes and sells craft beer under the name Stone Cow Brewery.

I thought that combination of enterprises would make a lightweight, fun story. Kind of. "Oh look, a dairy farm that brews craft beer. Isn't that cute?"

That was the story idea I sold to The Furrow, a 130-year-old magazine published by John Deere. It would be an easy story and, not coincidentally, would put me near my son and his family. At least that's how I went into the project.

But as I learned more about the farm, I discovered that the Stevens family was incredibly resourceful and determined. Not only had they adapted their dairy business to new ventures, they had done so during a family crisis that threatened their farm's existence. The real story, I came to understand, was that this family was illustrative of the fact that farmers can be resilient and ingenious, especially when their heritage is at stake.

I didn't discover any of this, of course, until I visited.

Sean DuBois, who had been quoted in the New York Times article, seemed pleased by my introductory phone call to Stone Cow Brewery. Sean proved to be an intelligent, articulate man of 37 who was the farm's front man with the public. He had a background in journalism and was eager to work with me. We discussed our goals for the story and set a date for me to travel to Barre.

To set the scene, the dairy industry was in a bind in those days, not only in Massachusetts but pretty much nationwide. Americans weren't drinking as much milk as they once did. But dairies were still producing millions of gallons of it every day. That led to oversupply and extremely low prices, which in turn led to many dairies—mainly small ones—selling their cows, boarding up their dairy parlors and finding other ways to make a living. The industry was consolidating the way much of agriculture had been doing for a century. Large farms capitalized on economies of scale and expensive technologies to thrive, while family dairy farms were headed for the endangered species list.

So it is not surprising that families look to supplement their milk checks with other revenue streams. Some make cheese. Some sell ice cream. Some deliver milk door-to-door.

For a rare few family dairies, craft beer seemed an offbeat—but enticing—sideline. For these few, the transition from milk to beer was aided by the fact that dairy farms already had large stainless steel milk tanks that could become part of the brewing process. These brewery dairies also benefited from a splash of youth. Small dairies are often endangered because their limited production volumes also limited income. Dairy families that are trying to transition from one generation to the next must find new revenue sources.

As Sean told the New York Times: "To succeed today as a dairy farm, you need to diversify. We found our passion for craft beer."

It wasn't that simple, as I learned when I arrived at the farm one sunny day in early November. Sean gave me a tour of the brewery, which was housed in a nearly-200-year-old hay bar. While we toured, we talked about the farm's history and how the brewery was born. It began like this:

The Stevens family had milked cows in the stony hills of central Massachusetts since the middle of the Great Depression. When Phil Stevens and his wife, Erin, took over the Carter & Stevens Farm in the late 1970s, they had 100 milk cows and a few acres of hay ground. Life was good, but money was scarce. By the early 2000s, their four kids were approaching adulthood, and questions of succession and the farm's long-term future were starting to rise.

Phil and Erin, of course, understood that the dairy industry in Massachusetts was rapidly declining. In the previous three decades, they had seen dozens of neighbors lose their dairies. The infrastructure for the industry itself had rapidly evaporated. As dairies vanished, processors and suppliers had closed their doors or moved to more fertile pastures.

The Stevenses also understood that, in the 21st century, a dairy as small as theirs certainly could not provide enough income to support multiple generations. And their four children had families of their own in the making. The Stevenses took steps to expand their income base, but the future of Carter & Stevens Farm as a family farm was nearing crisis.

Then Phil fell off the barn roof.

The path from that fall to opening a brewery in a dairy barn is convoluted, and to tell it, Sean passed me to his father-in-law, Phil Stevens, who was waiting for me outside the brewing barn. He shook my hand and offered to show me the rest of the farm.

Phil is a tall, wiry 60-year-old with 1970s sideburns hanging just below the ear. His wrap-around sunglasses and pulled-low farmer's cap do their best to hide his face. But I can see it is a friendly face.

He tells me to hop into his utility vehicle for a trip to the milking parlor and pastures. His dog, Shadow—a smiling black Lab mix going grey around the mouth—jumps into the bed of the vehicle. "He won't let me out of his sight. If I didn't let him ride with me, he'd just run along beside us," Phil says with a grin. Apparently, that's how Shadow got his name.

I've long known that farmers do their best talking while driving in pickups and UTVs. They like to take it slow and point out details and farm history as they drive. Driving tours give them a chance to brag a little without seeming to do so. Phil is no exception, and he is clearly proud of what his family had done on this rough and ancient land. He picks up the story of the Carter & Stevens farm where Sean had left off.

Phil's grandfather Donald Carter started the farm in 1938 and passed it to his son-in-law Dan Stevens, who was Phil's father. When Dan slowed down and Phil took over, he and Erin almost immediately began to diversify the dairy. They realized, even back then, that they would have to modernize the operation and grow its income potential if they hoped to pass the farm to the next generation.

The couple had a haying business on which to build, and they started selling sweet corn in a wagon by the side of the road. It was a self-service operation where customers put money into an honors can. "Then people started stealing the can," Phil tells me with evident disgust. "It's one thing to steal the corn. But when they started taking the can with the money in it, we knew we had to do something." They decided to build a storefront to slow down the theft and to give the farm a more professional retail appearance.

To build that store, they bought land with frontage on the main two-lane road between Barre and Petersham. There they sold not only sweet corn but vegetables, homemade ice cream and other farm-related products. As the kids got older and helped, the store's inventory expanded. Pumpkins. Cornstalks for fall decorations. Raw milk for sale directly to the public. By now—pre-accident—the whole family was involved in farm ventures. Phil's father, Dan, tapped the farm's trees and made maple syrup. Daughter Molly planted acres of vegetables to sell at the store, and she baked bread and pastries. Son Will took over the day-to-day dairying.

To lure city families to take a drive in the country, the Stevenses conjured a small petting zoo with ducks and goats and calves as the star attractions. Will, a genius with a welding torch, built a 10-foot-tall stainless steel smoker with numerous cooking racks stacked vertically inside. And the family started to sell smoked pulled pork and brisket sandwiches in a small patio area outside the store. To attract more passersby, the family commissioned a local artist to create a cow made of chunks of granite Phil had dug from the farm's fields. The 8-foot-long bovine sits by the road and dares travelers to pass without stopping to see what the farm store has to offer.

One autumn, the Stevenses got extra creative. Will built a 15-feet-tall wooden catapult. For a few dollars, customers could buy pumpkins and hurtle them at a target 30 yards away. Pumpkin-chucking they called it.

The plan to diversify was working. But it required everyone's labor. Phil's accident in 2002 blew a huge hole in the multifaceted operation.

As his rehabilitation stretched from weeks into months, the family's prospects for the future faltered. Not all the Stevens kids were onboard with the farm anymore. Without Phil's labor and leadership, the farm was functioning but not thriving. Phil was frustrated to see the family struggle. "At that point, I was pretty much ready to sell out," he tells me as we drive.

So he and Erin brought the kids together for a family meeting that would decide the farm's future. It was one of those ominous meetings where optimism, realism and pessimism all seemed to lurk in the doorway awaiting an outcome. To Phil's surprise—and not-so-secret joy—Will and Molly committed to gamble on the farm. They vowed to keep it going at least one more generation and said they could manage to do so even if Phil's disability continued to hamper him.

Phil tells me all this as we wander a half-mile through pastures, crop fields and woods. We make occasional stops so he can explain why the hayfields look so bad this year and how the family had to make adjustments to their plans almost every season. He points to a cornfield he had to replant in June because untimely downpours washed away young plants. He pulls to a halt to show the residue from the vegetable fields that Molly has planted and harvested despite poor growing conditions.

These all sound like minidisasters to me. But to Phil, they are a validation of how hard the family worked to wrest a living from the land.

LAY OF THE LAND

Central Massachusetts looks nothing like the Midwestern and Western dairy regions I know. It's all hills, dark woods, small ponds and quaint villages. And in November, it smells like smoke drifting out of fireplaces. It's beautiful countryside. But, "This is the armpit of the world for agriculture," Phil tells me as the UTV bounces and jolts on paths and roadways. "The weather is horrible. Our fields are all rock and clay. Stones just destroy equipment whether it's a mower, a harrow or a planter."

That explained why many of the farm machines we pass looked like they'd been in a fight with a quarry truck, and it also explains why Phil and Will are skilled surgeons with welding torches. They get a lot of practice performing metal-replacement procedures on battered equipment. With field conditions so hostile to iron and steel, the Stevenses long ago decided to buy only used equipment, preferably cheap at auctions. "We haven't had a new tractor on this farm since 1938," Phil tells me with a touch of pride. Having seen part of his machinery inventory, I believed him.

We reach the milking parlor, and as Phil pulls the UTV off the road and gets out to open a gate, I notice that he had an unusual gait; he seemed to walk on his tiptoes. I ask if that was the result of the accident, and he looks me in the eye.

"When you break your heels, let me tell you, mister, it is one serious thing," he begins.

The accident had happened while he was working on the roof of a tall barn and lost his balance in what he remembered as a "slow-motion fall." He was wearing a heavy tool belt hung with two power drills and a hammer. The extra weight increased the force of impact when he landed feet-first onto concrete. The fall broke both of his heels and drove bone fragments deep into the marrow. It sent him into nine hours of surgery and a painful recovery. He was incapacitated for months.

Phil spent much of that first summer in a wheelchair and had to learn how to walk again. The pain was so severe he considered a double amputation, thinking artificial legs would be easier to live with than his agonizing real ones. When he could endure the pain, he farmed, but mainly from the seat of a tractor. For a farmer, lack of mobility and an inability to work full out is mental torture. It's also somehow embarrassing, as if he were less a farmer than he had been. Phil lived like that for 12 years.

The trajectory of Phil's life finally began to swing up in 2014, when his daughter Nelly, who worked in the medical field, heard of a new exoskeletal prosthetic device for people with damaged heels. She suggested it to Phil, and he and Erin flew to Gig Harbor, Washington, to be evaluated and fitted at a medical facility called the Hanger Clinic.

"It was almost like a miracle," he tells me with real emotion. Two days after his fitting with a prosthesis known as an ExoSym, he and Erin were able to walk side by side in snowfields around Mount Rainier. "That was the first time my wife and I had walked together in 12 years. It was a big moment for us."

To show me his miracle cure, Phil pulls off his right boot and unstraps a device that wraps around his leg and foot. Its base is carbon fiber molded into the shape of a foot and calf, and embedded in its spine is a steel support rod. At the top of the rod is a strap and brace that wraps around Phil's calf. The contraption takes weight off the heel, which is why Phil walks more on his toes than his heel. But he can walk for miles.

Phil's had his ExoSym customized with the black-and-white spots of a Holstein cow.

"Ain't she a beauty?" he asks as he holds it up for me to photograph.

Back in the UTV, we head to a high pasture above the dairy's building complex, which consists of the milking parlor and two freestall barns. We climb and climb until we are above the bordering trees and find ourselves on a grassy, rounded plateau surrounded by grazing Holsteins.

Phil, Shadow and I exit the UTV so we can enjoy the view. To the east are lines of hills going blue in the late-afternoon haze. On the close horizon, the pasture flows downhill to deep old woods that had sheltered Nipmuc tribes before white pilgrims ventured this way. At the foot of the hill we just climbed is the white, two-story, hip-roofed house grandfather Donald Carter built and Dan Stevens enlarged. It has a widow's walk on the roof like those built on the Massachusetts coast so wives of ship captains can peer out over the sea and watch for their husbands' return. Phil and

Erin live there now, and Molly's daughter, Maple, is in the side yard tending her two pet white ducks.

The cows, curious creatures that they are, gather around us. I ask Phil and Shadow to sit in the grass while I take their photo, and cows gaze over their shoulders in a kind of benign bovine photobomb.

It is quiet on top of the hill as we finish the photos, and I can hear the cows munching as they slowly wander away across the pasture, moving together in the random way herds do. Phil explains that his cows feed mostly on grass and get some silage ration consisting of the farm's corn and brewers' grains. That simple, homegrown feed regime is part of the farm's quest for self-sufficiency.

At the crest of the hill is a new 15-kilowatt wind turbine on a 40-foot tower. It is slowly spinning in a small breeze and makes almost no noise. On the roofs of the dairy buildings below, we can see arrays of solar panels, also recent additions. It is with satisfaction that Phil tells me, "The milking operation is completely energy self-sufficient. If the area's power grid goes out, we can still milk our cows and cool the milk."

Phil and I have not yet talked about the family's brewery. He is more interested in the farm. Besides, the brewery's history is still missing a key piece, which involves another accident.

A few years ago, the Stevens' hay barn on the property near the main road burned to the ground. This was the same bad luck barn from which Phil had fallen. At the time of the fire, it had contained 8,000 bales of hay, for which the farm was not insured—a heavy financial loss. But like so many negatives in this family's history, the fire became a positive.

A neighboring farm just up the road had an 1820's post-and-beam barn that needed either restoration or demolition. The neighbors, whose name was Stone, offered the old barn to Phil if it would help the Stevenses recover from their loss.

Such are neighbors in rural America.

The Stevenses, always open to a challenge and an opportunity, jumped at the offer. It wasn't long before that ancient barn was loaded onto massive supports and carefully moved down the road.

Once they had the barn safely on their land, the Stevenses realized the full value of their neighbors' gift and set to work making it something special again. It is a 60 x 40 structure made from hand-hewn American chestnut trees, which had long since disappeared from the area. Its ridge pole is a full 60 feet of uninterrupted timber, as strong as the day it was cut from a single tree. Probably stronger, because hardwood that has been kept dry gets harder and harder over the years until it is almost impervious to age.

The Stevenses cleaned, replaced braces and patched holes in the structure's siding. In a matter of weeks, the old barn was ready for new hay. But because the Stevens family tends to see beyond the obvious, they never stopped thinking about other possible uses for their new old barn.

Why not somehow make it a part of the retail farm? That patio where they now served smoke brisket sandwiches is too small. Why not move food service into the barn? While we're at it, what about that craft beer we've talked about brewing? We could serve it with those sandwiches. Why don't we use the barn not only as a restaurant but also as a brewery? Why don't we convert that old barn into a brew pub right here on the farm? All of these "what-ifs" eventually became reality.

This is a part of the Stevens' story that Sean DuBois knows well.

At about the same time Phil fell off the roof, daughter Molly fell in love with Sean DuBois. Both were students at the University of Massachusetts at nearby Amherst. She was studying agriculture; he was studying journalism and education. They married in 2005, and she continued to work at the family farm while he taught high school English, history and video production. But he also worked on the farm in the summers and was delighted to discover he enjoyed the life. "I'm the city mouse who married the farmer's daughter," he tells me with a laugh.

Early in his college career, Sean had studied abroad in Dublin, Ireland. He was born into a nondrinking family but soon learned that pubs could be wonderful places. These pubs weren't places to slam down drinks and get rowdy. They were community and family gathering places. Kids came with their parents, and the generations mingled. Pubs were village focal points.

Looking back, Sean realized, "I fell in love with beer culture. I wanted to be part of it."

A few years later and before the reclaimed barn, when Stevens family discussions turned to new enterprises, he had suggested: "If we're serving barbecue sandwiches on the patio, why not offer beer?"

Those discussions didn't go far, in part because, well, where would they brew the beer?

But now they had a big old barn on the property.

Still, the family hesitated at what seemed a far-fetched idea. None of them had ever brewed beer, even for personal consumption. They certainly didn't know how to brew beer commercially or even what equipment that endeavor would require. The idea of beer on the farm was pushed to back of mind.

Then, in about 2012, Phil heard a craft brewery near Boston had closed and was having an auction. The old brewing idea came closer to front of mind. Phil, an auction aficionado and the just-plain-curious sort, decided to go. Just like at farm-equipment auctions, he couldn't pass up a bargain. "Of course," he laughs now, "we ended up buying the whole thing."

It was a much bigger brewing system then they envisioned to complement their barbecue, and the time didn't seem right. So they put the equipment in storage for a couple of years while they mulled over the possibilities. One day in 2014, it just seemed right, and Phil recalls, "We jumped in, hired a brewer and started making beer."

They named the business—and the brand—Stone Cow Brewery after that granite cow that sits at the entrance to the farm. Sean sees some deeper meaning in the name. "To think that we would be brewing beer in a place called Stone Cow Brewery in a barn that had been on the Stone family farm is just so perfect. It was meant to be."

RESTART

New plans were made. Hay came out of the refurbished barn, and the family constructed new walls to divide the space into specific work areas. The ever-industrious Stevenses decided a dairy farm, a farm store, a petting zoo, acres of vegetables and now a brewery weren't enough to keep them occupied. So they built a kitchen in the new/old barn and got into the restaurant business. The brewery filled its first kegs in 2015, and the restaurant began serving a selection of beers with its sandwiches and dinner plates.

Like the dairy, the Stevenses wanted the brewery and restaurant to be energy independent. So the beer tanks and the kitchen stoves now use wood harvested on the farm to generate heat. They use cherry wood for smoking meats. Chickens are locally sourced, hogs come from Vermont and vegetables on the menu come from the farm. In the same pursuit of self-sufficiency, they planted hops to give their beers flavor and aroma.

"We are the only place I can imagine where, in order to brew beer or serve you a sandwich, we first have to cut down a tree," Sean tells me.

At about the same time the brewery began to transform from fantasy to reality, Sean decided to go all in with his in-laws. He traded the teaching job he loved for his dream job: manager at a family brewery.

There is still something of the city mouse in Sean. Over the years, he has observed his in-laws and found that farmers are, indeed, different from city folk—at least the Stevenses are. Of Phil, Will and Molly, he says: "They think on some other level than most people. I have never seen the drive those three have."

As for talent: "Phil is an engineer without the degree. There is nothing he can't do. If he came in tomorrow and said he was going to build a spaceship to the moon, I would 100% believe it."

Will, who manages the dairy and farming portions of the operation, is "one of the smartest guys I have ever met" and can fix anything that breaks. His wife, Shayna, tends bar in the Stone Cow taproom and helps with a variety of other jobs.

Molly? She is the Energizer Bunny, running here, there and everywhere doing dozens of tasks. She is in charge of the store and of food operations. She oversees the restaurant staff, makes ice cream in season and bakes bread for the taproom almost daily. She also tends a vegetable garden of several acres both for sales in the store and to ensure the restaurant is truly farm-to-table.

She and Shayna attended a cheesemaking school in Vermont and came back wanting to add farm-made cheese to the merchandise inventory.

"When are you going to have time to make cheese?" Phil asked his daughter.

"I have plenty of time between 9 at night and 5 in the morning," answered the mother of three home-schooled children aged 5, 8 and 11.

Phil, meanwhile, jokes about his role on the farm: "I just irritate them all. I put out the fires, make sure the toilets are flushing and the machinery is running." In fact, he is a utility player and a jack-of-all-trades.

Why are they—farmers—like this? Sean-of-the-City muses: "It comes down to survival. Every day on a farm there is some kind of crisis, and you have to figure out how to fix it, because there is no one you can call to help."

By the time Phil, Shadow and I start winding our way down the hill, the sun is setting, and Phil has become philosophical. It's not easy to talk philosophy over the chatter of a UTV in rough terrain. But Phil seems to want to tell me why he believed farming was a special way of life.

First was the importance of growing food. "People today don't value food, and they don't value farmers like they should. Farmers should be almost a cartel that rules the world. But instead, there are cartels for oil and other things. You can live without a brewery, you can live without oil, but you can't live without food," he says without a hint of humor.

Turns out, Phil has mixed feelings about the brewery that "saved" the farm. While he appreciates the value the brewery income has for the farm, it galls him somehow that the family must rely on something other than food production to keep the farm running. "I think the most disheartening thing for me is that people will drive long distances for beer, but they won't buy milk while they are here."

On a positive note, he admits he has now been introduced to a culture he had not previously known. "Breweries—kind of like farms—are not in competition with each other. One of the nicest things about getting into the brewery world was to find out how friendly everyone is, kind of like farmers. If you have a breakdown, another farmer will lend you a tractor. Same way with brewers. Everyone works together for the greater good."

I ask him, now that he is both a brewery owner and a farmer, how he introduces himself to strangers. It's a thought that hadn't occurred to him. But he says, "It starts with 'dairy farmer' for sure. And then I say we have a brewery, too."

As we arrive back at the area of the farm that holds the old barn, the store and the petting zoo, Farmer Phil chuckles: "This part is kind of a pretend farm. Everything is beautiful; nothing is broke down. There is no grease, no oil or no manure. So they [visitors] can experience what they think is a farm."

With that, he drops me off to continue my interview with Sean, and he and Shadow spin off in the UTV to do final chores before the sun completely sets.

Sean invites me into the taproom to sample some beer and whatever looks good on the menu. It all looks good. There is beer-brined chicken, grass-fed beef burgers, smoked pork ribs and home-grown veggie sides. I order a "Roll in the Hay IPA" and smoked chicken wings that taste every bit as good as they sound.

Sean joins me, and we finish our talk as I gaze around the bustling room. Its 30-foot-high ceiling soars into the darkness above strings of white lights that hang like candles in a church from 200-year-old beams. A gaggle of young adults with glass mugs in their hands and laughter on their lips cluster around picnic tables. In an area set aside for them, kids play with Hula-Hoops and a beanbag game. Their parents sit at a corner table and converse. A couple of old guys sit at the bar and solve the world's problems.

The scene looks like an American version of the Irish pubs that had so fascinated Sean years ago. He seems pleased.

"The brewery subsidizes the farm now," he tells me with some satisfaction and pride. "I guess you could have the brewery without the dairy, but it wouldn't be the same."

This is a city mouse talking, a city mouse who has come to appreciate and love life on the farm.

We are about to say our goodbyes when Phil suddenly reappears. He wants to tell me a few things that escaped his mind. He wants me to know, for instance, that he understands the economic realities of his family-farm situation. But first, he shushes Sean away so he can't hear what he has to say.

"The dairy farm loses money," he concedes. "If you just went by the numbers, anyone would sell the cows. But the cows are what got us here."

He pauses for a moment and looks around. I have a feeling he is looking beyond the taproom. Maybe he is back at the hip-roofed house in the hills. "It is hard to put a value on what you see off my deck when the cows are on the hill grazing, and the hay is coming on. But we don't ever want that to go away, even if we have to subsidize it. I'd love to have the dairy break even, and I think in time people will value food more than they do now."

The faraway look leaves his eyes, and he turns back to me. "I just wanted you to know that we could have sold the land for house lots and become millionaires. My grandfather could have. My father could have. I could have. But to continue the farm is more important."

The Carter & Stevens Farm's 1,300 acres of land really is worth millions. Given the price of land in Massachusetts, it is probably worth millions in the double digits. But as Phil tells me this, I understand that, in his mind, the family farm has no price tag. How could it?

CHAPTER 5

PICK 'EM UP TRUCKS

A pickup truck is a manly machine, full of muscle and growl. It's power on wheels, and that's exactly the image truck manufacturers paint. Truck designers strive to create an "aggressive" look that tells potential buyers, "This is a workhorse. You'll feel masculine behind the wheel." Television ads for pickups show rough characters with a week's worth of beard growth, work pants and sweaty shirts climbing into their trucks after a hard day's work. They include a woman every so often in the ads, and she usually has to wipe the sweat off her brow at some point to show how hard she works.

A pickup, the image-makers also say, gives the freedom to break the bonds of the road. Go on trails, through deserts, up impossibly high mountains. A pickup gives the strength to haul heavy loads and pull trailers full of cattle. Getting dirty is part of its job.

For farmers and ranchers, a pickup is both a tool and a cultural icon; it is part of an identity. A pickup truck is as much a part of American agriculture as the soil itself.

I didn't recognize much of this iconography until I got my first pickup in 1997.

Suddenly, I felt taller, tougher and as manly as the farmers on whom I called. Now I belonged to a brotherhood of pickup owners. On the highway, I could now give the "pickup wave" to trucks passing in the opposite direction. The wave is the epitome of studly cool. It consists of nonchalantly raising the index finger off the top of the steering wheel and giving a slight nod to the guy going past you.

My truck gave me credibility when I pulled into a farmyard. I was among peers. Farmers and ranchers took me seriously in a way they hadn't when I parked my Oldsmobile Cutlass in front of the farm shop. I was a man in a truck now, not some city guy in a sedan.

My metallic blue GMC Sierra was a leased vehicle, given to me by my new employer, Progressive Farmer magazine. Editor Jack Odle, a Kansas rancher himself, understood the value of presenting a strong first impression to the magazine's story subjects. So he offered his field editors a choice of a leased pickup, a sedan or an SUV. Most of us chose the pickup.

Jack did put a restriction on the pickups: They had to be two-wheel-drive models. Four-wheel-drives, Jack said, invited stupidity. Unschooled farm editors might think they are invincible with four-wheel-drive and get stuck in wet, off-road situations or try to drive through snow they had no business challenging. Some of us resented Jack's edict, because almost all the trucks we saw on farms and ranches were four-wheel-drive models that had enough guts to plow through mud and manure. "Just stay on the road," Jack bluntly advised us two-wheel-drive editors. We knew that if we ever got stuck off-road, Jack would be unsympathetic, and there would be hell to pay.

Still, even a wimpy two-wheel-drive was an immediate conversation starter during farm visits. "You like your GMC?" was one of the first things a farmer would say as we exchanged greetings standing in the gravel drive, our opening handshake completed. One or more of his dogs already was nosing around the truck. A male would lift his leg somewhere around the

3 o'clock area of the hubcap to send urine dribbling down the rubber side-wall. A female might be satisfied with just a sniff.

I learned to fine-tune my truck conversations. If my initial observation of the farmer's trucks parked nearby indicated he also drove a GMC, I'd allow as how mine was a fine truck. If he drove Fords or Rams, I might demur and say about my GMC, "It's OK. Just a truck."

Farmers are notoriously brand loyal. Once a Ford guy, always a Ford guy. Likely, if the farmer drove a Ford, it's a good bet Dad and Granddad did too. Such loyalty made for some good-natured ribbing. Ford guys looked down on those who drove Rams and vice versa. Ford, a Chevy driver once pointed out to me, stood for "Found On Road Dead."

My relationship with a series of trucks I have owned has deepened over the years. A driveway without a pickup no longer seems a possibility. And trucks I have rented or ridden in were partners in stories I will tell until the day I die. Some of my adventures with pickups even changed my life.

FORM AND FUNCTION

Farmers of a certain economic size wear pickup trucks like they wear jeans: different ones for different occasions. There's usually "Ole Blue" or some variant, which long ago was top-of-the-line. But he has long since lost his "new" and has acquired some rust holes. Likely he's a two-door model whose seats have gone ratty and who is missing a tailpipe. His bed is filled with odds and ends—chunks of old wood, rusty rolls of wire, empty plastic chemical jugs. Several aluminum beer cans rattle around back there too, tossed out the driver's side window with the left hand while steering with the right. At least he didn't litter the highways with his beer cans.

Ole Blue is the truck the farmer uses for menial jobs like hauling firewood in the fall. He bumps and jolts across the pasture to the line of trees where the farmer cuts logs with a chainsaw and heaves them into the bed with a thud. What does a little abuse matter? Ole Blue's shocks are almost gone anyhow, and the bed is beat up. He hasn't been licensed since the turn of the 21st century, and most of the time, Ole Blue sits outside behind the shed waiting for the next dirty job.

The farmer has an everyday pickup too. He's not fancy but is in good shape and comfortable. He hasn't been around long enough to earn a name; he's just "the Chivy" or "the truck." The farmer hops into the four-wheel-drive vehicle first thing in the morning, and the two don't part company until late at night. The truck is new enough to be a mobile office: power outlets, Bluetooth for the phone, a wide console on which to set a laptop or tablet while working. The farmer will use him to drive to town for a quick errand or to pick up the kids from football practice if needed. The truck has four doors and plenty of room in the back. The seatbelts even work. But he's starting to accumulate some debris on the floor, and the farmer's winter jacket never seems to leave the back seat, even in the heat of summer.

Then there is the go-to-town truck. He's a new, big guy with nice exterior trim and leather seats. "The diesel," as he's called, has a great stereo system, power everything and room for the whole family. He stays clean, in part because the wife drives him too. He cost more than the farmer's first house. The family will take the diesel to town for dinner or to church. But he is supposed to be a work truck, after all, especially for IRS purposes. So under the hood is a diesel engine with plenty of pulling power. The diesel probably has duallies—two extra sets of wheels in the rear for better hauling capability—and a ball in the bed for hooking up a gooseneck trailer to cart around horses or the kids' show calves.

The family probably has a fourth vehicle—likely an SUV—which is the wife's main means of transportation. That's also the vehicle the family uses for those occasional trips to the city, because parking garages are not made for trucks of any size, especially the diesel. The parking slots are too narrow, the aisles too tight. And if the parking garage is one with those circular ramps, it is hell to be in a truck with wide turning radius. The driver turns the steering wheel all the way to the left and prays the rear will swing out enough to clear the bend. An SUV, however, is marginally easier to maneuver in parking garages, which makes it the date-night, goin'-to-the-city vehicle of choice.

POT SHOTS

Besides being great calling cards, I've valued my trucks as photographic tools. I use them to carry an 8-foot ladder in the bed, which I stand up to give me a high angle on a shot. That ladder and the bed of the truck put me and my camera more than 10 feet in the air. Great for landscapes or just an unusual perspective on a subject.

The pickup also can get me places a car can't. Despite Jack's warning about staying on the road, my pickup and I frequently venture into a pasture or crop field. How else are you going to get cattle pictures or shots of a combine coming up the hill that is 300 yards from the road?

On one memorable occasion, my pickup also served as a bunker against stray bullets.

I was in Garfield County, Oklahoma, doing a photo essay for the magazine's series "Best Places to Live in the Country." There is a lot to like about Garfield County. But if you have ever been there, you know it is flat as your mother's ironing board.

Getting a high angle for a panorama of the countryside is challenging, so I asked a waitress in a café in Enid where I might find a hill. She snorted a little and asked if a highway overpass would do? Maybe, but I had something else in mind, something more scenic. She advised me there might be some hills in the northwest corner of the county. Why didn't I drive up there and take a look?

An hour or so later, I did see some hills in that corner of the county. The light was decent as I drove to the top of a hill, parked and climbed into the bed of the pickup to see what I could see. The gravel road on which I sat wound down the hill then snaked back to the east. At the bend of the curve were a ranch house and some cattle pens. Beyond stretched more flatland, mainly pastures. Not a great shot, but it had the winding road to give it some nice lines and visual interest. It certainly was a better view of the county than I'd seen between there and Enid.

I decided I didn't need to set up my ladder and instead stood on the rim of the pickup bed with one foot on the top of the cab. As I raised the telephoto and framed a shot, I heard a snapping noise above my head followed by a pop. Then another snap and another pop. I've never been in combat, but I'd read that passing bullets bend the air until in cracks. Then the sound of the explosion that propelled the bullet catches up, and you hear a pop.

Crap! Was somebody shooting at me?

I dove into the pickup bed and listened for more. I heard a cluster of cracks and pops in rapid succession and knew that somebody had a semiautomatic rifle aimed in my general direction. I didn't think I was the target. But I wasn't sure. What if I had been standing on the ladder? Would that extra few feet of height have put my head in line with that passing bullet? My stomach started to clench, and my mind raced to figure out what to do next.

Just then, my cell phone rang, and I jolted onto my back to dig it out of my pocket. It was my 16-year-old daughter, Kathleen, calling. "Hi, Daddy, whatcha doing?"

"Punkin', I can't talk now," I said, keeping my voice as calm as possible. "Can I call you back in a little bit?"

The cracks and pops stopped. I crawled out of the bed and over the side, keeping as low a profile as possible. Crouching, I opened the driver's door, climbed in and started the truck, prepared to gun it down the hill if necessary. I rolled a few yards forward past the tall brush at the side of the road, and my view to the east cleared up. I saw another road branching off at the bottom of the hill, and sure enough, a sign pointed the way to a gun range. I'll never know why bullets had left the range and flown low over a county highway, because I didn't turn into that road to ask. Instead, I drove quickly away and back toward Enid.

Garfield County would have to give my camera a high angle somewhere else.

FOREIGNERS' TRUCKS

Turns out pickup trucks are universally popular in rural areas. At least, I've seen them on my reporting trips to foreign countries. Not so much in Europe, where farmers often use small tractors instead of pickups to run errands in town. But pickups are ubiquitous in Central America, for instance. I went there to report on food sustainability issues, i.e. how well were underdeveloped countries prepared to feed themselves? Not that I saw many pickups on farms. The vast majority of Central American farmers I met could not afford even motorbikes and certainly not pickup trucks. But estate owners, agricultural companies and touring Americans could buy or rent pickups.

In Honduras, I traveled with a group of Catholic Relief Services (CRS) personnel. We visited CRS project sites to see how farmers were handling new technologies or new crops. In some cases, we were there to learn the farmers' needs so the NGO (non-governmental organization) could design programs or offer grants to help. We traveled in a caravan of three to four vehicles, most of which were Hilux pickups made by Toyota. These small pickups are among the most popular in the world, especially in developing countries, and I saw them again and again in Central America and Africa. It seemed to me that Toyota only made Hiluxes in white and dust brown, because all the pickups I saw were either dull white or so covered in dirt, it was hard to discern their original color.

On one of these Honduran trips, we headed into the mountains north and west of the capital, Tegucigalpa, to visit coffee farms. The farmers there were moving higher and higher up the mountains as climate change made the lower regions too warm for coffee plants to thrive. The drive through the mountains was thrilling. Our little caravan wound on roads that, from above, would have looked like ribbons dropped onto balled-up, multihued green blankets. They rose and fell on the contours, intertwined with vegetative fabric. I was in the rear pickup, and round one curve after another, I watched the trucks in front of me disappear and reappear. At times, I had to turn my head so far to the rear to follow their paths that they seemed to be behind me.

When we stopped at one village, I noticed that another Hilux, not part of our group, was loaded with people and produce for a trip to a nearby market town. Burlap sacks and townspeople filled the bed—people on bags, bags in people's lap. Chickens in cages joined the retinue. Loose heads of cabbages filled woven baskets. It was quite a haul. Daring young men stood shoulder to shoulder and leaned over the back of the cab to keep their balance. With goodbye waves to those who couldn't fit into the bed, the half dozen people and their merchandise sputtered off down the road, dust whipping in curlicues around the Hilux.

It all looked very primitive to my eyes—and a little dangerous.

A few miles out of town, we passed a horse-drawn cart on that same road. It also was filled with people and their produce. With literal horsepower, it would take them hours to get to their destination. Meanwhile the trusty little Hilux I had just seen would get its passengers and cargo to market much sooner. I realized at that moment that pickup trucks are a sign of great progress. They indicate that antiquated farming is crossing a frontier and entering modern times.

In Kenya on a similar food-sustainability story, I also rode in caravans of SUVs and Hilux pickups containing members of NGOs assessing sustainability farming projects. Some places we visited were drought-stricken, and our caravan felt like a train of camels as we passed through parched landscapes of dust and red earth. But on a few days, blessed downpours fell in torrents. On those days, whatever we had in the bed—usually luggage but sometimes locals who were hitching rides—got soaked.

Once, when trying to climb a hilly slope made slick by new mud, one of the SUVs got stuck up to its hubcaps. All of us in the caravan climbed out of our vehicles and shouted advice as our comrades tried to free the SUV. To no avail. Finally, as I stepped away to capture the scene with my cameras, a Hilux maneuvered into position in front of the SUV. A rope mysteriously appeared from nowhere and was tied to the truck's rear bumper and the SUV's front undercarriage. The Hilux, which is light in the back, fishtailed as it tried to pull. It couldn't gain any traction, and its spinning wheels were the sound of futility. A couple of guys flung themselves into the bed to add ballast, and the driver gunned the pickup again. With more yelling, pulling from the front and pushing from the rear by several hands, the SUV finally was free.

The men who had been pushing the SUV were covered in mud as the rear wheels spun. They laughed at the ridiculousness of their situation as they wiped mud from their eyes, their noses and their mouths. I'd observed it all from a distance through a telephoto lens and remained quite clean.

That night we planned to check into a hotel in the port city Mombasa on the Indian Ocean. For the trip through the bush to the city, most of my companions jammed into an SUV. Rather than squeeze one more sweaty body into the SUV, I opted for the front seat of a two-door Hilux with a young driver named Isaiah, who grew up in a Migumomiri village we had visited that day.

As the sun sets, the group in the SUV is still saying goodbye to the villagers. Isaiah tells me he knows a road that leads into the bush in the general direction of the coast. So we set off ahead of the group, and I settle into comfortable silence as the little pickup wends its way through narrow paths closely walled by trees and vegetation. Isaiah inches the Hilux along through thickets that look impenetrable in the deepening darkness. But gradually, a way clears, and Isaiah picks up speed. I think he's going too fast for the rutted road. But I'm just the passenger and keep my silence.

I sway in the seat as we round curves and bounce over bone-jarring bumps. It's full-on dark now, and several times as we round a bend or top a hill, the truck's headlights suddenly reveal pedestrians, and Isaiah swerves at the last second to avoid them. The pedestrians are going home from jobs or from the market, and they hardly react to their near disasters. But the near misses send my heart racing. Meanwhile, in the light from the instrument panel, I can see that Isaiah has only one hand on the steering wheel and his face is impassive. I try to relax and mimic his nonchalance.

It seems hours, but finally, we break out of the rural roads and come to a busy freeway that leads to the city. The now-familiar rattling of the Hilux's fenders and the groans of its suspension on the rutted roads are overwhelmed by the roar of tires on pavement and the growl of big trucks. Through our open windows, the fecund smell of vegetation gives way to diesel fumes and rubber vaporizing on concrete. We have found the B8, a freeway that follows the coast for hundreds of kilometers. We are just north of Kilifi and have a little more than 70 kilometers to go south into Mombasa.

As we near the city a half hour later, we merge into heavy truck traffic. Suddenly, our Hilux has become a tiny Thomson's Gazelle in a herd of massive stampeding wildebeests. We're nimble; but the number and size of the semis and their trailers feel overpowering. The blare of angry horns scream danger. The highway seems alive with motion, noise and peril, and I feel a growing sense of apprehension. Will we be trampled?

The highway has four lanes and modern streetlights. But because of the volume and velocity of the traffic, the lanes seem incredibly narrow, just wide enough for our small pickup. Speeding semis spill into our lane and seem about to shove us either onto the shoulder or into the concrete barrier that protects us from vehicles in the opposite lane.

I sit rigidly upright. My fingers tighten around the armrest. The scene outside our vehicle is chaos on concrete with cars darting among trucks, semis snaking around each other and our Hilux surrounded by metal and noise.

Isaiah remains unphased. He casually steers the Hilux close to the rear of a semi pulling a flatbed piled high with cargo covered in canvas. He gets nearer and nearer. Way too close for my comfort. I look over at him, and his chin is resting in his left palm; his right hand is draped carelessly at 12 o'clock on the wheel. His half-closed eyelids nearly cover the whites of his eyes in his dark brown face. He looks bored.

Meanwhile, I'm growing more and more frightened by the insanity of the highway. OK, at this point, I'm scared shitless.

To make it worse, Isaiah suddenly decides to pass the semi in front of us and swings into the left lane with only a cursory glance at the sideview mirror. Going 110 kph, the right front bumper barely misses the steel frame of the flatbed, and now we're in the passing lane, hell-bent for somewhere. Isaiah floors it, and we pull even with the flatbed. Its tiedowns flap wildly, and I hear a strap snapping in the wind next to my right ear. I glance over at Isaiah again, and he's looking out his side window, not ahead. As he does so, we drift closer to the semi. We've reached the cab, and the support holding its sideview mirrors seems to lunge at me and misses our sideview mirror by centimeters. As we finally whiz past that semi, another blasts its air horn behind us. I turn in my seat and see the grill of a truck filling the rear window.

Now I'm truly terrified.

Miraculously, we roar into the night unscathed. Racing. Racing. Racing. The gazelle among the wildebeests.

For what seems hours, we continue on this road from hell with annihilation surrounding us in the form of deafening semis and careering flatbeds. I try to calm myself and just endure. It has been a while since I was this near to death.

Two years earlier, I had had a heart attack. It involved "the widow maker," the heart's left anterior descending artery (LAD). At the time, I thought it was merely indigestion. Then the room spun, and I hit the floor. Gretchen called 911. Our dog howled mournfully as paramedics loaded me onto a cart, and we sped through the dark to a hospital 40 minutes away. I remember the controlled bedlam in the emergency room. A whirl of noise and motion. Fluorescent lights streaming overhead as my gurney rolled down a hallway. I remember, too, experiencing a sense of calm curiosity. Where are they taking me? So this is what an operating room looks like. Is this what happens as you die?

Turns out only 70% of my LAD was blocked. So they left it alone and inserted a stent in another artery called the proximal RCA (right coronary artery), which my paperwork describes as 100% blocked and the "culprit lesion."

For years after, I was especially sensitive to anything out of the ordinary in my chest. Small pains became big reasons to worry. I avoided fatty foods and stressed about my cholesterol levels. I carried a vial of nitroglycerine tablets—just in case. And I worried a little about the next heart attack.

But even as I worried, I knew I needed to find a way to cope with my fear, a way to put it into the background.

As I think back on that African night of near misses and impending doom, I remember that something odd happened. In the glare of the headlights and the whoosh of vehicles, I had what I now consider a revelation. I realized I could die at any moment. It could all end right there in Kenya in some primordial scene on a foreign highway where tiny Hiluxes wiggle out of the bush and go rushing side-by-side with steel beasts. It could be over instantly. And there would be absolutely nothing I could do about it.

Somehow the combined senses of helplessness and inevitability brought me calm. I smiled. My heart rate slowed. My breathing grew more regular. I began to sit more easily in the truck seat. Whatever my fate, I'm was peace with it.

I'm thankful I did not die in a dusty Hilux that night. But the immediacy of obliteration that night changed me. Death no longer frightens me as it once did. If it happens, it happens, and I am no more.

Just make it quick.

THE SHOW CIRCUIT

Invitations to new pickup truck introductions are among the great perks of being a machinery editor for a farm publication. You get an email asking you to attend a two-day ride-and-drive event in an intriguing location such as the Arizona desert in the winter or the backcountry hills of Tennessee in the spring.

These events usually begin with an evening reception featuring an open bar and endless hors d'oeuvres. It's your chance to meet other journalists and to renew acquaintances with the automotive company reps. A cocktail party, in other words, with all the initial awkwardness and subsequent boozy conversation of most such gatherings.

I usually was the odd duck when I attended these truck events, the only agricultural journalist in the room. Most of the other journalists were from consumer magazines or trade pubs centered on the automotive or motor sports industries. They chatted endlessly about diesel minutiae and gear ratios. They were on-road and off-road geeks in the same way I was a farm geek. We just inhabited different geekdoms. Fortunately, journalists by nature often are facile socializers, and these things fly by with a few laughs and an expectation that tomorrow will be a fun day.

That day usually begins early with a brief breakfast at the hotel; then a shuttle takes you to a staging area featuring a large tent decorated with muscular new trucks and shiny engines on slowly rotating display stands. Company product experts lay out the goods with well-rehearsed scripts. They do a walk-around and describe why their new pickup trucks are a leap ahead of last year's model and light-years ahead of the competition's.

The main event, which is the ride-and-drive, follows. Outside the tent are rows of sparkling, clean trucks. Each journalist (or maybe a pair of you) picks a truck, signs a liability waiver and you're off.

The company reps have a precise route mapped out through the countryside, and they give you directions in a notebook so you don't get lost. It's usually a scenic route and has a dirt road component, some highway segments and some hills. They want you to experience all the conditions your readers might face.

The idea is to test the truck's mettle. How does it accelerate? Is it comfortable? How does it corner? Does it comfortably tow heavy loads?

Along the route, there are some rest stations to swap vehicles with other journalists so you can drive different truck configurations and maybe grab one with a trailer attached.

Lunch is usually in a wayside tent where you refresh and compare notes with the other scribes. Then more driving. Late in the day, you wind up back at the staging area with buses ready to take you to the hotel. Another cocktail party, which is much more relaxed now that the journalists and the company reps have shared a day. We are pals, comrades in Pickup World. Dinner follows. The next day, you're gone.

The variety of venues for these drives was amazing during my 20 years on the circuit. Once in Nashville, the truck manufacturer rented the home stadium of the NFL Tennessee Titans for the intro. The bus from the hotel drove us journalists onto the field where the test trucks sat waiting for us to drive off the field into downtown traffic and then into the countryside. Lunch that day was at a funky barbecue joint/country store in the hills. Dinner was at a Nashville nightclub complete with live honky-tonk music.

At an event that ended on the Torrey Pines golf course, in La Jolla, California, dinner was served on the fairway of the third hole. As a golfer, I was in heaven. It was the greenest, plushest grass I'd ever seen. The Pacific Ocean was a chip shot away and whispered a siren's song as its waves hit the shore. The hosts timed the event so that the sun set over the ocean as we journalists drank California wines in seemingly bottomless glasses.

It was tough duty.

HIGH-CENTERED, RED-FACED AND BUG-BITTEN

Here's something you don't want to do at a large media event for seasoned automotive journalists from all over the world: high center a dually pickup truck during a test drive—on an off-road trail where you are not supposed to have taken that kind of vehicle.

But that's what I did.

The scene was Chrysler's Chelsea Proving Ground, near Ann Arbor, Michigan. The occasion was the company's international "What's New for 2015" event. The embarrassment was all mine.

Here's how it happened:

Chrysler had dozens of new vehicles available at the event for journalists to test-drive, everything from Ram pickups to Jeeps to Fiat 500s. There also were sports cars: a sleek Alfa Romeo and a couple of evil-looking Viper SRTs. Those were for show and for drooling over only. Car companies know better than to let journalists behind the steering wheels of such high-horsepower dynamos.

The dually in this sad story was a gorgeous deep-blue 3500 Ram Laramie Crew Cab Long Bed 4x4 DRW. It's called a dually because it has two wheels and two tires on each side of the rear axle. It was my first truck of the day.

Initially, I took it through the road course, a long, flat loop with pavement hazards of all sorts, including chatter bars, uneven slabs and manhole covers. Some sections of the course reminded me of the roads around my rural Missouri home, broken blacktop that once was smooth but now dipped and slumped with old age and neglect. I also took the Laramie through the handling course: a couple of miles of S curves—and whatever is curvier than S. Maybe Z?

The truck had taken all of this with ease. It cruised over the bumps with no uncomfortable jolts and glided through curves without swaying. Credit the dually's three-link coil with track bar front suspension and the rear suspension leaf springs with air bags. Very impressive.

On my second trip through the road course, I noticed a sign pointing to an off-road trail. It lured me like the scent of pizza lures a teenager. I had been on this trail a couple of years earlier in a smaller truck and remembered it as tough but navigable. Without much thought, I made a left turn off the road.

The trail was both muddy and rocky. I avoided the manmade, boulder-strewn dry riverbed near the front of the trail. I knew this Ram was rugged, but it had standard ground clearance, and I didn't want to rip out the bottom of a $66,000 vehicle those nice Ram people let me borrow. Instead, I made another left turn and headed down a steep gravel slope. No problem. Once down the hill, I avoided the water crossing. No need to get wet. I made another left turn and drove up a steep hill complete with "steps" of half-buried railroad ties.

That was my big mistake.

The Ram roared up the hill, but once at the top, I realized the trail became seriously narrow. This is not dually territory. The truck was too long, and its turning radius would never allow me to weave among the trees that were closing in on all sides. But I couldn't turn around, and I didn't think it was possible to back down those steps. So, I edged forward looking for a way out. I saw another vehicle off to the left in front of me. It was a Jeep negotiating its way between two trees with its mirrors folded back to give it a skosh more clearance. Once through the trees, it would head down a rocky slope. No way the dually would fit between those trees.

I get out and on foot scout a trail to the right. It's muddy and bumpy but wide enough for the big truck. Eventually, I think, it must lead down the hill.

I turn into it and make progress for only about 10 yards. Then the truck's front end goes up and over a bump and comes down with an ugly thud. I gun the engine and begin to feel sick. The dually's frame rests on a rock. Both the front wheels and the rear wheels are barely touching the slick ground, and I have no traction. The wheels spin but gain no purchase. I try rocking back and forth. Nothing. I am high-centered and going nowhere.

The Jeep I'd seen by now is long gone, and I am alone with swarms of Michigan's hungriest mosquitoes, who have just heard the dinner bell. I swat and curse as I hike out of the woods and to the road. Finally, I flag down a Jeep full of journalists and a Ram staffer approaching the trail. Embarrassment and bug bites make me red-faced as I explain my predicament. Yes, I went into the trail without a guide. Yes, I knew a dually wasn't designed for that kind of off-loading. No, I wasn't crazy, just stupid.

I'll say this for the Ram guys: When I got back to base, they didn't mock me (visibly at least) or laugh. They did allow ruefully that their rival colleagues on the Jeep side of Chrysler would make their lives miserable. The rescue vehicle for the trail was a Jeep with a winch, and the Jeep people would be sure to take video of that small vehicle pulling that big, high-centered Ram out of trouble.

Nick, the chief honcho who rode herd on the Ram contingent of journalists, is a jovial, back-slapping kind of guy. But there was something serious in his eye when he told me—a strong hand squeezing my upper arm, his teeth smiling—"Next time, take a Power Wagon. It's meant for trails like that. A dually is not."

PostScript. I did take a Power Wagon back to the trail—as a passenger and with a guide. No problem until we got to that same narrow place between the two trees. At the bottom of that rocky slope was a Jeep lying on its side, its windshield shattered, its top caved in. The driver for some reason had swerved instead of going straight and had plunged over the edge of the slope. He was OK, as was his guide, both standing in the trail looking bewildered.

I hate to admit this, but looking at the scene, I smiled to myself. It is a recognized facet of human nature that nothing will more quickly heal the scars of embarrassment than someone else's misfortune, especially on the same off-road trail.

CHAPTER 6

APPALACHIA

Washington County lies on ancient folds of the earth near Virginia's southern tip. It's where Tennessee, Kentucky, North Carolina and Virginia share the Great Appalachian Valley. It's where the Blue Ridge, Great Smokies and Cumberland mountains nestle against each other to create a region of inland coves tucked among hills with rounded shoulders.

The bottoms of the coves are lush and sheltered, and on early summer mornings deer graze side by side with cattle in dewy pastures. Farmsteads shelter in the valley necks at the end of gravel roads. Some of the hillsides were farmed for too many generations and played out completely. They have a tired, exhausted look. The look is reinforced by abandoned old wooden barns that rest where they were built a hundred years ago, their formerly red or white painted sides now grey and weathered. The steepest hills are unfarmed and wear crowns of broadleaf and conifer trees.

This is not a prosperous area. Farms are numerous, but small and are mostly run by moonlighters who work them after their day jobs and on weekends. Washington County's 2020 median income was a mere $54,000, and the poverty rate was 13%. The county seat of Abingdon has about 8,000 souls and owes its relative prosperity to government jobs and tourism.

Fortuitously, it sits near the Appalachian Trail and the Virginia Creeper Trail, which attract thousands of out-of-state visitors and their money.

This is southern Appalachia, and Washington County is like so many others in the region: naturally beautiful but poor.

Still, Washington County is a proud area. Some residents wouldn't think of living elsewhere. This is home, and they understand Nature's rhythms here. Local jobs are scarce, and many commute to the nearby Tri-Cities area of Johnson City, Bristol and Kingsport just across the border in Tennessee. It can be a long drive on Interstate 81, but folks judge that it is worth it to live in their home county where housing costs and taxes are low.

Some can't wait to leave Washington County and flee to far-flung metropolises. Others do so reluctantly. They leave behind family histories that stretch back to White settlement days of the 17th and 18th centuries. It's a complicated history that includes the Civil War (or as some here call it, The War of Northern Aggression), which left deep scars. The Union Army burned the town of Abingdon, and starvation stalked the population. Some resentments never die, and today, Confederate battle flags hang defiantly from a few front yard flag poles.

This is a White county. In 2020 Whites made up about 93% of the residents. Before the Civil War, enslaved people comprised 15% of the population, many of whom left as soon as they were freed. Others left over the next century, and by 2020, only about 1.2% of the county was Black. Total population of around 54,000 has not changed much for the last 20 years.

FARM VISIT

It's the summer of 2017 and I'm here to visit Adam Wilson, a young farmer who has faith in the county. Adam is one of those energetic, optimistic farmers I love to meet because they have a vision for a future that is built around hard work and hope. Adam is a community leader, whose special emphases are improving the local cattle industry and reviving agricultural education in schools. He's busy looking to the future and doesn't have time to dwell on the past.

The afternoon I arrive, Adam is waiting in his Gator utility vehicle by the side of the two-lane farm road. He'd described the meeting spot as only farmers do: "Once you make that second S-curve and come down the hill, you'll see an old barn on the west side of the road. Pull into the drive just beyond that. I'll wait for you there."

We shake hands, and he invites me to hop into his Gator so he can check on some of his cows who are calving. It's rough, hilly ground, and from the road, we climb a pasture hill so steep the path needs switchbacks to lessen the slope. When we crest the hill, I see small groups of cows grazing with their heads down and their bodies heavy with calves. A few have already dropped their calves, who are pulling at their mamas' teats. We pause for a moment so I can admire and photograph the view and Adam can count calves. It's quiet on top of the hill, and I can hear a breeze in the grass and the lowing of cows calling their calves.

At the foot of one hill slope is a long-abandoned concrete block silo with a silver and rust metal conical cap. It's evidence someone once grew and stored corn here but gave up when the soils grew too weak to support a crop. Across the way is an old barn that might have been a dairy but now looks like it still serves as storage for hay. In a small draw nearby is a trailer home, which may or may not be inhabited. It's tough to tell if the owners have abandoned it or just don't like to mow the grounds around it. In the distance of another valley is a neat farmstead with a white clapboard house that has a green metal roof and several outbuildings. I find out later that that it is the farmstead where Adam stores equipment and works cattle.

Although there are no snow-covered peaks in the distance, there's an Alpine feel to the pastures, as cows stand on 30-degree slopes eating their way uphill. Off to one side is a structure of big round bales piled in a pyramid shape and covered with a white tarp that looks like the steep roof of a

Swiss chalet. In the late-afternoon light, the scene is charming. I'm happy to be here.

Adam is a good-looking, fit man in his 30s with piercing dark eyes and trim brown sideburns the jut from beneath his farmer cap. He's folded into the Gator now. But when he stands, he's a little taller than I and wears a button-down blue dress shirt, clean jeans and a big brass belt buckle. The smile he sports is comfortable. I fancy he wears it every day as an accoutrement to his relaxed, easy manner. His demeanor indicates he likes people and loves his life.

We hear a cow bellowing on the side of an adjacent hill, and Adam steers the Gator that way. "Sounds like a mama has a new calf," he says.

Indeed, when we spot her, the Black Angus mama is watching a new, wet calf struggle to its feet for the first time. Adam intends to drive over there to take a better look, and I ask him to let me out so I can stay here and photograph from a distance as he inspects the newborn.

I watch him navigate down one hill and up the next, where the mama and calf stand. She is not happy to see the Gator and makes aggressive motions toward it as it gets closer. Adam tries to steer close to her but not too close. The protective mama is having none of it. She lowers her head and charges. I can hear the thud from across the valley as she smacks into the side of the Gator. It shudders, and Adam guns it to get away. He circles the cow-calf pair at a distance as if considering his choices. Then he heads back to pick me up.

Adam has a wry grin on his face. "Some mamas are more protective than others," he says. "That one is really something. I still have to ear-tag her calf. But I think I'll wait until morning when Mama is a little calmer."

We wander the pasture more and talk about the vagaries of bovine personalities. Before long another Gator putters into view. In it are Adam's wife, Sarah, their 10-year-old son, Clint, and 7-year-old daughter, Madalyn. We pull alongside each other and exchange greetings. I'd asked that they meet us here so we could do family portraits in the pasture to catch the early-evening light. Which we do. The kids are friendly, smiley and willing to take directions, which means they are easy subjects. Sarah is an attractive woman with a brunette bob, a trim shape and a ready laugh. She fits well with Adam and is a delight to meet. I soon learn that she's also a cattle farmer with a separate operation of her own. While Adam's specialty is cows and calves, Sarah backgrounds older animals until they are ready to go to a feedlot for finishing. Tomorrow, I'll visit her cattle operation, which she runs with her family 25 miles over the nearest range of hills in Lebanon, Virginia. That's where she and Adam live. He commutes here to care for this herd; she works closer to home with the other herd.

After a delightful hour of photography, it's time for the family to finish its after-school chores and have dinner. And, it's time for me to head to the hotel in Abingdon. So, Adam drives the Gator back to the road where we left my rental car, and we agree to meet at 7 the next morning.

It's been a long day. After a 3 a.m. wake-up this morning, a flight from Kansas City to Knoxville with a layover in Atlanta, where I cadged a hurried breakfast, a two-hour drive through the mountains and about two hours work on the farm, I'm ready for a restaurant dinner, a glass of wine, a goodnight call to Gretchen and a hotel bed. Sleep is easy that night.

When I awake next morning, I'm recharged and eager to get back to the farm to watch Adam work again. I get a pleasant surprise as I check out of the hotel. Fog lies like white lace kitchen curtains on the Virginia hills. Shapes are indistinct beneath the fog, and there's a stillness all around. For most photo shoots, fog is at the bottom of the list of lighting conditions a photographer wants to see. But understanding the terrain I'm in and knowing that I already made some nice sunlit images yesterday, fog could be a welcome element. Besides, it's a morning fog and will be gone by mid-morning. The sun will shine again.

I'm a little early when I drive up to the cluster of outbuildings at the farm where I'm to meet Adam. He hasn't arrived yet. So I wander around a little in the farmyard and climb the hill of a damp pasture, playing with the camera's view of light and fog. The sun is making itself known now and casting eerie shafts of light through the fog. Dewdrops still glisten on grass tips and green is much richer with a moist sheen. These are times I love being a photographer. Beauty awaits anyone who looks, and a person with a camera looks more closely than most.

The peaceful morning turns hectic as soon as Adam arrives. He's in a hurry. But I've already told him to ignore me and go about his business; I just want to watch him work. First up is a trip back to the pasture where cows are calving. Adam expects to find a few new calves who were born overnight, and he's right. In a brushy draw, he finds a black calf still wet and shaky from birth. His mama is there, but fortunately, she backs away as Adam disembarks the Gator and walks cautiously toward the calf. If anything this mama is equally curious about both her baby and the man. She's not aggressive like the cow yesterday. So, Adam is able to wrestle the calf to its feet, check its soundness and insert an ear tag with a number he records in a tablet as soon as he gets back to the Gator. He'll keep track of this calf from the day of birth until it leaves the farm.

We putter through the pasture looking for more calves and making sure those already born have found their mamas and are nursing. Finally, reconnaissance of the cows and calves complete, we head back to the farm- stead where Adam gasses up a tractor that already has a baler attached and is ready to go. In a few minutes, he's headed to a hayfield just down the road where John, Adam's top hand, already is conditioning hay that was cut a couple of days ago and spread evenly over the field. The whirling machine with angled tines John pulls with a tractor is called a tedder, and this is probably its second trip across the field. During a previous trip on a previ- ous day its long tines picked up the hay that had been lying on the ground, fluffed it and laid it in rows to dry further. Now those tines are fluffing the hay once more to make it to easier for the baler to pick up.

Adam makes round after round with the baler, guiding it along the windrows. Pickup fingers feed hay into an interior chamber where a complex series of belts and chains compresses the material into 7-foot round bales that can weigh a 1,000 pounds or more. When the bale is formed, the clanging, dusty machine spins it around inside the chamber, wrapping it with twine. Then the baler lifts a rear hatch and the bale, now dressed in a pale green protective net, rolls into the field, ready for pick up. Back and forth, back and forth the tractor and baler traverse the field making hay bales.

After a couple of hours, Adam pulls to the end of the field. "Lunch time," he says as he climbs down from the tractor cab. "I'm going to take you to the Country Corner. I think you'll get a kick out of it."

Adam, John and I pile into Adam's pickup, which I'd driven from the farmstead to the hayfield behind Adam in the tractor.

"You sure you want to take him there?" John asks.

"Sure. It'll be a new experience for him," Adam says and chuckles.

I've been to lots of places like what I expect Country Corner to be. Most rural communities have something like it, an unofficial gathering place where old-timers and a few young folks—mostly men—congregate daily to gab and drink coffee. Most rural cafes have a few booths with Formica-topped tables and plastic and plywood benches. Some have tables for four that can be drawn together if a bigger group shows up. Waitresses are usually friendly with the regulars but can be suspicious of men who arrive with a camera bag on their shoulder and a notebook in their back pocket. Fortunately, they can be won over with a smile and a generous tip.

Country Corner turns out to be a general store and gas station that looks like it has been there since the roads leading to it were cow paths. I can tell it's had a recent face lift, because its walls and roof are the ubiquitous metal panels that now constitute so much of rural America's commercial architecture. Inside, Country Corner is mostly a convenience store with aisles of essentials such as air fresheners to hang from your vehicle's rearview mirror, canned soups, candies, a display of jersey work gloves, a bank of soft drink dispensers and coffee pots, a wall of refrigerated goods (everything from milk cartons to beer) and snacks of all sorts including four types of beef jerky. A deli counter sits along the left wall. Behind it is a sizzling grill operated by a woman with a greasy apron and a stainless steel burger flipper in her hand.

"We'll order over there," Adam tells me. "The food's really pretty good."

Indeed, the menu board on the wall behind the counter lists several hot sandwiches, a couple of dinner plates and some desserts. I'm intrigued by the patty melt, a staple by which I judge lunch joints when I travel. That's what I order from the friendly woman in the clean apron who waits on customers.

Adam and John place their own orders and guide me to the rear of the shop. I assume we're headed for dining room booths. Instead, what I see is an automotive parts department with hoses and belts hanging from the walls. There's also a bulletin board with posted notices for cattle auctions, firewood for sale and business cards for plumbers, carpenters and electricians.

"Welcome to the dining room," Adam says with a sly laugh as he waves a hand toward eight vinyl and metal chairs that line the area's walls. In front of each chair is a 5-gallon plastic bucket. A few diners are already seated there with Styrofoam shells filled with food atop their buckets. No tables or booths here.

Adam is enjoying the puzzled look on my face as he explains, "The local health department says every restaurant with tables must have two restrooms. One for men and one for women. The people who own this place only have one restroom, and darned if they are going to add another one just to satisfy some government regulation. So, instead of tables, they have these buckets. And everybody's happy."

I get the joke and laugh as I take a seat next to a low refrigerator with a couple of signs plastered on it: "Meal worms sold here." "Nightcrawlers for sale."

The "dining room" soon fills to capacity. There are eight of us, all men who look like they are on lunch breaks from work. They all wear work boots and faded jeans or work boots and bib overalls. All wear branded farmer caps except for the one guy with the red "Make America Great Again" cap cocked crookedly on his head. They eye me with only casual interest and nod. Must be some tourist or a friend of Adam's from the city.

These guys all know each other, and easy banter ensues with heavy doses of gossip thrown in. In the country, men claim to take second place to women in the field of gossip. But they're lying. Today's session starts with one poor farmer's name being dragged through the mud because of the sorry state of his farm equipment. "You know he's loaded. Why the hell doesn't he sell that stuff and get something decent? Why doesn't he at least put it in his machine shed so I don't have to look at that junk every time I drive by?"

"Did you hear about Charlie and his old lady? He might be looking for a new place to live soon."

"Anybody know if Ron sold that bull yet? I might be interested if he comes down in his price a little."

The man in the "MAGA" hat looks at me the way a lab tech might look at white rat before he starts an experiment. "You guys hear the latest 'Fake News' about Trump? They can't lay off him just because he called that Korean 'Rocket Man' at the United Nations. Bunch a bullshit. The best damned president this country ever had. Better'n that Obama for sure." He spat out the word "Obama" like it was something vile.

Just one month earlier, a "Unite the Right" rally brought together alt-right, neo-Confederates, white nationalists, neo-Nazis, Klansmen, and various right-wing militias into Charlottesville, just 250 miles up Interstate

81 from where we were having lunch. They marched through the night like so many "Brownshirts" from 1930s Berlin and chanted: "Jews will not replace us. Jews will not replace us." After the inevitable riot and after one of the White Supremacists drove his car into a crowd and killed a young woman, Trump said, "I think there are good people on both sides," and excused the racists.

I don't take "MAGA" man's bait. I'm working, and now is not the time to get into a political argument. I look at the floor, take another bite of my burger and chew.

Based on the 2016 election results for Washington County, which gave Trump 75% of the vote, most of my fellow diners voted for him. But nobody else in the room seems interested in discussing the merits of Donald Trump. Maybe they are tired of the subject. Maybe they don't have anything new to add. Maybe "MAGA" man is one of those one-note pests people don't want to encourage.

Stymied by silence, he gives up, and the gossipy chatter renews. All in all, a good lunch experience.

"How'd you like it?" Adam asks as we leave.

"That was one of the best patty melts I've ever had," I respond honestly. "And the ambience was…interesting."

We drive back to the hayfield, and the men bale for a couple of more hours. Then Adam and I pull out of the hayfield in his truck and onto the blacktop to retrieve my rental car from the farmstead. The plan is for me to take my rental car to Lebanon, where I'll meet Adam and Sarah, who have some cattle to work there. It should make good photos. Then we'll have dinner at Sarah's parents' farm, where Adam will convene a meeting of son, Clint's, Webelos pack. (Webelos means "We'll be loyal scouts" in the Boy Scout language.) Adam, of course, is the pack leader. Busy guy.

As we drive, he tells me about his dream to establish a cattle auction in this part of the state. He thinks it will bring better prices for locally grown animals. The producers here, he says, need all the help they can get, because many of them lack the knowledge to improve their herds generically or to improve their pastures with rotational-grazing techniques. That's understandable. Almost all the 1,000 Washington countians who raise cattle have other jobs. Their small cow-calf and feeder operations are weekend and spare-time projects meant to supplement incomes. They don't have the time or inclination to study animal science or pasture management.

Adam, by contrast, goes at his business full time and full bore. He's proud of the improvements he has made to his own operation. His cattle have top-of-the-line genetics and his pastures have fencing and water facilities that help him get the most out of marginal land. "This is my passion," he tells me. "I work at it."

He also shares another passion: vo-ag (vocational agriculture) programs. Russell County, where his kids go to school, didn't have a vo-ag program in its school until Adam went on a crusade. "We need to keep our kids educated about agriculture if we are going to have another generation of farmers," he tells me. Even those in the general population who don't farm should understand what farming is all about and how important it is to the nation, he says. It's the nonfarming public that writes the rules, and farmers must constantly make their case for reasonable regulations. That is more likely to happen if "Joe Six Pack" and "Senator City Boy" understand how agriculture works.

Adam easily convinced the county school board of the urgency of his vo-ag mission. But he got some pushback from the Virginia Department of Education. It didn't see agriculture as vital to southern Virginia's economy. Fortunately, Adam has some bulldog in him. He lobbied the county government, the state representative from his district and his state senator. With them onboard, the Department of Education eventually caved. Vo-ag classes appeared in the county's three high schools and proved to be popular. Enrollment in the county's career and technology center doubled as rural kids flocked to career paths that included agriculture.

Adam is proud of that. He thinks it puts the area on a path to a better farming future.

Optimism certainly is needed in besieged Washington County. As we drive through it toward Adam and Sarah's home, he points to a pale green ranch house. "Druggy," he says by way of description. A few minutes farther down the road, he says "druggy" again and nods to a farmhouse with peeling paint and an overgrown yard. "We have a lot of meth in the neighborhood. Not good. Not good at all. I think the guy who lives there makes it and sells it. But some of these places are just drug stores."

We pass another house set a little farther from the road. In its yard hangs a large, faded Confederate battle flag. This time, Adam shakes his head in disgust. "That tells you all you need to know about that idiot."

I've wondered ever since what that flag meant to Adam. He obviously disapproved. Was it because he doesn't believe the "Lost Cause" myth that so many who fly that flag cherish? Was it because he deplores the racism for which that flag stands? Or is the flag just a symbol of the past, and Adam is focused on the future?

Any one of those three explanations is okay by me. All three of them would be great. The fact that he said, "That tells you all you need to know about that idiot," makes me like Adam even more than I already did.

CHAPTER 7

THE BABY LADY

Life got off to a rough start for little Petey. He was born in prison to a mother serving time for armed robbery. His father already was dead, shot in self-defense by Petey's aunt. His older brother was only 10 years old when he was sent to a reformatory for assaulting a police officer. All of this before Petey was out of diapers.

Even so, some would say the 2-year-old got lucky.

Out of the blue, a stranger rescued him when he was a newborn. Frieda Weststeyn, a southern California dairy farmer who calls herself "The Baby Lady," transported Petey from behind prison walls to her home. She cared for him there for the next two and a half years until his birth mother was released from prison.

So lucky.

When I first saw Petey, there was no evidence of his unfortunate beginning. He had a smile that was pure, sweet innocence and a manner that was unencumbered by fear or worry. His pale blue eyes were as happy as you'll ever see in a toddler. Somehow, perhaps because of an extraordinarily high-functioning maternal instinct, Frieda had kept the little boy well and well-adjusted.

And Petey wasn't the only newborn Frieda rescued from prison. When I visited her in 1987, she also was caring for 9-month-old Ryan, whose parents both were in prison for arson, and 1-year-old Amber, whose drug-addled mother was doing time and whose father's whereabouts were a matter of conjecture.

I had learned of Frieda and her work with babies from an article in the Los Angeles Times while I was based in the Philadelphia offices of Farm Journal. Intrigued, I pitched the editors a story about this California farmwife who just didn't think it was fair that the crimes of adults should be visited on their young children's lives. This woman, I told the editors, apparently felt that when babies were born in the nearby California Institute for Women (CIW), it was her duty to give them shelter. The editors agreed the story had potential and decided that it could be part of an occasional series in the magazine called "Let's Be Neighbors Again."

So I made airline reservations, packed my bags and headed for LAX.

In the two years before I met her, Frieda and her husband, Pieter (Pete) Weststeyn, already had opened their home to 12 children of women in prison. They also were in the midst of raising their own eight children, some now grown and with children of their own. As if that wasn't enough children around the Weststeyn household, Frieda also babysat as many as 15 neighborhood kids while their parents worked.

For Frieda, motherhood bordered on obsession—in a good way.

When I drove up to the Weststeyn farm in Corona, I found a small ranch house surrounded by an 850-cow dairy on the outskirts of a megalopolis. The look of the house and the size of the herd told me that the Weststeyns were middle class but probably didn't have a lot of extra money. The farm was neat but dusty, alive with the bellowing of cows, the clang of metal gates and the mechanical buzz of a tractor in the distance hauling grain to feed bunks. It smelled of sour manure and sweet fermenting feed.

It was typical of Southern California dairies, but it seemed an unlikely spot to find batches of foundling babies.

At my knock on the front door, a tall, strong looking woman of 46 with broad, Nordic features that bespoke her Dutch heritage opened the door. Frieda shook my hand with a firm farmer's grip and invited me inside. Her welcoming smile mixed with an expression that said this was a busy woman. The house was spick-and-span but packed to the ceiling with evidence of a lifestyle dominated by children. In one tiny bedroom, I counted three cribs and a single bed. A clothes pole mounted high on one wall held neatly hung jumpers and onesies. Below that were wall-mounted shelves stacked with folded toddler pants and extra sheets. Even farther below was a line of 8 x 10 framed studio portraits of smiling babies. And below that were a couple of clothes dressers and a line of cribs. Every corner of the room was filled, and we had to enter sideways.

I asked Frieda how, with all she did with her own kids and her neighbors' kids, she found room in her life to care for babies whose mothers were in CIW. "I had to," she said simply.

Two years prior, she explained, she had joined a volunteer church group called Match 2, whose mission was to visit women inmates who had little social contact with the outside world. These were women whose families had turned their backs on them, whose husbands and boyfriends had vanished, whose friends had stopped visiting after the first few months of incarceration. Frieda and others in Match 2 would regularly go to the prison to chat with inmates to bring a sense that the outside world still cared.

On one of the Match 2 visits, Frieda noticed that an inmate was pregnant. At first, she was confused, then shocked. "I was so naive," Frieda told me. "I didn't think they would actually put pregnant women in prison."

That was a hard concept for a woman with Frieda's maternal instincts to accept. The thought of babies being born into a cold prison environment was more than she could bear. "Those poor babies had done nothing wrong," she told me, shaking her head in disbelief. "I prayed on it, and God dropped into my head that I had to do something."

Without much thought for the commitment she was making, Frieda hatched a plan. She told a guard: "I will take care of their babies. Tell them [the pregnant inmates] I live just down the road, and I will bring the babies to visit their mothers every week."

Such a simple idea. It was so simple that, in the real world of regulations and standard practices, it seemed impossible. Yet somehow, Frieda's persistence prevailed. After months of letter-writing and negotiations, California's prison authority gave its blessing. And that was how Petey came to live on the Weststeyn farm. He was Frieda's first prison baby. Over the years, a long line followed him down the road to the dairy.

"Most of the women in prison don't like foster homes," Frieda told me, "because they don't see their children as often as they'd like—and sometimes they don't see them at all. But we promised to take them all, black, brown or white. It don't matter to us."

Frieda's daughter Yvonne, whose appearance suggests how a 20-year-old Frieda might have looked, was also on child-rearing duty the day I arrived. She shrugged off the work as not much of a burden: "When you have a family our size, a few more really don't make much of a difference."

Yvonne was one of five Weststeyn children—ages 11 to 22—living at home at the time. As I watched them with the prison babies, it was easy to forget who was family and who was a guest. At one moment, Yvonne was nuzzling Amber's neck; at another, sister Michelle was rocking Ryan to sleep. Meanwhile, father Pete was feeding calves while Petey ran after him, yelling and cavorting as happy toddlers do. The dairyman said to me with a patient expression, "I'm used to it."

Frieda's passion for parenthood couldn't have happened without husband Pete. He was a Dutch immigrant who came to California as a teenager. Like so many other Dutch in California, he was a dairyman who brought his native skills to a new land and adapted them to a dairy environment unlike any he had experienced in the Netherlands. Dairying in his homeland was centered on rainy green pastures and homegrown hay. In California, dairies exist on land once considered desert, and water and hay must be imported. A large dairy in the Netherlands had fewer than 100 cows. One-thousand-cow dairies were more typical in California. But Pete adapted. He knew how to care for cows, and that was the most important thing.

In 1959, he met and married a woman named Frieda Van der Meer, another emigree from the Netherlands. They had their first child in 1960 and kept going. Pete didn't object when Frieda decided to open their home to the children of women in prison. It meant that Frieda would not be able to help on the dairy as much as she always had. But Pete was willing to accommodate to help the kids.

"We wouldn't have those all kids sleeping in our bedroom if it bothered him," Frieda told me. "He loves children as much as I do."

As I took it all in that day, it was clear that Frieda was the driving force behind this chaotic collection of children. She moved through the mayhem with a natural calm and grace, and seemed to know what the kids needed before they asked. She had the right combination of cajoling and scolding to keep them in line. She brooked no nonsense but tempered orders with love. To my eyes, these young children seem almost unbelievably well-behaved.

When I asked how she did it, Frieda looked a little puzzled. Finally, she said unself-consciously, "All you need is love in your heart."

That afternoon, Frieda changed into her prison-visiting outfit, and she, Petey and I went for his weekly trip to visit his mother, Sherry. The prison was, as Frieda said, just down the road from the farm. Surrounded by a high fence and concertina wire, the 120-acre campus lay in flat, brown terrain with purple mountains in the distance. It looked oddly out of place, as if it had been conjured there by some outside force and plopped down on a dusty plain.

CIW held all categories of California's female prisoners, from women in minimum security with no fence around their dormitories to those whose violent crimes warranted armed guards and an observation tower hanging over an exercise yard surrounded by razor wire. Near the main gate squatted a bland visitors center that looked like a 1970s middle school. That's where we were to meet Petey's mom.

We walked through a wide parking lot in a baking afternoon sun, Petey holding Frieda's hand. I trailed behind with my camera bag on my shoulder. As we walked through security, female staff smiled and greeted Frieda and Petey with familiarity. My reception had a more suspicious tone. But the administration had agreed to my visit, and no questions were asked. I had only to show my ID and nod that I would use my camera only in the visiting room and only to photograph Petey and his mom. After they examined every fold of my camera bag, I was allowed to follow Frieda and Petey down a dun-colored hallway.

The visiting room itself was much like a school cafeteria, with metal and plastic tables spaced far apart on a shiny linoleum floor. High windows let in enough light to overpower the fluorescent panels on the ceiling. Inmates and visitors clustered around the tables chatting in low, guarded voices. The room smelled of disinfectant and floor polish.

Petey's mother rose to greet him as he came through the door. She was in her early 30s and dressed for visitors in slacks, a white blouse and a knit sweater vest—no prison uniform today. She had long, curly dark hair, and her full face was lit with joy. Her empty arms spread open wide and begged to hug her precious son.

But Petey held back for a second or two, clinging to Frieda's hand. He finally looked up at her, and she nodded. Petey then walked cautiously to his mother and her welcoming hug. He returned the hug in his own time, and Sherry waved to Frieda and smiled. The two mothers talked briefly from a slight distance about what Petey had been doing since the last visit. Then Frieda and I retreated to a corner of the room to let mother and son become reacquainted.

Sherry had told a reporter from the LA Times, "I live from Thursday to Thursday." Without Frieda, she said, Petey "would probably be in a foster home somewhere. And I probably wouldn't know where he was. And I probably wouldn't see him."

I glanced at Frieda now and saw that she was watching the reunion closely and had in her eyes a mixture of love and regret. In ways she couldn't control, Petey had become hers, but not really.

When the visit ended and we left, the staff and guards gave Frieda and Petey an affectionate goodbye. On the short drive back to the farm, Frieda told me her relationship with the prison administration has been less cordial than it might now appear.

From the beginning, she said, she wanted nothing to do with the state bureaucracy. To avoid interference in how she cared for the kids, she refused to be classified as a foster parent. "I don't want anyone to think I'm doing this for the money," she told me through gritted teeth, "and I don't want state social workers sticking their noses into how I take care of these kids."

Nonetheless, she did accept food for the children through the federally funded Women, Infants and Children program, and Medicaid covered the babies' medical expenses. An occasional anonymous donation also helped, and Frieda did receive about $100 a month from a local church to assist in her work.

Financial expenditures were under control. But emotion expenditures were more problematic. Frieda knew that whenever she opened her heart to a child—something she could not avoid doing—it was a gamble. After all, these were children of criminals, women fully capable of making extremely bad decisions. So Frieda worried about "her" babies' futures. "We try to give them as good a start in life as we can," she told me near the end of my visit. "But I know that some of them will have a rough time of it when they go back to their mothers. I worry about them after they are gone, and I pray for them."

She recalled Stephen, a baby she had for eight months who was reunited with his mother when she was released. Four months later, the mother broke parole and wound up back in prison. Stephen was again motherless and probably scarred by having his life once more thrown into turmoil. It hurt Frieda to recount that lost baby's plight.

Just as painful were memories of babies she returned to mothers who were released then moved away and never contacted Frieda again. It was as if those babies had vanished into a dark expanse, a place she could never visit. Frieda was a little bitter about that. "After all we did for them, you'd think the mothers …." She caught herself before she let her grief and anger go any further.

As I listened, I imagined that it would be especially hard for Frieda when Petey left. He had been her first, and the bond between them was obvious and strong. What if he vanished too?

The same thought must have occurred to her. As we arrived back home, and Frieda unbuckled Petey's seatbelt, she cupped his chin in her hand. "You wiggled your way into our hearts, didn't you, Petey?"

Over the years, Frieda had to eventually say goodbye to a lot of Peteys, more than 120 of them by one account. And the Weststeyns still maintained room in their heart for their own 37 grandchildren and 14 great-grandchildren. When dairyman Pete died in 2017, his obituary read in part: "Pete loved and accepted all the children who came through his home. He taught them about Jesus, and he treated them as family."

Soon after I got back to Philadelphia, I sent Frieda some of my photos of her and the babies that inhabited her world. She sent me a card in return: "Thank you so much for the real good pictures. Everyone at CIW saw them. Thanks again for coming. It was nice to meet you. Sincerely, Frieda, 'The Baby Lady.' "

CHAPTER 8

BLACK GOLD RUSH

I wanted to see up close the Black Gold Rush. From a distance, North Dakota in the 2010s looked like a modern version of California in 1849, when thousands stampeded to a frontier region in search of yellow gold and quick riches. Of course, the fortune hunters in 21st-century North Dakota were not going to stake gold claims; multinational corporations already had a lock on the real riches in the form of shale oil deposits. This wave of adventurers was hunting for high-paying jobs, quick cash and a new life.

In my imagination, they had much in common with the forty-niners: young men and women who left behind meager jobs or no jobs at all and rushed north in hopes of striking it rich. Some brought their spouses and children. Some left them behind. Some had no one to leave. They all were drawn by the promise of big bank accounts and a bright future.

It was mainly oil field roughnecks I imagined in North Dakota's oil fields. But I soon discovered that roughnecks were just one part of a mosaic of fortune hunters in the Bakken Basin. All sorts of folks sprinted to North Dakota. Truck drivers, accountants, waitresses, barbers, gas station attendants, strippers, prostitutes, bartenders, nurses, lawyers, heavy-equipment operators, linemen and more. They might not work in the oil fields, but they did create—almost from scratch—an oil industry and a boomtown society.

Some of this assortment of roughnecks and other folks made good money north of Interstate 94. But as always, the real money was reserved for men and women in executive offices who wore fine suits and dress shoes, not greasy jeans and muddy boots. And if oil company execs made good money, investors and owners made millions and billions.

It didn't take much to convince The Progressive Farmer editor Gregg Hillyer that the Black Gold Rush would affect our readers, especially farmers and ranchers in North Dakota. The story I proposed to Gregg also had implications for farmers in other areas, including Ohio and Pennsylvania, where new drilling technology produced new oil fields and a collision of cultures. I sensed that new oil production in rural areas would be laden with contradictions. Some would love it for the wealth it created. Others would hate it for the peace it destroyed and the environment it violated. Some would welcome the oil boom because it gave them an opportunity to change their lives. Others would abhor it because it did, indeed, change their lives forever—and not just in ways they welcomed.

Once I got permission from Gregg to pursue the story, I did background research and then began the 900-mile drive from home to Stanley, North Dakota, in July of 2013. I expected to see a new Wild West where old and new lifestyles rear-ended each other, where transplants rushed to find quick fortunes, and farmers and ranchers labored patiently as they had for generations.

I'd been to North Dakota several times on reporting and photography trips. But I had never been to the northwest corner of the state, the area known as the Bakken Basin or, simply, the Bakken. Heading almost due north through northwest Missouri, western Iowa, and eastern South Dakota, I was in familiar territory. I recognized the names of farming communities hugging the flanks of I-29 and as I crossed I-90 still headed north. The farther north I went, the greater the distance between exits and the fewer towns and farmhouses I saw. A full 400 miles from home, I pulled into Watertown, South Dakota, for dinner and a motel.

Next morning early, I am back in the pickup and passing a few miles east of the Cheyenne River Reservation and then the Standing Rock Sioux reservation, which sits nearby. Farm villages are even scarcer here, and in all directions are broad wheat fields and soybean fields. At Summit, South Dakota, I leave the interstate and start angling northwest on two lanes finally finding the North Dakota state line near Ellendale. Six hundred miles into the trip, I cross I-94 at Jamestown and angle northwest toward Minot. As I go farther west, I notice the landscape subtly change. Hardy canola replaces soybeans, and canola flowers decorate the hillsides in a yellow carpet. Scattered clusters of Black Angus and white-faced Baldies graze treeless hills once home to an ocean of bison. American coots, blue-winged teals and canvasbacks cruise lazily on the waters of prairie potholes left by receding glaciers in another epoch. A great blue heron floats on the surface then flaps its Jurassic wings and breaks into flight with sparkling water dripping from its feet.

Minot is still 50 miles from my goal of Stanley. But I know it is as close as I'll come to the Bakken oil fields and still find an open motel room, because oil field workers had filled them all in the Bakken. So I stay in a Minot Holiday Inn, planning the next day to drive to Stanley and see my first fracking operations.

OIL BONANZA

Until recently, some had written off North Dakota as a place of empty spaces and few people. One academic school of thought said you might as well convert it and the rest of the High Plains into a huge national wildlife reserve and call it Buffalo Commons. But you didn't hear that in the early 2010s. North Dakota, especially the northwest quadrant, was suddenly booming, filling with new people and new construction. Oil pumps were sprouting on the landscape like toadstools after a spring rain. Everywhere

I look in the Bakken are derricks for drilling, tanks for storing and trucks for hauling black gold.

Road crews are laying new pavement and repairing potholes. Housing for the immigrants is materializing like magic. Within city limits, housing means new frame homes, some large and opulent, most small and frugal. It also means apartment complexes being built lickety-split on any vacant lot and on the edge of town. In the raw and windy countryside, housing is called "man camps," quick and dirty construction with no frills. Plop down some Quonset huts. Convert old barns into condos. Pull in a bunch of travel trailers and connect them to makeshift power lines and lagoon waste systems. Take two shipping containers, cut doors and windows in them, stack them on top of each other and, voilà, you have a duplex. Bring in more shipping containers, and before you know it, you have a man camp.

As I drive toward Stanley, I see man camps of all descriptions and sizes. "Not for me" I think but understand that for the men and women who occupy them, they are essential. They are also temporary, places to abandon when the boomers have saved enough to afford something more permanent—or the last stops before moving back home either flush with cash or flat broke.

FREQUENT BOOMS

This corner of North Dakota is known as the Bakken because oil was discovered in the 1950s on land owned by a farmer named Henry Bakken. That triggered a miniboom, but one that was short-lived. Another more substantial boom struck in the 1980s, when spiking oil prices and tax incentives made the Bakken attractive again. But the second boom also petered out when oil prices dropped. The current boom is the product of high oil prices, political rhetoric about "energy independence" and technology. How long it will last is anyone's guess, because a "boom" usually comes back as an echo—that sounds like "bust."

The twin technologies behind this boom are hydraulic fracturing (fracking) and horizontal drilling.

In the Bakken, the middle layer of three strata of rock is the target. It is a porous shale layer of dolomitic sandstone and siltstone that has trapped within it valuable low-sulfur oil. But the oil doesn't lie here in easily accessible pools; it must be forced from the shale before it can be pumped. That is where fracking comes in.

Millions of gallons of pressurized water, sand and various chemicals are pumped into the shale layer. The intense pressure they create fractures thin channels in the strata through which oil can flow. The sand's role is to prop those channels open so the oil can be extracted.

You could drill straight through the upper layer of rock into the middle layer, which is only 30 to 70 feet thick and rests on bedrock. Placing a pipe in that middle layer would be like poking a soda straw into a shallow bowl. You'd get a brief pull but not much oil. That's where horizontal drilling comes into use. In fracking, the drilling process starts vertically and can travel up to two miles deep. That takes pipe through the upper layer of rock into the middle layer of shale. There, the pipe is made to do a miraculous 90-degree turn, which can extend up to three miles. The horizontal pipe is thus in contact with the shale layer for a much greater distance than if it were poked vertically down into it. It can suck a lot of oil.

When I arrived in the Bakken, dozens of drilling companies—large and small—had set up shop to drill thousands of wells. At the end of 2011, North Dakota had 6,202 oil-producing wells. The oil fields exploded after that. In 2013, the state issued permits for 42 more wells per week. Some say growth is slowing, but you'd never know it by the number of trucks on the road.

Estimates of the amount of oil stockpiles in the Bakken vary greatly. Deposits of up to 50 billion barrels are possible, with perhaps 30 billion being recoverable by current technologies. Some say fracking wells could be pumping in the Bakken for the next 30 to 40 years.

Lynn Helms, director of the North Dakota Department of Mineral Resources, was more optimistic. He told The Atlantic magazine: "Your grandchildren's grandchildren will be working in the Bakken."

There are ecological downsides to fracking in the Bakken, of course. Use of chemicals in the fracking process has many residents worried about aquifer contamination. Others are concerned that fracking of substrata rock can lead to earthquakes. Oklahoma has had plenty of them because of fracking. But by 2013, none of these concerns has stopped or even slowed the boom in North Dakota.

MONEY BY THE BARRELFUL

"There is a lot of money in the country, and a lot of people are getting wealthy off of it," Powers Lake rancher Doug Feiring told me after we shook hands outside his ranch house. "I've seen a lot of oil booms and busts. But never anything like this."

Doug is 50, wears a dusty cowboy hat that once was white and has on a blue, long-sleeved denim shirt with pearl stud buttons. His two breast pockets are jammed full of notebooks and pens he uses to write himself reminders. He wears grimy jeans held up by a belt with a big brass buckle. He's a quiet-spoken man with wire-rimmed glasses and a trimmed mustache that is going grey. Doug is friendly but perhaps wary of talking to a journalist.

Tentatively, he admits to me that he has oil wells on his land and receives royalties from oil leases. He admits he has a vested interest in the boom. But Doug also has reservations about it. Tanker and construction trucks beat up the rural roads around him and his ranch. "Roads weren't great before the boom but now … " he shrugs and shakes his head. "I used to be able to trail cows for three miles and be lucky to see one car come down the road. Now it's a hundred-some cars in one mile."

The influx of money and people has changed the landscape. Temporary housing facilities appear in the most unlikely places, and shipping container condos have ruined the pastoral scenery he has loved all his life. Man camps were built for oil field workers after they had occupied every existing domicile in the area. If you can find housing, Doug tells me, prepare to be gouged. It costs $850 a month to park an RV, and a one-bedroom place will set you back more than $1,500. Prices like that pushed locals out of what little low-cost housing had been available. "Only old folks and unwed mothers can get into subsidized housing now," he tells me.

And if you are a farmer or rancher like Doug, the oil boom has pushed wages way up, making it difficult or impossible to hire and keep good employees. "It costs $50,000 a year to keep a good employee up here. I can't pay that and stay in business," he says.

Law-breaking is an unwelcome newcomer to the area. FBI statistics indicate aggravated assault reports rose 55% during 2011 in boomtown Stanley. Doug tells me: "Crime and violence in this area is unreal compared to what it was before. Now we have murders. We have people who go missing. It's just unreal. People don't feel safe anymore."

He's especially worried about oil leaks and chemical contamination that could pollute the groundwater. Pipes used in fracking are supposed to be encased in concrete to prevent leaks. But that works only if the concrete is properly installed. "It's OK if you're pouring concrete on a nice summer day," Doug says. "But in the winter when it's 20 below zero, and the wind is blowing, guys aren't going to be as careful as they should. All they want to do is get the job done and get inside. It's human nature."

This oil boom, Doug tells me frowning, is "changing things and changing them dang fast. Everybody used to laugh at western North

Dakota being 'Hicksville.' You know, Buffalo Commons. We kind of liked it that way. But we have been turned upside down, to put it bluntly."

Doug and I wander his ranch in his pickup. It's not one of the new, fully accessorized ones that have become popular in the Bakken. Instead, it's like a cowboy's trusty horse—nothing fancy but it will get you where you are going. It takes us out of the sheltered draw where his house sits amidst trees and into rough pastureland where trees can't stand up to the cold winds that blow unabated from Canada. He shows me a pod of three pumpjacks in one of his pastures. Their painted yellow heads rise and fall like slow-motion cartoon birds pecking at seeds on the soil. With each rise and fall, they pull oil from the ground and push it into storage tanks that could be a mile away. The pumpjacks make a mechanical squeaking noise that seems out of place in a land where the wind is usually the only sound.

We get out of the truck and walk toward the pumpjacks so I can take pictures. Doug sits on a rock and gazes into the distance. His expression is glum. He looks for all the world as if he's contemplating how his life has changed. And he's not happy about it.

PROSPERITY'S FACE

Fred Evans is a happy man—and he should be. He lives in a stunningly beautiful valley formed millennia ago, when cascading water from melting glaciers created coulees that now form a large bowl with rolling hills at its fluted edges. Fred and his wife, Joyce, moved to the Little Knife River valley, just south of Stanley, in 1960 with not much to their names. They have since acquired several thousand acres of ranchland and turned cattle and other business ventures into affluence. TTT Ranch has given them a comfortable living. About 10 years ago, the oil boom began making their lives even more comfortable.

Fred and Joyce's frame ranch house is handsome and well put together. It looks to be just what it is: home to a prosperous family. Fred greets me at the door with a large smile and a ruddy, open face, and ushers me through the living room into an open-concept dining room and kitchen area. Large windows open onto a view of the valley. Joyce is behind a kitchen counter and greets me with the same enthusiasm and warmth as Fred.

The couple are in their late 60s or early 70s, and seem fit and active. We chat for a while about their family and trips they have taken to places far from the Bakken. Joyce offers me some iced tea, and the conversation flows easily. I like the fact that they are curious about me and my travels. I judge people by their interest in strangers like me. And I judge the Evans couple to be fine folks.

At last, Fred and I get down to business. Mostly he is satisfied with the way the oil boom has treated him and the community. Sure, there are some negatives. But the positives far outweigh those, at least for him and Joyce.

"Want to look around?" he asks after a while, pointing to the camera bag I left strategically on the dining room floor.

"Let's do it," I say.

He puts on a crisp white cowboy hat that sports a stitched band where crown meets brim, and we head outside.

Fred's brand-new pickup is a shiny midnight blue that is inexplicably free of dust. The interior is tan leather with chrome fittings and has that new-vehicle smell that doesn't last long. We ease out of the drive and onto a gravel road that leads into the heart of Fred's ranch.

Several oil wells—which Fred has named for his children and grandchildren—now dot the beautiful valley. "Savannah TTT" is here; "Ramona TTT" is there; and in the background is "Joy" (no TTT for some reason). The pumps' presence on the landscape does not bother Fred at all. In fact, while cruising in his new pickup, Fred has nothing but praise for the way the oil companies have treated him and the land. He points to where pipelines lie buried below the surface. Wheat grows lush over them. Proof, Fred tells me, that the pipeline company did a good job laying the pipes and restoring the land above them.

Inside and outside his valley, "the roads are the best they have ever been," Fred says.

That's not what I have heard, but I don't disagree.

"I think it's funny," Fred continues. "All these people who drive new pickups bought with oil money and yet complain about dust on the roads."

Indeed, a lot of new pickups sail through the Bakken. The oil boom has created millionaires, 2,000 a year by one estimate. People are reluctant to talk about newfound wealth, but a 2012 report cited by Reuters indicates that many Bakken landowners with mineral rights reap royalties of $50,000 to $100,000 a month. The annual average income of citizens in Mountrail County, which sits at the epicenter of oil activity, doubled in five years as of 2010 and has risen more since. It now ranks in the top 100 counties in the U.S. for average income. I suspect Fred and Joyce earn a lot more than most.

As our tour comes to an end, Fred drops me at my pickup, which looks shabby and unkempt next to his.

"If you're ever up this way again, be sure to stop and visit," Fred says with an affable smile and a wave.

MONEY DOES NOT EQUAL HAPPINESS

Greg Tank is an oil patch millionaire. Not only does he make money from mineral leases, he also has used the legal system to harvest money from oil companies. Almost as soon as I arrive on his ranch, near Keene, Greg tells me that years ago he won a multimillion-dollar lawsuit settlement against an oil company that had done him wrong by slow payment, lack of payment and environmental destruction to his property.

Greg and his family have had raw relations with oil companies since the boom of the 1950s. "The companies deceived us" about mineral rights and leases, he tells me. In the 1980s, the second oil boom brought more confrontation for the Tanks, and Greg pursued more legal action against rogue oil companies. This latest boom might be even worse for the environmental havoc it has wreaked.

"Unfortunately, I live right in the middle of this crazy thing," Greg says.

His home doesn't look like a millionaire's abode. It's modest but homey. Like so many ranch homes I've seen in North Dakota, it's tucked into a draw to protect it from winter winds, and it is far from the nearest neighbor. It has a few outbuildings around it, a horse corral next to a barn and a busy gravel road in front of it. A few hundred yards away, a highway roars with trucks coming and going from oil-drilling sites. In other times, the gravel road and the highway would have been rarely traveled. But now, "this crazy thing" has them alive with traffic.

Greg's attitude toward the latest boom is the polar opposite of Fred Evans'. Anger and frustration are key emotions for him. But not helplessness. When he invites me inside his house, I see that his desk and office area are buried beneath file folders and papers related to his lawsuits—past, present and future.

Included in Greg's complaints is a well site that was abandoned on his property five years ago and has not yet been reclaimed. "They just walked away from it," he tells me, still fuming about the affront. He also rails against pollution he says taints his water well. He now triple-filters water from his kitchen faucet before drinking it.

Despite his loathing of oil companies, Greg has figured a new way to profit from the boom. Money earned from leases and lawsuits is one thing. He also is part owner of a company that recycles fracking wastewater by removing salt and chemicals with centrifuges. The company sells the water back to the drilling companies for reuse. Tank's business card features both cattle and an oil pump.

"Come on. I want to show you something," he says.

We climb into his small pickup and wait a few moments for traffic to clear on the gravel. Then we wait for more traffic to clear on the highway. A mile down the road, we turn into a rough field road. What Greg wants to show me is a moonscape. This is the land that an oil company walked away from five years ago. What once was pasture ground is now covered in clay so sterile that even weeds eschew it. Widening furrows show where rainwater has eroded the clay and runs into a small basin that has become swampy. Along the treeless horizon, I see piles of red rock that drilling crews left behind like heaps of garbage after a party. In the distance, two or three pumpjacks work incessantly in the remnants of what once was a busy field.

"This is what they left," Greg tells me with his arms crossed as he sternly surveys the view.

SCENES FROM THE OIL FIELDS

Early one morning, I set out to explore the landscape on my own. I want to capture with my cameras what western North Dakota looks like now that the latest oil boom has found it. It is—or used to be—a lovely land: infinite rolling hills under a vast sky. On sunny days, the water in prairie potholes gleams blue under that sky. When clouds roll in, the waters turn gray but twinkle when winds disturb the surface. Pastures and farm fields flow in all directions and lap around farmsteads planted well apart from neighbors. Small islands of hardy trees shelter homes and lounge in low, wet areas. Though beautiful in the summer, in the winter, this land is not for the faint of heart. Snow blows like a demon's breath across these same fields. Sun dogs hunt in winter skies, and frigid nights linger for 17 hours. The natives love it, summer and winter. The fact that they survive proves their strength and endurance. The fact that they can prosper proves their ingenuity and their deep understanding of the land.

Today, it is a scarred land. Deep trenches have been cut into the side slopes of hills. Some trenches already have been filled with pipes and covered with unnatural-looking gravel—they look like wounds that have yet to heal. Other trenches are still open, and beside them lay large steel pipes with gaping mouths that will be welded together and rolled into the holes in the earth. Cows graze near the pipes but keep their distance. The pipes create a barrier to their wanderings.

Down one gravel road is a new drilling site. Workers' trucks are parked near the road, and I see the men a few hundred yards away operating heavy equipment and trucks carrying more pipes. The entire area along the road is fenced, so I pull to the side and climb into the truck bed to take photos from a higher angle. There's not much to see. But I take a few frames and consider the scene that includes alien steel frameworks against a backdrop of unspoiled pastureland. I'm about to climb down when a company truck speeds past on the gravel and comes to a dusty stop nearby. A young man in a hard hat and safety vest exits and walks quickly toward me.

"What the hell do you think you are doing?" he yells at me as he comes abreast of my truck.

"I'm taking pictures."

"You can't do that. You didn't ask permission."

I've seen this act before. Some yahoo takes offense at my taking pictures and wants to bully me into stopping.

"This is a public road," I reply.

"Yeah. But that's private property over there, and you didn't ask permission."

He's getting angry now. He probably thought I'd wilt under his first verbal barrage.

"Doesn't matter. I can see it from a public road. I can take photos. That's the law."

"The hell it is! How'd you like me to take that camera and shove it up your ass?"

He's taking it to another level now. But as I said, I've seen this act before.

"Why don't you calm down and go talk to your supervisor before you do something rash," I say as evenly as I can manage.

He stares at me, and I can tell he's pondering his next move. Does he really want to get his supervisor involved? Or should he let it drop?

He's a young guy. Probably had a fight with his wife or girlfriend this morning, and is mad at the world. I happened to cross his path. Even so, I doubt he'll do anything stupid. In any case, I have finished what I wanted to do here. So I turn away from him, take a few more quick frames to prove I can be prick too and say to him, "All done. I'll leave now."

The guy kind of snorts and stomps back to his truck, work boots kicking up dust like a little boy who has just avoided a fight.

I'll admit my adrenaline is flowing as I get behind the steering wheel. My hand shakes a little as I turn the key in the ignition. I take a deep breath and put the truck in gear. While I drive, I wonder about the young man's state of mind. Was his anger, as I suspected, because of domestic troubles? Or was he, like so many young men in the Bakken, unattached, lonely and always on edge? Too much testosterone bottled up and doing nothing? I'd heard about rampant violence in the man camps and saloons. Maybe violence is always just below the surface in oil boomtowns. Maybe I'd been tempting fate back there.

I keep driving, mulling the possibilities.

After a while, I notice flames shooting out of a tower in the distance. It's a natural gas flare at a well. Flares are common practice wherever oil is produced. Natural gas that accompanies oil deposits is set alight because it sometimes is more economical to burn the gas rather than capture and ship it. The Bakken oil fields are still so new that natural gas pipelines do not exist, and the drillers have little choice but to burn the gas as it comes out of the ground. It's a horrible sight when carbon dioxide is ruining our atmosphere and climate. But that's the dirty nature of the oil industry.

Down another road I see flames boiling out of the ground near some storage tanks. I pull over to investigate and look around to see if there are any oilmen to ask about the fire. Seeing none, I can only guess this is either an accidental fire or an alternative way of flaring natural gas. In either case, it is frightening. I hesitate then decide to trespass to get closer. As I approach on foot with my cameras, I see the fire is contained in a man-made bowl of earth. This is something planned, not an accident. I find that somehow reassuring.

The heat licks at my face, and I shield it with my arm as I get nearer. Hotter and hotter. The heat is now so strong, it warps the light coming through the flames so the storage tanks beyond seem to bend and twist. Amid the snapping of the flames, I hear a hissing sound and think, "Explosion?" I start to back away but stop when I hear no blast. I move forward again because I'd like to capture an image of flames erupting as if from hell onto the desecrated North Dakota prairie. Finally, the heat is too much. I retreat, having taken only a few mediocre frames and none that show the hellish vision I'd hoped to capture.

I stumble back to the truck and drive away.

In time, I find the main highway and an enormous truck stop. Tankers, dump trucks and semis with flatbeds loaded with pipe also have found the truck stop. They funnel in and out like bees at a hive. There must be 50 diesel and gasoline pumps here. Trucks that already have filled up move to one side; trucks that await their turn stand idling in long lines on a concrete pad as big as an airport tarmac. Drivers stand beside their rigs socializing with other drivers. Some of these guys are long-haulers who don't often have face-to-face conversations. They trade war stories about the road. Some are short-haulers who work the area regularly and know each other on sight. They talk about families and shared friends.

My pickup seems like a toy compared to most of these trucks, and I park it near other small trucks and go inside to find a booth in the diner. This complex is much more than a filling station or convenience store. From its expansive entrance doors, I see aisles and aisles of goods for sale— everything from snack food to truck parts. I see two-way radios, books on CDs, windshield scrapers, bibles, Bluetooth earphones, washer fluid, jugs of antifreeze, work gloves, sunglasses, ball caps, soft drinks, winter coats, boots, replacement antennas, comic books and greeting cards.

Over the intercom comes a computer voice: "Driver No. 52, your shower is ready." A room to one side has a sign over the door: "Professional drivers only." It is filled with lounge chairs and couches. Another room is crammed with video games. A kiosk selling coffee drinks stands alone, and a young woman in a low-cut top wipes the counter, her swinging breasts entertaining customers. On one wing of the complex is a McDonald's. On the other is a Subway sandwich shop. In between is a diner.

I prefer the diner and seat myself, just as the welcome sign commands. A middle-aged woman in a burnt orange uniform and white apron lays a laminated menu in front of me and asks, "Coffee, Hon?"

I love busy truck stops. The sights and sounds are like the midway at a small-town carnival. Imagine a trucker stereotype, and he'll walk by in a minute, his wrinkled clothes and unshaven face evidence he's still waiting to be called for the shower. Want to see a family tableau? Watch for a bit, and you'll see a grumpy couple of married travelers rehash an argument that began decades ago. Want greasy comfort food? Close your eyes and point to the menu. Order whatever your fingertip touches.

But this truck stop near Williston is singular. It combines all the usual truck stop culture with a huge diversity of customers come to fill up with food and fuel in an energized oil boom area. There are locals standing at the checkout counter next to truckers from the Twin Cities. Indigenous folks from the Fort Peck Reservation drink coffee at the counter next to Guatemalans who made the long, long journey looking for North

American wages. Ranchers and roughnecks. Farmers and field supervisors. Lot lizards and itinerant evangelists. The truck stop's clientele is as varied and interesting as its merchandise. I watch, intrigued, from my perch in the diner as dozens of small worlds come together then spin apart again headed into different universes.

TRAFFIC

Among the crazier aspects of the Bakken boom is the traffic it has spawned. Greg Tank told me he has counted as many as 3,300 trucks in one day rumbling past his house on the small gravel road. And the two-lane Highway 23 at the top of the hill near his ranch is alive day and night with the constant whining of tires, squawking of air brakes and belching of exhaust pipes.

Traffic accidents are frequent. The oil counties of North Dakota now lead the state in traffic fatalities. "It's not a matter of if you are going to be involved in an accident, it's when," Curt Trulson of Stanley, a fourth-generation farmer, tells me. The 61-year-old plants several thousand acres of spring wheat, durum wheat, canola, flax, field peas and other crops. He owns his land's mineral rights and leases them to oil companies, so he shares in the boom. Like Greg Tank, he also plans to start a business to recycle fracking wastewater.

Despite his financial interest in the boom, Curt is concerned about its negative effects on the area, especially on its infrastructure. When you see a "Rough Road" sign in western North Dakota, he tells me, take it seriously. Between visits by county maintenance crews, the roads are quickly beat to hell and strewn with potholes that scrape car bottoms and blow tires. Plumes of dust create a gray haze in summer skies.

School overcrowding is another concern for Curt: "When I graduated in 1970, my class had 70 students. Now the high school gets 120 to 130 new students every year." While the school district is struggling to keep up, it can only build and staff up so quickly.

The same is true with hospitals, housing and services of any sort.

Counties depend on the state for financial support to cope with the boom. About 11.5% of oil revenues go to the state, which has created "energy impact funds" to distribute to local governments so they have the resources to build and repair infrastructure. But the boom so far has outdistanced the funds, and some in the North Dakota legislature are concerned. Former state Senator John Warner, who is a farmer, told his colleagues in 2013, "My hope is that we will finally be able to get our hands around the issue, that we will be able to get ahead of the cascading collapse of our western infrastructure, stabilize our communities and finally, after this long slog, begin a systematic rollout of the future we want for our beautiful state."

Curt Trulson is not so optimistic. As he and I stand in a canola field that is draped in gorgeous yellow blooms, black oil storage tanks loom on the horizon. "We'll never get back to normal," he tells me. "But I guess I don't know what normal is anymore."

NO GOING BACK

There are other, more primal, reasons to be wary of the boom. The Bakken has become a land of strangers. When a newcomer walks into a café in most rural American communities, the regulars turn to get a look at the stranger. Not in the Bakken. Nobody turns and looks, because everyone is a stranger. The sense of community is gone, and no one is sure what will replace it.

Also gone is the quiet solitude of western North Dakota.

Aaron Jacobson, 43, went away to college before returning to Noonan to run the family farm and ranch. He came back because he missed the peace and isolation he loved about his hometown. The boom "is destroying my life," he tells me. "The roads are wrecked, and I'm losing pasture to pipelines and power lines."

Worse, an oil company built a new tanker truck depot three-eighths of a mile from his house. The traffic it begets is constant, loud and dangerous. If that weren't enough, a well only a mile from his house flares natural gas all day and all night. "It's never dark here anymore," Aaron says woefully.

Heightening his frustrations, perhaps, he does not own the mineral rights to his land. Under North Dakota law, mineral rights and surface rights are separate. A farmer might own the soil he tills, but the resources below the ground might belong to someone else. In previous booms, many Bakken farmers sold mineral rights to speculators. Or they lost mineral rights in family disbursements or even foreclosures. Landowners like Aaron, whose families sold mineral rights long ago, cannot cash in on this boom's prosperity.

It's what rancher Doug Feiring told me was a "double curse." If you don't have mineral rights and don't reap oil's benefits, all you have is the obliteration of your way of life.

My last stop of the day is a railyard out in the country. On its six sets of tracks sit dozens of black tanker cars waiting beside storage tanks to be filled and sent on their way. They will wind up at refineries as far away as California, Illinois and Louisiana. Bakken oil will then be turned into gasoline, diesel or heating oil, the forms of black blood that throb in America's veins. Back in North Dakota, more migrants will heave into man camps, more wells will be drilled, and more farmers and ranchers will wonder how long the boom will last.

I take pictures of the tanker cars and of the setting sun glinting off the rails, get back in my pickup and head to the motel in Minot.

The next day, I begin the long drive home.

THE ROAD HOME

When I take a lengthy road trip, I usually fill the time with audio-books. Local radio stations that carry only whiny music and right-wing talk shows depress me. On the way up to the Bakken, I listened to two books, one a John Grisham mystery, the other a Harry Potter book. But I had miscalculated the length of this trip, and halfway back home, I had no book to take my mind off the drive. Instead, I contemplated what I had seen in the oil fields and tried to make sense of it.

First, I acknowledged that I had begun the trip with the notion that the oil boom will dramatically alter the region and the lives of farmers and ranchers. A journalist is supposed to be free of such preconceptions. But I doubted from the beginning that the oil industry and traditional farmers and ranchers could exist side by side in the Bakken without dire consequences. My bet was that farmers and ranchers would lose out. I think I was correct in that assumption. The oil industry's environmental impact is massive wherever it plants its rigs. And the Bakken is no exception. Everywhere I looked in the Bakken, I saw environmental degradation.

Just as bad, the boom has distorted the familiar warp and weft of the fabric of the ag community. It is a society forever changed.

The trip also reaffirmed what I always have known about farm communities: They don't welcome change. They don't adapt well when the outside world stretches a long, grasping hand into the neighborhood. They just want to be left alone.

Farmers in the Bakken had told me:

"We are not opposed to oil, but we want responsible development and want to know what it will be like when they are done."

"We are getting flat run over. Even the guys in the oil fields will tell you this is the Wild West. There is no regulation out here."

"What price do you put on the quality of your life? Even if you have a big bank account but spend every day living in fear of your safety and health, you will have nothing."

To a large degree, then, the trip had confirmed my preconceptions that when oil interests meet farm interests, oil money wins.

And if the boom busts? I remembered what Doug Feiring told me: "We will look like a city slum with empty houses and weeds growing up everywhere."

As I drove home, I also wanted to count reasons for hope. Pipelines eventually will get buried, and scars in pastures and farm fields will heal. Equilibrium will arrive, and infrastructure will catch up to growth. Newcomers will create a diverse population that eventually will enrich the community.

I reasoned that Oklahoma and Texas had survived oil booms. I had visited farmers and ranchers in those states who do not give oil derricks a second look because they have become part of the landscape. Money from oil wells subsidized the lifestyles of generations of farmers and ranchers. Oil in Oklahoma and Texas was just part of the landscape—for better or worse. Maybe it would be so for North Dakota.

POSTSCRIPT

Years later, I read that the Bakken oil boom had stalled not long after my visit. In 2015, a drop in oil prices blunted the boom's momentum. Oil field employees were laid off and moved away. Rents dropped, and houses sat vacant. Schools lost many of the students for whom they had built new schools and hired new teachers. The boom had not quite become a bust, but the rush to dig new wells had ended.

A few more years, and oil prices shot up again. But by then, the oil industry categorized the Bakken as "mature," which meant exploration dollars had dried up and would be allocated elsewhere. In 2022, Lynn Helms,

North Dakota's director of natural resources, told the Associated Press that he didn't like the Bakken's rebranding as "mature" because it meant that, "We are looking at very low rates of growth, and some companies are just holding their production flat."

Helms admitted that fracking wasn't as productive as it once was in the Bakken. To even retain current oil output levels, new technologies must be discovered to squeeze more oil out of the rock where wells already had been drilled.

This is the same Lynn Helms who, a few years earlier, had said, "Your grandchildren's grandchildren will be working in the Bakken."

Maybe they will. But they won't be part of a black gold rush. And with climate change pushing the world away from petroleum, the long-term future of the Bakken cannot depend on oil forever.

CHAPTER 9

CLYDESDALE HEAVEN

Three giants and their three babies stand at the crest of a hill on a golden spring evening and gaze into the valley. A utility vehicle putters through the pasture at the foot of the hill. It stops, and two men get out. The giants watch the men from afar, gently shaking their black manes and twitching their bobbed tails. Soon—when they decide the men are no threat—they saunter down the slope, keeping their bodies between their foals and the visitors. Mark Boese stands to greet the Clydesdales, while I crouch with a camera to frame photos as the horses descend. Before long, we are encircled by muscular bay bodies, and I squint in the sun to look up to them.

Six feet tall at the shoulder and weighing 2,000 pounds, the three brood mares tower over us. Their hooves are as big as dinner plates, their heads are huge. Despite their mammoth stature, when the mares dip their heads toward us, they aren't intimidating. Instead, they exude an aura of—politeness. It's as if they are saying, "Nice to meet you."

I'm mesmerized gazing up at the mare closest to me whose enormous brown eyes contemplate me. We connect in a way I can't describe. The other mares, in turn, make eye contact, and I feel each is as curious about me as I am about them. A preternatural quiet settles over the scene.

Mark, who has a long history with these horses, whispers in wonder, "It's surreal, isn't it?"

I must agree. The mares are somehow magic.

Welcome to Clydesdale Heaven, also known as Warm Springs Ranch, in Boonville, Missouri, where Mark is herd manager for the famous Anheuser-Busch Clydesdales. After more than 20 years of working with the breed, he has come to believe that these majestic horses are somehow special.

"We call them gentle giants," he tells me. "You can walk into a field with Clydesdales and, unlike most horses, they don't run away; they come to you." In fact, they seem to welcome you.

HISTORY

August Anheuser "Gussie" Busch Jr. was a marketing master. His family has brewed beer in St. Louis since the Civil War, though they took a break from 1920 to 1933 during the Prohibition era. To survive, the Anheuser-Busch brewing company had diversified into nonalcoholic malt beverages, restaurants and a shortline railroad. It endured, if barely, until the country came to its alcoholic senses and welcomed back beer.

Gussie moved into upper management during the dry period, and it was his idea in 1933 to celebrate the end of Prohibition by delivering a wagonload of beer to President Franklin D. Roosevelt. Gussie didn't settle for just any wagonload. He made sure his publicity stunt drew attention by arranging to have the wagon march up Pennsylvania Avenue to the White House. As an extra gimmick, he hired a team of spectacularly beautiful Clydesdales to pull the wagon. The buzz the Clydesdales created that day was loud, and Gussie decided to make them a symbol of the company, which even today uses their images in advertising and on marketing materials and labels.

By the 1950s, Gussie was president and CEO of the company St. Louisans fondly call "A-B." To solidify its hold on local affections, Gussie and A-B bought the St. Louis Cardinals baseball team in 1953. You must understand that in St. Louis, baseball is the dominant religion. It cuts across ethnic, economic and political lines. By purchasing the Cardinals, Gussie placed A-B at the heart of the city's cultural identity. He also tapped into a regional audience, because the Cardinals were the only team west of the Mississippi until the New York Giants and the Brooklyn Dodgers moved to California in 1957. The Cardinals also were the team farthest south until the Braves moved to Atlanta in 1966. To fill much of that geographic void, the Cardinals teamed up with KMOX, a radio station with an enormous broadcast reach. Even today on cloudless nights, you can pick up KMOX in the middle of Kansas. The Cardinals created a vast network of local radio stations that fed fans in Arkansas, Kentucky, Illinois, Indiana and Tennessee. As a result, the St. Louis Cardinals were the major league team for millions, and Gussie Busch loved it.

In another stroke of marketing genius, he wove the Clydesdales into Cardinal culture. He made the big horses part of the baseball team's special events. Come opening day, a Budweiser Clydesdale team pulled a beer wagon around the ball field. When the team won a World Series, the Clydesdales had a prominent part in the victory parade through downtown St. Louis. And it wasn't just St. Louis parades. The Budweiser Clydesdales became part of parades elsewhere, as well. My wife, Gretchen, remembers perching on her father's shoulder as a girl to watch the Budweiser Clydesdales parade in Chicago. "That's when I fell in love with horses," she says.

Later, the breed became part of Super Bowl lore. Budweiser commercials featuring Clydesdales are intertwined with the nation's annual football ritual. The whole country associates Clydesdales with Budweiser.

Growing up in the St. Louis suburbs, I've been enchanted by the big, beautiful horses my entire life. Not only did I thrill to see them as accoutrements to my beloved Cardinals baseball team, I also got to see them at Grant's Farm, another brilliant marketing idea from Gussie Busch.

In 1904, his family purchased a farm on the south side of city that had once belonged to Ulysses S. Grant. The Busch family built a mansion there and turned it into their residential compound. In 1954, Gussie decided there must be some marketing value in Grant's Farm and converted part of it into an exotic animal sanctuary, which he opened to the public for free tours.

One of my earliest memories is of riding a small train through the rolling hills of a pastoral deer park section of the farm where buffalo, camels, elephants and kangaroos roamed. In the distance, floating like a castle in the air, we caught sight of the Busch family's opulent "Big House." Closer to the tracks was a log cabin built by Grant. The train took us to a petting zoo with donkeys, goats and peacocks. There was even a trained bird show. But the main attraction was the stables complex, where the magnificent Clydesdales resided. It was built to resemble a regal cobblestoned German bauernhof and featured brick arches, red tiled roofs and fountains. On one roof perched a good luck stork's nest, complete with stork statues. The stately Clydesdales lounged in brick and dark-stained wood stalls with brass fittings. Their glorious heads swiveled to watch us as we trooped in awe down the stable passageway. Outside, Gussie had arranged a further bit of marketing magic. Adults were treated to free samples of A-B's finest brews.

With that background, I already was in love with Clydesdales by the time I arrived at Warm Spring Ranch in 2019.

CELEBRITIES

A believer in reincarnation might be forgiven for wanting to live his next life as a Budweiser Clydesdale. Their celebrity entitles them to royal treatment. Everywhere they go, people gather and crowds cheer.

At Warm Springs Ranch, they have the run of 300 acres of lush pastureland. Think of it as a horse resort and spa. The 50 to 60 pounds of timothy hay they eat each day—whether in the ranch barns or when they travel for parade business—is imported from a single farm in Eden, Idaho. The 8 pounds of daily supplements they consume contain the highest quality oats. Their pristine stalls are bedded in shaved wood. The aisles between the stalls are swept, then vacuumed. A farrier comes every six weeks to pamper their feet, which are a weak point in Clydesdales' physiology because they support so much weight. A veterinarian is on call 24/7 should they feel out of sorts. When they are on the road, the traveling staff has a network of veterinarians across the country on speed dial—just in case.

When they prance in parades pulling the Budweiser beer wagon, the Clydesdales wear leather and polished brass harnesses custom-made by an Ohio family and costing $12,000 each. The teams travel in a caravan of three red and silver air-conditioned semitrailers emblazoned with their breed's name and the beer brand logos. Sophisticated suspension systems and cushioned flooring in the trailers ease the rigors of traveling, and drivers stop every two hours so the horses can take breaks. If an overnight stay is necessary, one of the trailers carries custom stalls for the horses' sleeping comfort, and reservations are made for a paddock to serve as a horse hotel.

Warm Springs Ranch is the primary breeding and training facility for the Budweiser Clydesdales. When a mare is ready to mate, she is washed and led into a large breeding room. An eager stallion is showered in a room down the hall. The breeding room itself is tall and airy with springy rubber floor mats. "This is where the magic happens," Mark tells me. But the mating ritual is not as romantic as it might sound. Staff watches the proceedings to make sure nothing goes wrong. When it is not in use as a honeymoon suite, the space is a visitors reception hall, complete with a bar that rolls in carrying Budweiser on tap.

WORK FOR THEIR LIVING

Clydesdales must earn their unique Budweiser celebrity. To be a part of the eight-horse hitch, a bay-colored gelding Clydesdale must be at least 4 years of age, stand 18 hands (72 inches) at the shoulder and weigh between 1,800 and 2,300 pounds. He must have a black mane and tail, a white blaze on his forehead and four white stockings with feathery hair that is groomed daily. He must have an even temperament and be a team player.

Mark tells me future team members begin training at birth. "Handling, touching, being around people" is part of the regime, he says. Major training starts in earnest at 3 years old. Horses have pulling practice every day, two hours a day for at least a year. Each gelding learns to pull in all positions of the eight-horse team. The pair of horses closest to the wagon are "wheel" horses. Then come "body" horses, "swing" horses and "lead" horses. Each position requires special skills, and each member of the team must be prepared to pull in any position. The body and swing horses, for instance, must be nimble, because their turns are sharpest.

In recent years, Clydesdale training has become as structured as spring training for a pro baseball team. Mark shows me a training chart that details each stage of the students' training and what drills they have performed: How many times on the left side of the team? How many times on the right? What positions—lead, middle, rear? How did each student execute at each position?

When strung together, the team is 40 feet long, which means the driver must have the lead horses start turning a long way before the wagon reaches a bend in the route. Drivers, too, must be well-trained and strong. Each driver must be able to hold four leads in one hand and four in the other for a total of 40 pounds in each hand. He also must be familiar with the principles of geometry to steer around corners. "It's kind of like shooting pool," Mark tells me. "Because you have to understand angles to get that bend going from a long way off."

Once a gelding Clydesdale graduates, he is assigned to a hitch based either in Colorado, Missouri or New Hampshire. Three strategic locales help the teams span the country to annually appear at 120 to 150 events—parades, sporting events and beer wholesalers' promotional campaigns.

While their boys are on the road, female Clydesdales continue to earn their keep at Warm Springs Ranch. Pregnancy lasts almost a year (about 340 days), and foals weigh about 140 pounds. Once they struggle to their feet, they stand 3 feet tall. They nurse for about six months.

During my visit, I was fortunate to see a 1-day-old in a stall with his mama. He was all knobby knees and awkward legs. He lay flat on his side on the shaved wood floor and eyed me curiously. His mother bent down and nosed him until he rose, forelegs first, to stand. She backed away to give him room to maneuver until he found her teats. This year, he is one of 20 foals to join the Budweiser Clydesdale herd.

Brood mares not only give birth, they also serve as ambassadors for the ranch, where they greet thousands of tourists each year. The day I arrive at the ranch, there are two scheduled public tours. Dozens of cars pull into Warm Spring Ranch's parking lot, and occupants file into an impressive red metal barn with gables, high pitched roofs and decorative dormers. It's not as grand or as old as the stables at Grant's Farm. But this is a working ranch, and utility takes precedence over opulence.

Tour guides named Kayla and Lana await the visitors and form the 50 or so folks into two groups, who walk in separate lines through the barn and out to the corrals. For many, this is the first time they have seen Clydesdales up close, and kids and adults ooh and aah at the stately beasts. When they get to the stalls containing foals, a woman puts her hand to her mouth and whispers, "Oh my god, they're adorable!"

Kayla and Lana keep up an informative chatter about the Clydesdale breed's Scottish origins and its place as fourth-largest breed behind Shires, Percherons and Belgian Draft horses. They point to displays of gear the horses wear and pause the tour groups to watch a petite female groom stand on a stool and reach high to brush a mare's mane. Another groom uses a comb on the feathered fetlocks of a mare.

The two tour groups finish in the large reception hall (formerly the honeymoon suite). A beer cart has been rolled out, and a tall mare stands patiently awaiting her fans. Some of the adults head for the beer cart for free samples of Budweiser. But all the kids gravitate to the mare. An attendant loosely holds a lead while the kids reach up to stroke the mare's muzzle or run their hands over her flanks. The kids are awestruck, and the mare turns her curious eyes to them and considers the faces one at a time.

Mark and I have our own tour to finish, and he leads me to some distant corrals where randy young stallions are kept away from general tour groups. These guys are the only Clydesdales I've met that inspire any fear. They are so hyped on testosterone they could be dangerous, Mark tells me. Which is why he doesn't allow tour groups near them.

When we hop into the utility vehicle again, it is to visit pastures where younger male Clydesdales play. Like any youngsters, they have energy to burn, and I watch bemused as they gambol and gallop through the lush grass. One day, perhaps, they will use that energy to pull beer wagons.

Our last stop of the day is a pasture where fillies are maturing, waiting their turn to blossom into brood mares and bear their own foals. They are much more sedate than the colts we saw and seem almost to preen for us, batting long lashes over big, mahogany-colored eyes. One day, perhaps, they might saunter down hills in golden evening light with babies of their own to inspire wonder in men standing by utility vehicles.

CHAPTER 10

CENTRAL AMERICAN CAMPESINOS

She is 20 years old, beautiful and dignified. On her hip is a chubby 9-month-old son, who hides his head on her chest rather than look at the strangers arrayed in front of them. She stands in the doorway of a cement block storage building explaining to the strangers in a steady voice that she is determined to hang onto the 5 acres of rough land she farms in southern Nicaragua.

Her name is Flora. She is dressed in a yellow tank top, and her bare brown arms are muscular yet feminine. Her countenance is patient and smiling, and she seems so much more self-assured than most 20-year-olds. She quietly answers questions from the eight strangers and laughs sweetly when they compliment her son.

The strangers are men and women from three international NGOs (nongovernmental organizations), a Nicaraguan government agency and me. Flora already has shown us the stick and thatch shack where she cooks and the lean-to where she stores tools and from which chickens and turkeys erupt as we approach. The storage building, which has a corrugated metal roof, is brand new, paid for in part by one of the NGOs. She is proud of it. A partition inside the building creates a small space that serves as her bedroom. It's empty except for four sacks of grain and a wood-framed bed with a thin mattress where she and her son, Yasser, sleep.

Flora tells us she plans to one day tile the concrete floor to make the place more attractive. She will add a table, chairs and a chest to store clothes—the kind of simple things that are necessary dreams for a young mother on her own.

I am on Flora's farm as part of a tour of agricultural development programs, including one named El Manantial (The Spring). Its stated goal is to bring training, crop improvement and land ownership to Nicaragua's peasants. Its underlying goal is to enable simple dreams like Flora's.

Two years ago, she and her husband, Roberto, took out a loan with El Manantial and became landowners. In southern Nicaragua, 5 acres can be enough to make a family secure. But two drought years have hit hard, and the family has not been able to make this year's loan payment. Roberto, in an act of desperation, has gone to Costa Rica to labor in sugarcane fields and earn money to pay his debts.

His timing was questionable. The family's cassava fields are now ready for harvest, which should produce much-needed money. But Flora tells us she cannot harvest it alone. The work is too much for one person. The best she can do is hire someone to help while she guards the crop against thieves. "If anyone tries to steal it, I will chase them away," she says and points to a nearby machete. There is steel in her voice, and I imagine her grabbing a weapon and challenging an interloper.

For reasons I will never understand, Flora begins to tell us intimate details of her life. She lost three pregnancies in her teen years but wanted a child so much she kept trying. Finally, she had Yasser. She reveals all this with startling simplicity. She also admits that she understands that Roberto might never come back. Many men who leave Nicaragua for work never return. "I told him the day he left that if he does not come back, I will go my own way. But I will survive." There was no fear in her voice.

As she speaks, she slowly rocks her son on her hip and strokes his thick black hair. She is in profile to me, and light from the doorway falls on her face in a caress. It is a determined face with the high cheek bones, full lips and mocha skin of her indigenous heritage. She is someone's wife, someone's mother and someone's daughter all at the same time. Strong but vulnerable. Optimistic but aware of realities. Her head is tilted slightly upward, and her dark eyes catch the light. Through the lens of my camera, she is a Madonna, pure and resolute. I trip the shutter, and my heart goes out to her.

It is a moment that has stuck with me. Over the years, I have returned to my photos of Flora many times and wondered what happened to her. Did Roberto return? Did they save the farm together? Or did he vanish? Did she and Yasser forsake the farm and move back to her home village to start a new life?

In cynical moments, I've even wondered if Flora had fabricated the story of her husband's leaving to earn the sympathy of the El Manantial officials so they would extend the family's loan. Maybe.

But when I look at her picture again, I see dignity and courage. I want to believe every word she said. And I want to believe that Roberto returned, Yasser grew into a happy young man, and Flora had more children to cherish.

I'd come to Nicaragua for a second installment of a series of articles on international food security issues for The Progressive Farmer magazine. The concept was to examine how farmers in developing nations met—or did not meet—the nutritional needs of their families. What did the future hold? I'd been in Kenya and Ethiopia 18 months ago and decided that Nicaragua and Honduras would be my next targets.

When planning my trip to Central America, I turned for help to the redoubtable Bev Abma. I'd first Bev on my way to Africa. She'd invited me to join a tour of aid agricultural projects in Kenya. Bev was one of the founders of Food Resource Bank (FRB), a charitable organization built on donations by American and Canadian farmers. Its mission was to lend money to projects that help farmers in developing countries learn food production methods adapted to their own climates and circumstances.

The small, congenial Bev was FRB's eyes and ears. She spent most of her year visiting and assessing FRB-funded projects. She could say "yay" or "nay" to further FRB involvement but always leaned toward "yay." She was a force for good.

A widow in her 60s, in another life Bev would have been an extraordinary second-grade teacher; she had that sort of patience and kindness. Or her Christian faith would have made her an excellent pastor. As FRB's representative, she traveled to more than 80 countries for advocacy work and for adventure. Bev told me once that her religious convictions initially caused her to serve others. But she wound up devoting her life to service because of "the dignity of the people I meet. The work just grabs hold of you somehow. It gets into your heart; the people get into your heart. It becomes part of who we are."

When I contacted Bev months earlier to discuss a planned reporting trip to Central America, she told me I was in luck. She was planning a visit to FRB-sponsored projects in Nicaragua and invited me to join her and some colleagues. As she had in Kenya, she paved my way, made introductions and opened a new world to me.

In January of 2013, I met Bev in Managua, Nicaragua, the capital, and she introduced me to members of several NGOs with projects in the region. In a conference room in Managua, they gave me the lay of the land.

Many of the Nicaragua's five million people live in poverty, and malnutrition is rampant, especially in the countryside. Smallholder farmers here live by their wits and survival skills. In good weather years, they can grow enough food for their families. Sometimes they even have enough to sell and get ahead financially. But there are many bad weather years, especially now that climate change has scrambled planting seasons and brought an increase in severe weather events. In those years, smallholder farmers and their families have weeks of hunger.

The NGO projects I will see later are based on two concepts: the ability to improve the crops grown in specific regions, and the opportunity for small farmers to own land.

The projects attack the first goal with on-farm education and small agricultural experiment stations, which can boost productivity and give small farmers better odds, especially when the weather cooperates.

Landownership is a trickier issue because Nicaragua has a tangled history of government confiscation of land. It's almost impossible for a small farmer to purchase land because of the legal quagmire surrounding a sale. But a partnership of NGOs and funding organizations has gained title to parcels of farmland, which they put into land banks and offer to small farmers. It's a way around government control. Prospective landowners must meet rigorous criteria to qualify for this program. They must be poor, married, debt-free, landless, honest and willing to make a commitment to live on the land. If they qualify, the land bank sets up a strict loan payment schedule. If the farmers fail to make regular payments, they forfeit the land.

Over the next few days, I traveled with Bev and other NGO representatives as they inspected farmers participating in their projects. We visited an experiment station that contains rows of planted crops, a greenhouse and storage buildings. Partner farmers operate the greenhouse to grow and test alternative crops to replace or supplement maize. A new solar-powered pump makes water more available for both irrigation and for drinking. New storage bins preserve grain for food for sale in the off-season.

Middle-aged Gilberto Lopez is one of the partner farmers. He wears wire-rimmed glasses, a Masonic lodge baseball cap and a confident look. He greets us as we climb out of our vehicles and takes us on a tour of his farm. His two-room house is corrugated metal with a thatched roof. The inside is covered with yellowing newspapers that serve as wallpaper. Framed family photos add personality. I see a man in a wide sombrero astride a white donkey, a young woman in a graduation cap and gown, and solemn twin girls in pleated skirts.

Gilberto is proud of his solar-powered water pump and turns on a hose to demonstrate how much water pressure his pump can achieve. He also is proud that his drip irrigation system conserves water. The modern poultry house he built contains birds of several species that lay eggs and provide meat. One of his sons cradles a large white rabbit with black markings. It's a pet now but one day will be dinner or cash in the pocket.

Despite two consecutive years of drought that would have devastated maize, Gilberto tells us, experiments with new crops—grain sorghum, amaranth and cassava, among them—have paid dividends. He has money he might not otherwise have had. Gilberto's wife, Maria, has used some of the proceeds to open a small shop next to their house where she sells fresh-baked goods and necessities like toothpaste and soap. Neighbors walk the dirt roads for miles to the shop, which is the closest thing in rural Nicaragua to a convenience store.

Leaving Gilberto's farm, I felt optimism. The NGO programs had given at least one family a chance for a brighter future.

North Nicaragua. The day after our visit to Gilberto, Bev and I say goodbye. She and two FRB colleagues are going to visit two villages in the deep bush along the Rio Coco. They will spend days traveling by canoe and slogging through muddy roads. Bev had invited me to join them. But my time was limited, and I decided it would be better spent visiting a larger variety of projects. Besides, based on past misfortunes (capsizing on lazy Ozark rivers, for instance), canoes and I don't get along.

I had another option. Weeks prior I had contacted the Howard G. Buffett Foundation and Catholic Relief Services (CRS) and learned that some of their personnel would be touring food-security projects in the same region at the same time as my trip. I had convinced Emily Martin of the Buffett Foundation to allow me to travel with her and Gaye Burpee, a senior CRS advisor, as they visited projects that the Buffett Foundation funded and CRS administered. On this trip, they were going to northern Nicaragua and then the highlands of Honduras.

I met the two women at the airport in Managua as Gaye arrived from the States, and we piled into three rugged little Toyota Hilux pickup trucks along with drivers, translators and local NGO operatives. We headed north for the Jinotega area near the Honduran border.

Our destinations were two hilltop villages that had been without a reliable water supply until recently. Every morning for as long as villagers could remember, women or children had walked down the hill to get water, almost 10 kilometers round trip. Five years prior, the Nicaraguan government, CRS and the Buffett Foundation helped the villagers start building a system of pipes and pumping stations to bring water up the hill. For lack of funding, the first phase of the project ended 2 kilometers below the villages. Still, the walk for water was much shorter. A year ago, the project was finished and water was as close as the nearest outdoor spigot.

After a warm welcome by villagers and a tour, we listen as president of the water committee, a no-nonsense young woman named Ivania del Socorro, explains what the water project has meant to her people. First, there are fewer illnesses, she says, because people no longer drank untreated water. Second, nutrition has improved because kitchen gardens produce more food now that villagers use rainwater catchments for irrigation rather than for drinking. Third, the villages' children have more time and energy to go to school since they don't have to haul water every morning.

When del Socorro finishes her presentation, she and about a dozen villagers lead us among the adobe and wood houses to demonstrate a series of communal water spigots. The water system means an easier life for the village, a healthier life, a life with a better future. Del Socorro and the villagers are proud they worked together to make this possible. The fourth benefit to the water system is that it has united the community.

Our visit ends at a municipal center. It is a concrete block building with naked openings that serve as windows and doorways. It has an earthen floor and a green fiberglass roof that provides light. There are sweet cakes and bottles of pop on a table, which the villagers offer to us. We chat, ask more questions and laugh together. Then, Miguel Aparicio Lopez, a mustachioed middle-aged man in a plaid shirt and clean blue jeans takes a guitar out of a battered case and begins to strum. He sings us a song he wrote about the water project. He calls it "Community Progress," and the lyrics celebrate the fifth benefit of the water project: Villagers learned that if they work together, they can accomplish much. Now they are ready to tackle more community problems.

By the time we get back in our vehicles, I am reassured that progress is not only possible, it does happen.

Welcome to Honduras. The border crossing to Honduras is in the middle of nowhere. Our pickup trucks maneuver up a slope and around a bend in the dirt road, and we find ourselves suddenly halted in a long, stationary line. We're at a border checkpoint. A dozen vehicles idle while border guards check papers and collect bribes.

Ahead of us are box trucks and open trucks loaded with goods headed for Honduras. A few passenger cars and a couple of motor scooters are also in line. I notice that many of the vehicles have no drivers or passengers. They are milling around in the dust or have gone to the small frontier store that's doing a brisk business selling trinkets, snacks and drinks. Our driver tells us we might as well join them; it will be a wait before we can clear the paperwork at the border checkpoint.

I get out with one of the local CRS guys, and we mosey over to the store. It looks like something out of an Old West movie set. It has a broad plank porch under an unpainted wood roof. Inside, travelers of all sorts are examining merchandise or buying Cokes and sandwiches. Women in colorful tops and long skirts; men in torn shirts and faded jeans. A quiet buzz of Spanish.

As we leave the store with Coke bottles in our hands, the line hasn't budged. Manny, one of the CRS guys, approaches us. "Don't go too far," he says. "I'm going take care of this."

"Where's he going?" I ask the driver. He shrugs and says, "He's going to pay a bribe."

Manny walks toward the head of the line, and I see him approach a uniformed man who has a gun on his hip. I see them move toward the checkpoint with Manny leaning toward the man and gesturing. They disappear into a group of soldiers who have long guns slung over their backs or cradled in their arms.

In a few minutes, Manny comes back walking quickly. "Get in. Let's move!" We pile into the trucks, pull out of line and head toward the board crossing. The guards don't even look at us as we breeze past them.

Welcome to Honduras.

We make our way out of the bush and head for the capital of Tegucigalpa. We have business at the CRS headquarters there.

Teguz, as it's called, is a grimy city set in a bowl of mountains that trap wind currents and produce a yellow haze of air pollution. A constant drone of traffic echoes off the sides of the bowl, and the population of more than a million navigates streets that snake down from the hills toward an ugly downtown of concrete office buildings and hotels. As we drive into the city, I see a statue of Jesus, 100 feet tall and spreading his arms wide over the bowl. In another spot, I see a massive Coca Cola sign made up of individual letters set into a hillside. It reminds me of the iconic Hollywood sign in Los Angeles.

The CRS compound is on the edge of a business district and atop a small flat area surrounded by houses that cling to the hills. The compound's high walls are topped with razor wire, and serious men with assault rifles guard the parking lot. Tegucigalpa is a dangerous city in a dangerous country.

Juan Sheenan is in charge of CRS operations in Honduras. He oversees development projects and relations with both the U.S. and the Honduran governments. A strikingly handsome American with Latin features, he's around 40 years old. He stands to greet us, waves the six of us to chairs and sits again behind a desk that has a view of the city.

"Welcome to Teguz," he says. "Welcome to Honduras."

As we go through the inevitable introductory chitchat, Sheenan inquires about our trip so far and tells us he is glad we are interested in CRS's work. He is friendly and encouraging as he explains his duties and the status of aid and NGOs in Honduras. A coup in 2009 caused the U.S. government to pull some funding for humanitarian projects in Honduras. But he hopes funding will return when conditions allow. He is pleased that the Buffett Foundation helped pick up some of the slack, and CRS projects are moving forward with the foundation's help. There is much work to be done.

As we travel, he wants us to understand where we are. "Teguz," he says, "can be dangerous, and the countryside can be even more dangerous."

Whole swaths of Honduras, he tells us, are controlled by narco gangs. To consolidate their power and keep the populous docile, the gangs provide medical care and schools for regions under their control. But they rule with guns and threats. The central government rarely ventures into drug lord territory.

To emphasize the point about how dangerous Honduras can be, Sheenan tells us a story straight out of "The Godfather." It starts with Cardinal Óscar Rodríguez Maradiaga, Archbishop of Tegucigalpa, who is a prominent prelate of the Catholic Church. From his outpost in Honduras, he presides over Caritas Internationalis, a global Catholic relief agency. He has served as the Vatican's spokesman with the International Monetary Fund and the World Bank and, according to insider Catholic rumors, was a huge political factor in Jorge Mario Bergoglio becoming Pope Francis. Unfortunately, this powerful cardinal had run afoul of the Honduran president and now might be in peril.

To illustrate the cardinal's peril, Sheenan recounts a series of secretive lunch meetings he has had with Rodríguez Maradiaga to discuss CRS work in the Honduras countryside. When Sheenan arrives at the appointed restaurant, he always is searched by guards at the door, and a metal detector wand is waved around his body. The restaurant itself is empty except for the cardinal, who beckons Sheenan to join him. In the movie, they would have sat in a kind of spotlight with the room dark around them. In Teguz, they have a quiet meal, discuss the violence that threatens Sheenan's colleagues and depart the restaurant separately to vehicles guarded by armed men.

Sheenan follows that unsettling story by telling us that the previous year, gunmen had stopped the car of a female member of his staff. They shot her husband dead because he had refused to pay protection money to narco gangsters. They wounded her but let her live.

That year, too, a Peace Corps volunteer was wounded by gang members, and the agency evacuated the rest of its volunteers. CRS and other development agencies stayed, even though Honduras was then ranked as the most dangerous country on Earth, "and it is only getting worse," Sheenan says.

"Our first priority is the safety of our people." So he has moved some of his people off projects and stationed them in more secure locations.

Our group needn't worry, he tells us as we prepare to leave. The violence is targeted, not random. And the projects we plan to visit are in safe areas. If we are careful, we will be OK. Oh, he says as an afterthought while looking at me, lots of journalists have been killed—but they have all been Hondurans.

I can smile at this now. But I'll admit to being shaken by Sheenan's welcome. I'm an ag journalist, not a war correspondent. I was aware of Honduras' reputation for violence before I made the trip. But now that I've heard it firsthand, I was glad I had not discussed the potential danger with my wife, Gretchen. There'd be time for that when I returned. Meanwhile, I resolved to relax and enjoy the ride. What else could I do?

Indeed, the first village project we visit after Tegucigalpa is a scene of peace and pastoral beauty in the La Paz region. It is just the respite I need, and soon all worry about gunmen vanishes.

We're gathered on the side of a mountain slope in a new community building with a tin roof, a concrete floor and half walls of shiny corrugated metal. Archemia Garcia, a tiny, middle-aged woman with skin the color of polished bronze, looks up from her notebook as she addresses our group and a dozen farmers who have joined us. Garcia is treasurer for a project at El Naranjo, a farming community consisting of several villages who collaborate on development projects. In a clear voice, she is making an accounting of the group's savings fund.

It's a positive report. The two-year-old savings fund, which consists of deposits from community members, has a balance of about 26,000 lempiras ($1,200). Another 19,000 lempiras are on loan to members at 5% interest. They use the loans to buy seed and supplies. Production loans are vital to survival for these farmers as they are for farmers everywhere. Without them, next year's crop doesn't get planted.

Establishing the savings fund is a key part of a multifaceted CRS/ Buffett Foundation project at El Naranjo. The community also has launched several microenterprises to bring extra income and self-suffi- ciency. Members bake breads and cakes, and make marmalades and jellies, as well as vinegars and fruit wines, which they take to town to sell. The community also plants kitchen gardens to improve members' diets, and it sponsors programs to help youngsters learn how to make and save money.

Working with outside agronomists, El Naranjo farmers learn new planting and fertility programs for maize and edible beans. They also experiment with modern production technologies, including crop rotation and drip tape irrigation. We saw evidence of this as we drove up the moun- tain. On a hillside so steep I think of mountain goats, a farmer in a cowboy hat and tattered jeans uses a hoe to cultivate between beans and maize that are watered by a black drip tape. The field had been contoured to prevent soil runoff by a team of El Naranjo farmers.

Jiménez Sánchez, a development specialist with the Caritas who mentors the project, tells me later: "They have learned that by working together, they can get things done."

An hour's drive away through winding mountain roads, El Sauce farming community sits near the town of Florida, in southwest Honduras. This group, like El Naranjo, has an active and successful agricultural edu- cation program. Some of its components include a model vegetable gar- den/test plot and a pond for growing tilapia, which villagers eat and sell locally. A thriving poultry operation includes layer hens and egg pro- duction. Beekeepers place hives in the forests and harvest the honey for extra income.

A large demonstration plot a few miles from town tests maize- and bean-production methods. Farmers plant coffee bushes, bananas and mahogany trees on some highly erodible slopes to conserve the soil and to make the most use of the land.

The crown jewel of El Sauce is its coffee plant nursery. Sprinklers water young plants nestled in the trees of a cool valley. When older, the plants will be transplanted to production fields, where they will bear beans that brew some of the best coffee in the world.

(An increasing amount of Honduran coffee is sold to fair-trade markets, which pay higher prices to farmers than large commercial buyers. Fair-trade coffee costs more in the U.S. But some American consumers are willing to pay more to not exploit villagers for corporate profits.)

At the coffee nursery, I ask Gaye to do a video interview to describe her role with CRS. She is naturally reserved and not comfortable speaking into a camera. But with some prodding from Emily and me, she agrees. We set up a shot with her in the foreground and a large patch of potted young coffee plants in the background. Emily stands off camera and offers support and encouragement, while Gaye and I go through the torturous process of doing take after take until we feel confident we have something that can be edited into a smooth, three-minute video.

Gaye is tall and thin, and wears a floppy jungle hat to protect her fair skin. She is in her 50s or early 60s and has a doctorate in agronomy. As a member of the Burpee family (the world's largest home, garden, seed and plant company), she could have done anything with her education. But a stint with the Peace Corps in the West Indies shaped her career. One night over dinner, she told me the Peace Corps experience taught her the valuable lesson that, "It's just an accident of birth that causes people to have different lives. If we are born lucky, we must share that luck."

In her position at CRS, she travels often from her safe Maryland home to wild areas of Central America. That is where she can use her agronomic knowledge to help farmers develop better, more efficient ways to grow crops and feed their families. "I want to help," she tells me. "I want to fight for them."

On the video, she explains: "We [at CRS] use a learn-by-doing method in which trained agronomists work with leaders of a community. Then these community promoters work with their neighboring farmers to help develop farming skills. It's like the ag Extension system [at land-grant universities] in the U.S., which has helped make our farmers so productive. Using that method, 53 agronomists on our staff and the staffs of our partner agencies have trained 16,000 farmers throughout Central America."

The merging of idealism with practicality is a hallmark for many of the NGO agency people I have met. They have dedicated themselves to using agriculture to improve the lives of struggling folks in neglected parts of the world. I admire their work, and I admire them.

Another Checkpoint. It is late in the day when we start for our next destination, a hotel in the mountains where we will spend the night before one last village visit. Then I will leave the group and head home.

Our caravan has three vehicles now. I am in the rear seat of the third, which is a four-door white Hilux. A driver named Felix and a local CRS employee named Jose sit in the front and carry on an easy conversation in Spanish. As we climb higher and higher into the mountains, the road becomes a series of switchbacks. Looking out the rear side window, the trucks in front of us emerge from around a bend so sharp, the vehicles seem to be behind us. They disappear, and at the next bend, they are in front of us again.

We descend into a valley of wild banana trees and scrub trees beside a mountain stream. The vehicles in front of us are out of sight, and for a moment, we are alone on the road.

Suddenly ahead of us, two men appear on either side of the road. They have ugly long guns pointed in the air, and each has a hand extended to signal us to stop. My two companions go silent and glance at each other. As we slow to a halt, Jose looks over his shoulder at me. "It's OK," he says. "Just a checkpoint."

The young men with the guns are dressed in military-style clothes. But they are not in uniform. The man to the left of the truck has drab olive cargo pants and a long-sleeved shirt. The man on my side of the truck has camouflage pants and a white T-shirt. They begin to converge on our truck.

I've been in a few situations where I've had to pull over and watch in the rearview mirror as a highway patrolman walked up to my car. This has a different feel to it, and frankly, I am starting to get scared. I remember what I'd heard at the CRS office in Tegucigalpa about violence in the countryside. I don't know whether these men approaching our truck are government soldiers or narco gang members. Maybe it doesn't matter.

The gunman on the driver's side now is standing a few cautious feet from the car and talking to Felix. I don't sense any tension. But this surely isn't a welcome-to-the-neighborhood stop. Felix is gesturing forward as if he is explaining where we are going. Jose in the passenger seat is staring out the windshield, not at either of the gunmen. And I wonder if he is too afraid to look at them.

It is my habit to have at least one of my cameras on the seat beside me so I can grab it quickly and shoot. But for some reason, I'd zipped both my cameras in the backpack, which sits on the seat beside me. The gunman on my side sees the backpack and, before I realize what he is doing, reaches in the window. His gun is now strapped around his shoulder, and it catches on the window frame so his outstretched arm can't quite reach my backpack. His head and one arm are inside the truck, and he's almost in my lap. He starts yelling something, and my fear level quickly goes from five to 10.

Jose turns in his seat and starts yelling loudly at the gunman. I don't understand what he says, but I hear "Americano" and "fotógrafo." I discover that my hands are half raised and shaking. I try to look the gunman in the face. When our eyes lock, I slowly lower my left hand to my backpack and start to unzip it. I can feel the gunman tense up as he pulls his head and upper body out of the window and stands crouching, both hands on his gun now. I am still staring into his eyes, and Jose is still talking, but his voice is calm now and has a soothing tone.

I finish unzipping the lid to my backpack and reveal my cameras and lenses. I tilt the backpack to the gunman so he can see there is nothing dangerous about it. Gradually, his face relaxes, and he nods. That nod feels like a door has opened and warm, life-affirming air blows onto me. I exhale and nod in return. My heart rate begins slow.

Only then do I look at the other gunman. He has backed away and has his gun pointed at Felix. His compadre says something to him. The two have a short conversation over the truck as the one on the left lowers his gun. Then he waves us past him, and Felix puts the truck in gear again.

It takes me five minutes before I trust my voice not to quaver. "Who were those guys?" I ask. Jose casually answers: "Who knows?" It had been no big deal to him. Just another traffic stop in Honduras.

By the time we arrive at the hotel a couple hours later, I'm calm and thinking of myself as quite brave under the circumstances. It will make a story to tell, if not to the magazine readers then at least to my colleagues at the next farm show I attend.

The hotel sits on the shelf of a steep hill outside a medium-sized town. It is a walled compound with a guard at the gate and a series of one-story white buildings spread around an office and swimming pool. Luxurious by local standards, I guess.

We check in and are directed outside and to our rooms in a building at the back of the compound. As we start to leave the office, the manager calls us back. "We have armed patrols around the hotel at night. If you see men with guns, don't worry. It is our people," he says.

Still in Honduras, I thought.

There are gardens and a decorative pond along the path to our building. We lug our luggage to the building and go to our separate rooms, agreeing to meet at the office later for dinner. "We" now are Gaye, Emily, Paul Hicks and me.

Paul had joined the group the day before we went to Tegucigalpa. I hadn't had much chance to talk to him. But I liked him already. He was fortyish with a graying goatee and a casual air. I learned that he was stationed in El Salvador with CRS as a water project specialist. He was a former Peace Corps volunteer who had served in Honduras before returning to UC-Davis to earn a master's degree in international agricultural development. He'd been with CRS for more than a decade and had joined us in part because he had once worked with the villagers we were going to visit in the morning. He wanted to check on his program's progress.

That evening, Emily, Paul and I, along with a couple of the drivers in the caravan, ventured into town to find a cantina and dinner. Gaye decided to eat at the hotel and turn in early. The cantina we found was dark and almost empty. But it gave the impression that on payday, it was crowded and lively. I had a memorable evening learning about the local culture from my companions and the woman behind the bar. It was later than expected when we returned to the hotel, and the morning came before I was ready for it. But the cantina visit had been worth it.

I discovered that night that Paul was one of those earnest sorts of men and women who populate the NGO world and dedicate their lives to making others' lives better. Some are committed bureaucrats who keep the service agency running from an office in a foreign capital such as Tegucigalpa. Others travel the backroads to remote villages and work beside campesinos on water projects and farming test plots. Paul was in the latter camp.

His stints with CRS had taken him to Afghanistan, Albania and the Philippines before he settled down with a wife and family in El Salvador. Now he makes excursions in Honduras and other Central American countries to set up and maintain sustainable agricultural programs.

Like many who enter the foreign aid world, Paul is an adventurer at heart. Roughing it in remote areas has its own rewards. But he also is serious about the mission. It is important to him that he help others. Over the years, he tells me, he has learned that while work in backcountry villages is vital, it must be seen in a wider context. At first, Paul thought each mission was local. The goal was to help a particular village build a water system or grow a better crop. Eventually, he says, he came to understand that local problems are never solely those of the villagers themselves. Rather, the fault usually lies in the armed conflicts and political warfare that roil the lands outside their villages. Paul understands that villagers are people of dignity and intelligence. Left to themselves, they survived for untold generations. Now they lack the resources to battle outside influences, and they need help to meet the challenges of the 21st century. Many of them decide nothing can improve their lives if they stay. So they become immigrants. Some wind up at the U.S./Mexico border, swimming the Rio Grande toward what they hope is a better future.

For people like Paul, regional peace and better governance are better long-term solutions to poverty than chaotic immigration. In the short term, Paul says, he can help with local details.

The next morning our caravan continued to climb into the mountains. The air was cool and damp, and it turned to fog. The higher we climbed, the thicker was the fog. It hung like veils along the hillsides and the cloaked valleys below.

Our destination was the Paniaguara Watershed Management Project, in the Santa Ana municipality. The villagers here are predominantly Lencans, descendants of an indigenous ethnic group that has lived in this Miramar region for more than 2,000 years. It has always been a hard life among the high winds, treacherous mountainsides and rocky soils. But recent difficult times have made a hard life unsustainable.

For generations, the villagers had thrived on food crops like maize and beans, and had raised livestock like goats and chickens. They also grew coffee bushes to earn money for modern necessities like electric lights, an occasional bus trip to town, maybe even a cell phone with which to access the outside world. But the climate has grown warmer and stormier over the last few decades, making cropping seasons uncertain, especially for coffee growers. To compensate, people moved higher up the mountains, cutting down virgin forests to sell mahogany timber and to create fields where they can grow coffee bushes. That deforestation has had dire consequences. Rains now rush unchecked down the slopes, washing away what little topsoil there is. And some water supplies have disappeared because rainwater no longer soaks into aquifers.

The narrow rocky road we ascended has at last led our caravan to our destination. We park and see below us a cluster of adobe houses, some with tin roofs, some covered with thatch and leaves. As we walk down to the village, people come out of the houses to welcome us. Some remember Paul from his last visit and hurry to meet him. A family he knows well calls him to their front door and hands him a child of about 2. Paul lifts him into the air and parades him around like he is a lost nephew.

I follow as villagers give us a tour. I see a storage building where maize, still on the cob, is hung by its husk from wooden racks. I go inside a two-room house with a smoldering fire in an adobe oven, pots hung from the wall, a bag of grain tucked in the rafters. A proud man in a stocking cap with a Nike swoosh welcomes us and introduces his stair-step three children and his wife. Outside, I see a toothless but beaming old woman in a red top, a white lace sash and a faded blue flowered dress standing beside her half-built home. Beside it is a pile of adobe blocks with which her neighbors will finish the last wall.

We walk to the edge of the village where a middle-aged woman picks coffee beans from a cluster of wet bushes. She is wearing a plastic bag around her lower body to keep her dress dry while she drops brown and red beans into a cloth bag tied around her waist.

It is cold in the fog, and the villagers soon usher us into the village's largest house, which has four rooms. The front room is set up for us to sit on a bench against the wall, and a little girl of about 7 years old brings each of us a cup of hot milk with rice. It is time for a meeting of the water committee.

Jose de La Paz Mendoza Chica opens the meeting with a prayer. He spreads his arms wide and opens his palms to heaven. He prays that God will bless this meeting and bless the committee's work, which is to bring this village clean water and a sustainable food supply. He prays for a better life.

After moving about the room to take photos, I sit next to Paul and Emily, and listen as members of the community describe their progress. Each talks with enthusiasm and pleasure. What they tell us is good news, surprisingly good news.

"This is friggin' cool!" Paul whispers to me.

In aid-worker speak, "friggin' cool" is high praise. It means the village has made great strides. In this case, they have gone beyond Paul's expectations and innovated in ways he had not envisioned. Drinking water is more available, crops are flourishing, hunger is receding. The village has taken solid steps toward ecological and food security.

"This is why we do this," Paul says.

I'm glad Paul had said that. I carried that positive sentiment with me when I flew from Tegucigalpa home the next day.

On the farm with Howard Buffett. A few months after I returned from Central America, I drove to eastern Nebraska to visit Howard Buffett as he planted corn on his farm there. I had met Howard once at a farmers meeting and was impressed by his down-to-earth demeanor. As the son of legendary investor Warren Buffett, he is a millionaire, though his father reportedly gave him only a one-time lump of cash. But Howard's soul is a farmer's soul. He loves farming, and does so both in Nebraska and central Illinois. Like many of the farmers I knew, he is more at home in a tractor than anywhere.

I met Howard the first time in the ballroom of a fancy conference center hotel in downtown Chicago. He was there to give a presentation about his foundation's work with subsistence farmers in Africa and Latin

American. He seemed uncomfortable on stage before an audience of 300-plus farmers. But he was passionate about his topic, and he illustrated his talk with gorgeous and compelling photographs he had taken himself. The photos grabbed my attention, but his ag development work intrigued me even more. After his talk, I introduced myself and shook his hand. When I planned my trips to Africa and later to Honduras and Nicaragua, his foundation's name, The Howard G. Buffett Foundation (HGBF), was the first to come to mind.

As I arrive on his farm on this spring morning, Howard is at the wheel of a 325-horsepower John Deere 9230 four-wheel-drive tractor pulling a 16-row planter across the far side of a large, flat field. I turn off the highway into the machine shed parking lot at the end of the field to wait for him to complete the pass that will bring him to me. When he stops in a cloud of dust, he climbs down the tractor ladder and greets me with a friendly smile and handshake.

Howard is a middle-aged man with a jovial, round face topped by a thinning patch of uncombed sandy gray hair and framed by 1980s-style glasses. His tattered and stained blue T-shirt and well-worn blue jeans don't give off a millionaire vibe. He's the easygoing sort of guy I'd like to sit beside in a bar and share a beer or two.

The object of my visit is to record a video interview to post on The Progressive Farmer website at the same time we publish the account of my trip to Central America. Howard has been gracious enough to accept that proposal. So we set up the shoot in front of a small John Deere tractor in the doorway of the machine shed.

I ask Howard about the scale and purpose of his foundation's work. With a slight chuckle at the immensity of the number, he tells me his foundation has spent more than $300 million over the last decade on aid programs around the world. Much of that went to the Central American countries of El Salvador, Guatemala Honduras and Nicaragua. African nations have received some of the allocations, but Howard seems less enthusiastic about results there.

In Central America, Howard tells me, most of the HGBF funds go to projects aimed at bringing "50,000 farmers out of poverty and into the market to sell to local processors. That's a big step, but we've made a lot of progress." These projects are three- to five-year collaborative efforts that HGBF funds and NGO partners administer. Primary partners in Central America are Catholic Relief Services and the World Food Program.

Early on, some HGBF projects focused on bringing better nutrition to families through food programs. There is "an amazing rate of child malnutrition in pockets of Central America that can rival rates in Africa," Howard tells me. But after a few years, the foundation decided that nutrition programs were too expensive and required too much manpower. They weren't efficient uses of resources, and they seemed endless. So HGBF moved away from them.

Improving small farm production became the primary goal. Help people feed themselves.

With the world's population predicted to expand by nine billion people in the next 30 years, Howard tells me, "A lot of the small farmers around the world are going to have to increase production. We in the developed agricultural nations will not be able to ship enough food around the world to people who don't have the money to buy it or the transportation infrastructure to distribute it. Thirty years ago, I didn't understand that.

"But now, having been to 115 countries and having spent a lot of days with a lot of farmers in those countries, I understand we need to help them improve their productivity. They are not going to be selling food for export. They will be feeding their own families and selling to local markets.

"Most farmers in the world grow to feed themselves, and a lot of them don't grow enough. So they have times of hunger every year. The flip side of that is that it is absolutely going to take increased productivity in this country, too. We have the technologies to do that. We can grow more, but we also must be more environmentally sensitive."

Changing the world is not easy, and that is a lesson Howard Buffett says he learned early in his philanthropic career. For instance, he learned that you need local government support. But in seeking the best ways to attain that support, you must not be complicit; you must "fight lawlessness, corruption and cultural differences."

Consequently, the foundation is changing directions to emphasize advocacy programs more than in the past. "We've learned that without government support and integrity within those governments, you just can't have long-term success. So we have kind of changed our opinion over where we want to spend our money over the next 10 years versus where we spent it over the past 10 years."

How would Buffett assess his foundation's success over those past 10 years? Here, Howard gives a little shrug and a laugh. He's just an ordinary guy trying to do his best. "My wife calls me an optimistic pessimist, and that's probably a good description. I don't ever feel like I want to give up or that I can give up. But there are some big obstacles, and our foundation is only so big.

"Sometimes it's discouraging. But every time I visit places like Nicaragua or Honduras, I remember that I just love the people. They are amazing. When I sit down with a group of 20 or 30 farmers who are trying to eke out a living on 2 acres fighting all sorts of obstacles we don't even think about ... you can't give up on them. You have to believe there are ways to solve the problems. We have to keep pushing forward, and that probably makes me a bit of an optimist. But I am pessimistic much of the time, as well."

CHAPTER 11

RACE, RESILIENCE AND CONFEDERATE FLAGS

One November day in the late 1970s, I tagged along with a veterinarian as he made his rounds to farms in southern Minnesota. Like all vets who treat large animals, he had a stressful, physically demanding practice. Vets like him are subject to kicks in the gut, broken legs and puncture wounds. It's tough work.

Dr. Carlos Alvarez looked well-suited to the work. A dark-complexioned handsome man, he was tall and strong with a manner that was quiet and calm. As we drove, he explained with just a hint of a Hispanic accent that he had emigrated from Argentina to this small, ethnic-German town a decade ago. It took him a few years to get used to the cold. But this was home now, and his practice was healthy.

Earlier in the day, I had watched him do surgery on a dog in the controlled environment of his clinic. Now we are driving to a farm under a gunmetal sky and chilled air that bespeak the beginning of a long winter. Mixed-practice veterinarians in Minnesota must be adaptable.

As we pull into the farmyard of a small dairy, Dr. Alvarez parks the truck and sits quietly for a moment. He turns to me and says, "I have all kinds of clients. This one is … " He stops, sighs, shrugs his shoulders and eases out of the truck.

The farmer comes quickly toward us from his freestall barn, his limbs pumping furiously like a bantam rooster who sees an intruder in his yard. The farmer is bundled in a dirty coat with a hood that hides all his head except for his middle-aged red face, which is covered in three-day-old whiskers. The brown stains around his mouth are likely from chewing tobacco. "You were supposed to be here an hour ago," he immediately yells at Dr. Alvarez. Then he points at me. "Who is this?"

Dr. Alvarez explains that his previous stop—to look at a cow's stomach abscess on one of the neighboring farms—had gotten complicated and took longer than expected. He also explains that I am a reporter from the local newspaper and am doing a story about veterinarians.

The farmer doesn't seem to like either explanation. He looks me up and down like I was some alien form of life. He sees my camera. "You ain't takin' any goddamn pictures on my farm. Got it?"

I nod, and he barks at Dr. Alvarez: "I'll show you the calf."

The bantam rooster turns on his heel and heads back to the barn with Dr. Alvarez and me in his wake.

The black-and-white Holstein calf we find there is probably only a week old. It lies on its side in a bed of sawdust and dried manure. Its breathing is labored, shallow and fast. Dr. Alvarez kneels beside it and does an examination, beginning at its lolling tongue and working his way down to its palpitating chest. He considers for a few minutes then stands up to face the farmer, who has been peering over his shoulder.

"It's pneumonia. We can give it some medications, but it's pretty far along. I don't know if we can save it."

"Can't be pneumonia," the farmer spat out. "It was fine a couple of days ago."

"I'm sorry. That's what it is."

"I ain't ready to lose it. How much do the medications cost?"

Dr. Alvarez gives him a number, and the angry farmer explodes.

"You goddamn nigger! You think you can come out here and rob me blind? I ain't paying that much."

"Then you'll lose the calf," Dr. Alvarez calmly says.

"Get off my farm, nigger. And don't bother to send me a bill. You're worthless. I'll get an American vet out here who knows what the hell he's doing."

Dr. Alvarez shrugs. We turn and walk back to his truck. It isn't until we are in the cab that I notice his hands are trembling. "He'll lose that calf," he says.

A few moments later as we drive off the farm lane and onto the blacktop, he adds, "I'll send him a bill for my visit, and the hardhead won't pay it."

"Are any more of your clients that nuts?" I ask.

"Only a few. Thank God. But they make my life miserable."

That's the first and only time I've heard a brown-skinned Hispanic called a "nigger." I guess in some minds, what isn't white is Black, and what is Black is a nigger.

Decline of black farmers. In my long career, I haven't visited many Black farmers. Because America doesn't have many to visit. History accounts for why there are only about 45,000 Black American farmers, and racial inequity is a large part of that history.

Take the American tale of "40 acres and a mule" you might have heard in history class. As the story goes, U.S. Army Major General William Tecumseh Sherman paused long enough during his 1865 march across defeated Confederate Georgia to hold a meeting with a group of formerly enslaved people. He wanted to ask how they would take charge of their own lives as freemen.

One of the Black leaders, the Rev. Garrison Frazier, reportedly told Sherman and Secretary of War Edwin Stanton, who also attended the meeting: "The way we can best take care of ourselves is to have land and turn it and till it by our own labor ... and we can soon maintain ourselves and have something to spare ... .We want to be placed on land until we are able to buy it and make it our own."

That sounded like a reasonable vision for the future. After all, plantation slaves surely knew as much about growing crops as their white overseers. Given land and opportunity, newly freed people probably would survive and prosper as farmers.

Sherman and Stanton appear to have concurred, and Sherman issued Special Field Order No. 15, which set aside thousands of acres in the South so that "each [formerly enslaved] family shall have a plot of not more than 40 acres of tillable ground." He later threw in some surplus mules, and the phrase "40 acres and a mule" became part of our national lexicon. It came to symbolize reparations of a sort for rural Blacks whose families had endured more than 250 years of enslavement.

Field Order No. 15 as a transfer of land ownership was not unprecedented. Four years earlier in 1962, President Abraham Lincoln signed the Homestead Act, which gave 160 acres of surveyed "public land" to white settlers for a filing fee and a commitment to live on the land for five years. Of course in that case, the distributed land was home to indigenous peoples who did not have any say in the matter. At the time, there was little controversy about the transference of homestead land from one set of owners (Indians) to another (whites); it was within the government's power.

The Homestead Act was wildly successful. It granted about 80 million acres of farm- and ranchland (mostly in the West) to immigrants both from the eastern states and from other countries, especially Germany and Scandinavian nations. The Homestead Act changed the face and the culture of the Western Plains.

Turns out Field Order No. 15, by contrast, was mostly symbolic. A few months after it took effect, John Wilkes Booth assassinated President Lincoln, and new President Andrew Johnson reversed the order. He gave the land back to its white owners and, in essence, kicked Black farmers off the farms before they had time to reap their first harvest.

Despite the false promise of 40 acres and a mule, thousands of Blacks in the Old South did manage to remain in farming. They became tenant farmers, often renting land and sharing their crops with landowners who had once claimed them and their kin as property. It's not hard to imagine the dynamic of the new tenant/landlord relationship was heavily weighted toward the whites.

Remarkably, Black farmers persevered and expanded their holdings. The USDA Census of Agriculture reports that by 1910—only 48 years after the Emancipation Proclamation—Black farmers numbered close to 1 million and owned 16 to 19 million acres of farmland. But those numbers, like 40 acres and a mule, proved transitory. By 2017, the number of Black farmers had plummeted to below 50,000, and the amount of the land they owned had fallen by 3 million acres.

Multiple factors contributed to the demise of so many Black farmers' dreams, including systemic racism by no less an actor that the federal government.

For all American farmers, the U.S. Department of Agriculture is the gateway to federal funding in the form of loans and subsidies. Such funds can be crucial for farmers' economic survival during stressful times. And American agriculture has always experienced periods of economic stress. It's part of the bargain when you become a farmer.

The 1950s were one of those stressful periods. The number of all American farms declined from 5.9 million in 1950 to 3.7 million in 1957, according to the Census of Agriculture. Mechanization had decreased the need for human labor and made it possible for one farm family to plant many more acres. But to employ those new machines most efficiently and to justify their costs, farmers needed more land. So farm families with deep pockets bought out neighbors who either were poor managers or didn't have access to the capital required to buy machinery and land. An economic struggle of neighbor against neighbor ensued, and survival of the fittest became a way of life in rural America.

In such an environment, which continues today, government loans and subsidies can make the difference between economic success and selling the farm to take a job in the city.

To access those government services, farmers must apply at a county USDA office. It's perhaps not surprising that African American farmers often face a different reception from county agents than do their white counterparts. This was especially true in 1950s and 1960s Southern counties, where most Black farmers resided. Court documents reveal that African American farmers routinely were denied loans and subsidies based on their skin color. As a result, they could not plant, fertilize or harvest crops as they planned. They certainly couldn't expand their operations. With income restrained or dried up, families chose to look for work elsewhere. They sold their farms, and many became part of the Great Migration north to Chicago, Detroit and other cities where Black farm families hoped to start fresh in new industries.

The blatant discrimination in the administration of federal programs continued for decades, and by the 1990s, most Black farms had disappeared. Those that remained were under increasing economic pressure. They began to organize to fight for survival. For instance, the newly formed National Black Farmers Association marched on the White House and met with President Bill Clinton in 1997. African American farming groups also began seeking redress from the judicial system. Multiple lawsuits against the USDA claimed intentional discrimination both on a local and national level. Testimony from aggrieved African American farmers painted a portrait, especially in local USDA offices, of bald-faced racism that caused irreparable economic damage to Black-owned family farms.

In 1999, the racial discrimination class action suit of Pigford v. Glickman (Timothy Pigford was a Black farmer, and Dan Glickman was U.S. Agriculture Secretary) reached a settlement. The case involved African American farmers who had filed for assistance from the USDA between 1981 and 1996. With the settlement, those farmers and subsequent plaintiffs in the case were to receive more than $1 billion in cash, tax payments and debt relief.

The settlements helped stabilize some African American farms. And the number of Black-owned farms has increased. But the settlement could not resurrect family farms that had been killed by systemic government malfeasance.

As with any major class action lawsuit settlement, new claimants came forward—Blacks, Hispanics and American Indians. The total cost of settlements ballooned to $4 billion, and charges of rampant fraud emerged. Conservatives took this as proof that restitution was never a good idea, especially when it comes to cases involving race.

Echoes of the Pigford cases were heard in 2021. As the COVID pandemic ravaged the country, Congress passed the American Rescue Plan and designated $10.4 billion to assist farmers. It assigned about half of that to "disadvantaged" farmers, which largely meant Black farmers. This was only fair, Agriculture Secretary Tom Vilsack said: "For generations, socially disadvantaged farmers have struggled to fully succeed due to systemic discrimination and a cycle of debt."

Conservatives in Congress objected to the payment plan saying that funding African American farmers' recovery was a form of reverse discrimination. Worse, it was "reparations," a word fraught with divisive overtones.

So it goes. One segment of the population thinks that reparations are a way of placing blame for slavery and racial bias on generations that had nothing to do with it. Another segment says Blacks deserve compensation for four centuries of slavery and for the 150 years of segregation and systemic racism that followed emancipation. Still others say we should all just be color-blind.

America's struggle with racial inequality continues.

A DAY IN LOUISIANA

During a trip to Louisiana, a rancher and I hop into a utility vehicle to tour his cattle pens. On the way through a pasture gate, we pass an elderly Black man who wears tattered bib overalls and keeps his head down until we pull up next to him.

"Mornin' Jeremiah," the rancher says as we glide to a stop.

"Mornin' Mistah Grant," the man replies, barely looking up.

"I want you to get 20 feed sacks from that barn over there and take them back to the barn near the house. You can use the other Gator. You think you can do that for me?"

"Yessah."

"Make sure you get it done before lunch, OK?"

"Yessah."

Jeremiah never looks at Grant or me during this exchange.

As we drive off, Grant gives me a nudge with his elbow. "Ole Jeremiah. I kind of inherited him from my daddy. He worked for us for years, and when Daddy died, Jeremiah just never went away. We just kind of understood that he'd stick around. I find odd jobs for him to do. So he just keeps showing up, and I keep givin' him money every week." Grant laughs and elbows me again. "I'd feel bad if I just let him go, ya know? I have no idea how he'd get by."

On the one hand, it is admirable that Grant is generous and throws work Jeremiah's way. Grant is a Christian person who does good deeds.

On the other hand, it seems Grant would adopt a stray dog with about the same amount of compassion as he's adopted Jeremiah.

I don't say anything as we continue to the cattle pens. But I have a sour taste in my mouth. I'm not surprised by the racial chasm that exists between Grant and Jeremiah; I've seen it on other farm visits. I am just saddened that caste and privilege continue to coexist in adjoining, but separate, universes.

Racial inequality is engrained in rural America much as it is in every corner of this country. As a child of the suburbs, I saw it from a distance. When I lived in the city of Philadelphia, I saw it on the news and in the slums of north Philly. When I moved to a small town in Missouri, I was surprised—and shouldn't have been—to see it was endemic in the countryside, too. Racism takes different forms in rural areas and maybe is less evident because there are fewer minority people beyond big city limits, at least in the Midwest. But rural racism is no less pernicious than its city cousin.

HOMEGROWN RACISM

Like many rural communities, our town of Plattsburg has its white areas and its Black areas. About 10% of our inhabitants are African American. A smaller percentage are non-white of other ethnicities. The rest are white. Most times we are tolerant of each other and convivial. We're such a small community (2,300 souls), there isn't a lot of room for pointless animosity. Sometimes, however, stupidity prevails.

The road that leads to our town from the south is C Highway. It's a curvy, hilly two-lane that snakes its way through crop fields and pastures. It has almost no shoulder, and that has contributed to its reputation as a widow-maker. Over the years, C Highway's contours have occasioned scores of rollovers, missed curves and one-car crashes, too many of which have been fatal. A mile before you get to town on C Highway is a pasture where an old single-row corn picker lies permanently rusting. Mounted to its frame by a short vertical stick is a Confederate battle flag that flutters in the strong winds that whip through the treeless pasture. Over time, the flag gradually tatters and eventually falls apart. Inevitably, a new one replaces it in a few days.

I know the farm family that owns that ground. They tend to be loners and are protective of their land. One of them once accosted me as I was taking photos of his cattle herd from the road. "What the hell to you think you're doin'?" he yelled through the rolled-down window of his pickup.

"Taking pictures," I replied.

"Did you ask permission?"

"This is a public road. I don't have to ask permission."

"Those are my cows, you dumb son of a bitch. You can't take pictures of them without my permission."

I got back into my truck and left.

It was totally in character for that farm family to display a symbol of grievance and self-righteousness such as the Confederate battle flag.

The first time I saw that flag, I was infuriated but not surprised. That was the summer of 2017. Donald Trump had been president for only a few months, but already, white supremacists had started to poke their heads up from the shadows and demonstrated that they'd been emboldened by Trump's racist pronouncements and inuendoes.

Plattsburg is a multiracial town. But racism slithers in the shadows. It was home to slave trading in the mid-19th century. A statue of a slave owner sits in front of the county courthouse in our downtown. And during the 1950s, Plattsburg had an active Ku Klux Klan chapter.

I didn't know any of this history when we first moved to town. We bought a house on Broadway, a main residential street with well-kept homes of many varieties, styles and ages. All our neighbors were white except for the family that lived in the house next door. That family was African American. I didn't know until weeks after we moved in that the Guy family was a boundary buster. By some unwritten rule, Plattsburg's Blacks lived in the north part of town. The Guys were the first Blacks to move as far south as Broadway, and it was a cause of consternation for some.

"Did you know there were Blacks next door when you bought the house?" a townie asked me one day.

"I did," I said and received a puzzled look in response.

A neighbor told me that as she and her husband unloaded the moving van the day they moved to town, a pickup truck pulled to the curb, and the driver got out to offer a welcome. During the course of the friendly chatter, the driver offered: "We do have a lot of niggers here. But they mostly keep to their side of town."

In those days, too, Plattsburg had a country club pool but no public pool. A white teenage boy who was new to town invited a Black friend to go swimming with him at the country club. The friend looked amazed. "You know I can't go there!" he said.

"Why not?"

The friend laughed. "I guess you didn't notice I'm Black. No way they'd let me swim in that swimming pool."

Plattsburg's race issues usually stayed below the surface, and over the many years I lived there, I think the racial divide has closed considerably. More Blacks moved from the north side of town into the white parts of town and vice versa. Interracial marriage became almost commonplace. And Blacks and whites in general lived in quiet harmony.

So seeing that Confederate flag on the town's doorstep bothered me. A lot.

As a means of catharsis, I wrote an overheated open letter to the owner of the property where the Confederate flag blew in the wind. I sent it to the local newspaper where it appeared on their letters to the editor page:

To the person who placed Confederate flags along C Highway south of Plattsburg:

I'm sure you know the history of the Confederate battle flag you chose to honor. But in case there are gaps in your memory, here is a brief reminder.

- *The flag is a symbol of the Confederate States of America, which broke from the United States of America and started a war on its fellow Americans. People who flew the flag were traitors to the United States.*
- *The Confederacy was created by 11 Southern slave-holding states to protect the right of wealthy whites to own other human beings. These human beings (Blacks only) could be bought and sold; whipped and killed for breaking an owner's rules; and made to breed like livestock to increase an owner's wealth and to improve bloodlines.*
- *The Confederacy's constitution (Article I, Section 9) leaves no doubt about why the rebel union was formed. It states explicitly: "No bill of attainder, ex post facto law, or law denying or impairing the right of property in negro slaves shall be passed."*
- *The war the Confederacy killed as many as 750,000 Americans. Soldiers fighting under the Confederate battle flag you display eventually lost and surrendered unconditionally.*
- *The Confederate battle flag faded from public view after the war but reappeared almost 100 years later when it became a symbol of resistance to the Civil Rights Movement in the 1950s and 1960s. The Ku Klux Klan flew it at rallies, and segregationist George Wallace used it on his campaign buttons, billboards and license plates.*
- *Recently, the flag popped up again as a symbol of racial hatred in photos of a young white man who slaughtered nine Christians in a South Carolina church merely because they were Black.*

As a student of history, you also know that the U.S. Constitution—which the Confederacy sought to destroy—guarantees your right of free speech, including the right to fly that miserable flag. The Constitution makes that guarantee because all flags—including yours—are symbols of ideas and therefore protected speech.

Some people think the Confederate battle flag symbolizes heritage or a bygone way of life. They say it's all about a genteel South populated by polite gentlemen and cultured ladies. You can believe that if you want. Just remember that the wealth of those gentlemen and those ladies was based on slavery. They owned other human beings; they traded them like cattle and treated them as subhumans.

Considering its history, the Confederate battle flag symbolizes to me the dual atrocities of slavery and racial hatred. I don't know what it symbolizes to you.

My letter had no discernible effect on the flag waver, who continues to replace flags as they disintegrate in the wind. But I did hear from neighbors who appreciated my effort.

The summer before the 2020 election, Plattsburg became festooned with Trump flags and signs. One house displayed both a Trump flag and a Confederate flag. Trumpian displays were a disappointment to me but not a surprise. I had no doubt that our county would again vote for Trump because in 2016, almost 70% of my fellow Clinton countians marked the box for him. Still, it was discouraging to be reminded that I was so outnumbered in my town by people who wanted four more years of racism, division and fearmongering.

At about this same time, a young man in Plattsburg began parading around town in his old pickup. On the right side of the tailgate, he had installed a large American flag. On the left side of the tailgate was an equally large Confederate battle flag. For about two months, he drove slowly up and down our streets, the two flags flapping behind him. I wondered if he understood that, had the Confederacy won, the Stars and Stripes would have disappeared from Southern states. Missouri being a border state, there's no telling which flag it would have flown.

Eventually, the flags became torn and dilapidated, and the young man removed them. Much to my surprise, a few months later his rusty pickup truck displayed a new bumper sticker. It reads simply: "Coexist."

Perhaps there is hope.

CHILD OF THE SUBURBS

I was raised in the mid-20th century in a suburb of St. Louis, which was a racist city then and still has its turmoils even as it has grown increasingly Black. Many of our suburb's residents were "white flight" families that left St. Louis because their neighborhoods were becoming blacker. They feared that crime, lower property values and general degradation were inevitable results when Blacks moved in. So thousands of families headed for tract homes in the suburbs that were pure white.

My mother's family moved to the North County community of Black Jack, Missouri, in the 1940s, predating most white flight. I think my mother's family just wanted to get back to my grandfather's rural roots, and they bought a small acreage that had a dairy farm and orchards for neighbors. My father joined them when he returned from the war. He and my mother moved our growing family (my older brother and me) to nearby Florissant in 1951.

Many in my mother's family displayed classic symptoms of racism. I never heard my grandpa use the word "Negro." To him, Blacks were either "coloreds" or "niggers." Growing up, I didn't consider those words racist. That's just what you called African Americans in 1950s Missouri. Although some things gradually changed, Grandpa's vocabulary stayed the same. His son Jack was more actively racist. Even as a child, I understood there was cruelty behind his Sambo jokes and the malicious laugh that accompanied them. My mother was not overtly racist. But she was uncomfortable with people of color. When I was 23 and preparing to leave for the Peace Corps and Fiji, she had tears in her eyes as she said, "I'm afraid you'll marry a native girl."

My father was out of synch with his in-laws on matters of race. First, he was a man with a generous heart, and hate of any sort was foreign to him. Second—and this is just a guess on my part—his being a first-generation American moderated his beliefs about people who did not fit into the white-bread stereotype. I'm sure that in his early years, he must have experienced bias and disrespect because his parents spoke Italian and still practiced Old World customs. He was a "wop" or a "dago" to some. So he understood what it was like to be different. Yet Joe Patrico rarely said a harsh word about anyone. If he had a racist thought, it never escaped his lips. He was a neutral observer. By the time he was an old man, the racial character of Florissant had changed. I remember driving the streets with him and hearing him say as if commenting on the weather, "There sure are a lot of Black people here." No judgment. No animosity. Just an observation.

I didn't really know an African American kid until I went to high school, and then there were only three in my graduating class. In those days, Brazil nuts were "nigger toes." Eeny, meeny, miny, moe led to "catch a nigger by the toe." Amos 'n' Andy were cultural touchstones. I was a teenager before Diahann Carroll's television series "Julia" for the first time brought a Black woman into our living rooms who wasn't a maid, a nanny or a cook.

Even the sports world of my childhood was vastly white. Although Jackie Robinson had broken baseball's color barrier in 1946 with the Brooklyn Dodgers, my team—the St. Louis Cardinals, which was the southernmost team in the major leagues at the time—couldn't seem to find a talented Black athlete until 1954, when they signed Tom Alston.

The 1960s Civil Rights Movement opened my eyes to a pervasive evil I didn't see in my own neighborhood. Fire hoses. Attack dogs. Beatings. Murders. All in the name of segregation. The images in the newspapers and on television destroyed my blissful ignorance. I became confused, anxious and angry about what I saw.

Advancements slowly have taken place. "Colored" transitioned to "Negro" during my teens. And when I was in my 20s, the Black Pride movement gave permission for us whites to call people "Black." "African American" eventually came into common use. And "nigger" became "the N-word" because it was too hateful for most to say out loud.

But race division never disappeared. I remember with embarrassment that my cousin once refused to return a soul handshake I offered. "Let's keep it white, Jim," he said.

The first Black I came to know personally was T.C., my dorm roommate at Mizzou. On check-in day, I found my assigned room but not my assigned roommate. He apparently had arrived earlier, claimed a bed by piling clothes on it and left for other activities. On the dresser, he had left an Afro pick and some curly black hairs. "This should be interesting," I thought. And it was.

Over the next year, I found myself immersed in an American culture that was somehow foreign to me. I learned some dialect, found some new music to love and got an idea about what it meant to be "cool" in a parallel society. It was an introduction, not a master class. But the experience broadened my horizons.

While I learned about them, T.C. and his friends saw me for what I was: a suburban white who had not a clue about their world. Still, with all my limitations, they accepted me. We were friendly, and we kidded about each other's racial peculiarities. We smoked pot together and traded observations of the universe.

Although we didn't become fast friends, T.C. and I were considerate roommates. We each kept our side of the room in order and tiptoed in at night so as not to wake the other. We didn't, however, socialize outside the dorm except when T.C. asked me to drive him someplace. I was the only guy he knew who had a car, and he quickly learned exactly how to get a ride when he needed it. T.C. could be very persuasive. Once, he even convinced me to lend him my car for a date. Late that night he called to ask for help because, he told me in a peevish tone, my car had run out of gas.

I came to know and like T.C.'s Black friend Clarence when he spent part of a semester sleeping in our dorm room. He arrived one day in Columbia from the Missouri Bootheel, where he and T.C. had shared a boyhood. Clarence found a job as an orderly at the university hospital and planned to enroll in nursing school after he earned enough money to pay tuition. In the meantime, Clarence made himself a little nest between my bed and T.C.'s.

T.C. was at Mizzou to play basketball, and many of his friends were athletes. One of them, Hiawatha, was the coolest of the cool. He looked at me and my white friends with a kind of casual skepticism. We were OK in his eyes. But we were clumsy and alien. Definitely not cool. Still, he found us interesting enough to engage in conversations.

Hiawatha once invited me to his family's home in St. Louis. What he really did was ask for a ride. If I was going to St. Louis that weekend to visit my family anyway, Hiawatha reasoned, I might as well drive him, too. Even though his family's home was well out of my way, I agreed.

I don't remember our conversations on the 125-mile drive. But I remember we shared stories and laughed together. During long, but comfortable, silences, we looked out the windows at endless stretches of farmland sweeping past. We smoked a joint and laughed some more. We crossed the Missouri River twice as it wound its regal way across the state, taking its time to enjoy the scenery as it made its way toward its meeting with the Mississippi. Farmland turned to suburbs; suburbs turned to city.

As we drove toward Hiawatha's St. Louis neighborhood, I remember thinking, "Will it be a ghetto?" Suburbanites like me didn't visit inner-city neighborhoods; we quickly passed by them, sticking to main thorough-fares where we felt safe. I admit to nervousness. Would this be as danger-ous and decrepit a place as what I saw in news reports? When we rolled off Interstate 70, the entrance ramp dropped us into a neighborhood that indeed looked tired. Here and there were abandoned shops and homes. Broken glass. Bent sidewalks. Weeds.

But the neighborhood had good bones. There were two-story row houses of red brick with front porches and tiny yards. This was north St. Louis, where my parents had grown up. Maybe they had played on some of these same streets. Maybe they had leaned against some of the same trees that today clung to small parcels of soil and reached up for sunlight.

When we pulled to the curb in front of his house, Hiawatha could have just gotten out of the car and said goodbye. Instead, he surprised me and invited me inside to meet his mother and grandfather. We climbed the stairs to their second-story apartment, and I followed Hiawatha. He kissed and hugged his mom as I would do soon with my own mother. He called for his grandfather and hugged him, too.

This was my first time in a Black home, and I noticed how ordinary it was. Small but neat. Family pictures on the end table. A faded couch. Food smells coming from the kitchen. A dining table with place settings waiting for action.

I watched from the doorway as the family made their greetings. It occurred to me that I had never seen a nontelevision African American family interact. I was surprised by how familiar it was. They motioned me inside and made room for me on the couch. Turns out, they were as curious about me as I was about them. We chatted for a bit the way people who have no inherent connection but are intrigued by their similarities do. I declined a polite dinner invitation and didn't stay long. I had my own family to visit. I left and drove to the suburbs feeling as if I'd had a great adventure. Hiawatha had opened a door to his world, and I thanked him for it then and now.

I opened a door for myself when, after graduation, I volunteered for the Peace Corps and an assignment to the Pacific island nation of Fiji.

Nothing informed me more about race than my Peace Corps experience in Fiji, a multiracial country whose population is evenly split between indigenous Fijians and Indians. There is a smattering of whites and Asians thrown into the mix for seasoning.

Fijians are African by heritage. By physique and coloration, they strongly resemble African Americans. Over millennia, their ancestors incredibly migrated from East Africa 10,000 miles away across the Indian Ocean, through Timor Sea and the Coral Sea, and into the South Pacific, where they found the uninhabited archipelago of Fiji.

Indian heritage Fijians are more recent transplants, having been imported by the British to work sugarcane fields beginning in the 1870s. The British themselves arrived after Captain James Cook and Captain William Bligh separately mapped the Fijian Islands in the late 18th century. Fiji became part of the United Kingdom in 1874, and a sugar industry soon took shape on the islands. Fijian culture is of a hunter/fishermen/gatherer sort with a small amount of farming thrown in. But the indigenous people were not inclined to do the monotonous work in cane fields set up by the British. So British companies began importing hundreds of laborers from India to do the work Fijians would not. Some of the immigrant farm workers came willingly. Some were indentured. Some were tricked. A hundred years later, Indians made up half the population of the country.

During the first few weeks of my in-country Peace Corps training, I lived with Indian farm families and with Fijian villagers. It was the first time in my life that I was a minority all day, every day. I like to think I learned from the experience what it is like to be the "other" in a society. It taught me how to adapt and how to see the world from another point of view. Most important, it taught me humility. The cultures I experienced in Fiji were rich beyond my dreams. They offered joys and fulfillments unlike—but equal to—those in my own culture.

Fiji set the stage for a lot of foreign travel during my career, which has delivered me to more than 20 countries on five continents. One key attraction that travel holds for me is the sensation of "otherness." I've come to enjoy being the one on the outside looking in. I am the one whose body shape and skin color flag me as out of the ordinary. In any crowd, I am the one at whom people stare. I value these experiences, because they give me some small sense of what it must be like to be the "other" in American society.

I understand that for most of my life, I have leapt to conclusions about non-whites solely based on their looks and their language. In the end, I am a product of my time and place, and—to my regret—race is still an obstacle for me. I do have African American and Hispanic friends. But even in the most casual conversations with them and with other people of color, I still am conscious of our mutual "otherness." It's revealing that I find myself sometimes describing a person as a "Black" man or a "Hispanic" woman even when those adjectives are superfluous to the story I am telling.

On my pessimistic days, I regret that I am not color-blind and cannot ignore racial differences. On my optimistic days, I rejoice that I do see color, because it is a key component of the world's diverse cultures just as it is part of what delights the eye when it sees Nature.

BLACK FARMERS

My good friend and colleague Dan Miller introduced me to most of the African American farmers I've met. Dan was a senior editor of The Progressive Farmer when I was on staff there. In the early 2000s, he had a genius idea for an annual series of articles on America's Best Young Farmers and Ranchers. He would seek applications and cull from entries and industry leads five farmers or ranchers under the age of 40. He would visit their farms and write stories about their lives and their operations. The series took our magazine readers to places they'd never been and introduced them to young farmers who faced both similar and unfamiliar challenges on their paths to success.

I was involved in many of these stories as a photojournalist. I'd spend a day or two with each of the winners, visually documenting them and their families. We wanted candid images of everyday activities. So I was to be a fly on the wall as they worked, as they interacted with their families, as they lived their unique lives. It was a tremendous opportunity for me to go behind the scenes of farms from South Carolina to Southern California.

In the early 2000s, Dan consistently and consciously found African American farmers for the program. And I had the pleasure of working with three of them.

Gary Coleman is a cattle farmer in South Carolina, where he has pastures and hayfields spread over several counties. Gary did not have a farm background. He was a suburban kid from Ward, South Carolina, who fell into farming when a neighbor got him a job on a dairy. Although he was still in high school, Gary saved his money and started buying, feeding and selling bull calves. He could buy those calves for a pittance because bull calves are expendable critters on a dairy. They don't produce milk, and cows usually are bred from a semen tank, not a bull. But if you castrate bull calves and feed them to maturity, they have value at the packing plant. That's what Gary did, and he made money and diversified his farming operation. "By the time I was in college," he told me, "I had enough money to buy 75 mama cows. They weren't the best mama cows. But it was a start." Gary used the mama cows offspring to background as beef cattle, which he sent to Midwest feedyards for finishing. By the time I met Gary, he had acquired land, begun a new cow/calf operation and started his own direct-marketing brand of locally processed, packaged beef that was hormone- and antibiotic-free. Gary is quite the entrepreneur.

Lamont Bridgeforth, of Tanner, Alabama, traces his farming heritage to enslaved people in the 1830s. His great-, great-, great-grandfather George Bridgeforth acquired a few acres after the Civil War, and the family kept and increased their landholdings against heavy odds. Today, the Bridgeforth name is one of the most respected in Alabama agriculture.

When I visited, Lamont told me that finding a work/life balance was difficult with three kids and more than 9,000 acres to tend.

My third Best Young (Black) Farmer was P.J. Haynie (Philip J. Haynie III). He was the most intriguing to me. In 2014, I visited him and his family at his farm headquarters in Virginia's Northern Neck region, which lies between the Rappahannock and the Potomac rivers where they flow into Chesapeake Bay. This is low country where flatland and short hills live comfortably together, and where tall groves of trees mark the many rivulets and creeks that drain into the big bay just beyond. There are no large farm fields here, just a patchwork of irregularly shaped tracts threaded among asphalt two-lanes. P.J. farms with his father, Ricky (Philip J. Haynie II). The two have pieced together small patches of acreage that form a quilt of land spread over four counties.

They are part of a long line of Haynies, who trace their farming legacy through five generations to Robert Haynie, an enslaved man born in 1823. After emancipation, he scraped together a living for his family on 60 acres of land he somehow managed to acquire. Today's Haynie farm is several thousand acres. But it didn't come easy.

During some rough times in agriculture, Ricky had to declare bankruptcy. He gradually recovered and started rebuilding. After graduating college, P.J. came back to help. Part of the rebuilding process involved a discrimination lawsuit against the USDA, which the Haynies won. They wouldn't be farming today, P.J. told me, if they had not won their case.

Today, the family's farming operation is on solid financial footing. To diversify their income and risk, they own and operate an over-the-road trucking company with about a dozen vehicles. These are busy folks.

The October morning I arrive, I find both P.J. and Ricky in the farmyard getting crews and equipment ready for a day of soybean harvest. P.J. is a big, handsome man with a wide and ready smile, intelligent eyes and a cell phone in his hand. He's gracious and accommodating. But I can see he's busy, and I keep our introductory chat short. "I'm just here to watch you work," I say.

I explain that I won't be in the way. I'll just use my rental car to follow him to his various stops. P.J. glances over his shoulder at the shiny sedan I arrived in. "Would you rather drive a pickup?" he asks.

"Sure would. That way I can drive out into the fields with you."

"Thought so." He grins and points to a pickup parked nearby. "Keys are in it," he says.

Then he's off.

First, P.J. ducks under a tractor and scoots through the gravel on his back until he joins one of his employees at the rear axle. I hear them talking about a quick repair that must be made before the machine can get to work. Next, P.J. is giving three other employees their assignments for the day. In the meantime, he's on the phone talking to his truck drivers deployed across the region. He's interrupted by a semi coming down the lane with a tractor on its flatbed.

Seems the Haynies have bought a new 8360R John Deere tractor, which they plan to equip with dualies on the rear for more traction when pulling implements. They are trading in an 8330 Deere, which is a fine machine but accommodates only single wheels on the rear. The equipment exchange tells me P.J. has both a need for more pulling power (which implies large tillage tools) and the financial wherewithal to make a discretionary upgrade to one of Deere's latest models.

It takes his crew only a few minutes to roll the new tractor off the flatbed and run the trade-in tractor into its place. Meanwhile, P.J. chats with the tractor dealer's delivery man, whose dealership is in Hopkinsville, Kentucky, more than 700 miles away. As he checks out the new 8360R, P.J. tells me he tries to buy local. But if he can't find what he needs at an attractive price, he buys equipment wherever he can. This tractor probably cost more than $180,000.

As the dealer's man pulls out of the yard and heads back to western Kentucky, P.J.'s men start the laborious process of putting new 8-foot-tall tires onto the new tractor's second set of rear hubs. They use a forklift and chains to maneuver the 600-pound tires and wheels into place.

His men know how to do that job unsupervised, so P.J. moves toward a grain bin with me in tow and a cell phone to his ear. His father, Ricky, and another man are making repairs to an auger that needs attention before use today. Ricky is in his 60s and is a spitting image of a bespectacled James Earl Jones. He acknowledges my presence but is too preoccupied with his task to engage in friendly chatter.

Apparently he and the employee have had trouble with the auger repair, and Ricky does not appreciate P.J.'s suggestion about how to solve the problem. Ricky is a little snippy, but he, the employee and P.J. wrestle with the auger and eventually get it into place, which is snuggled under the discharge chute of a small grain bin.

That issue resolved, P.J. heads to his next task as he pulls the cell phone out of his pocket again. It's like that all day. P.J. moving, his cell phone plastered to his ear, me following.

We don't have much time to talk because, in the course of this one day, P.J. will oversee a liming operation, a soybean harvest and the spraying of a field with a preemerge herbicide.

The liming involves using a front loader and a 20-ton-capacity spreader truck. P.J. uses the front loader's bucket to transfer into the spreader a mountain of rock lime that lies at the end of a harvested cornfield. The truck then races off into the field, its rotary fan at the rear broadcasting a spray of dusty lime over cornstalks. It makes patterned 80-foot-wide passes until it runs out of lime then returns to the mountain for more. As soon as the last of the lime is spread, the driver hops into a tractor with a 30-foot-wide tillage tool. He repeats the same pass pattern to lightly incorporate the lime into the soil so it is available for plants next spring.

A few minutes later and a few miles away, P.J. is in a combine ready to begin the soybean harvest of a 40-acre field. Almost immediately, he runs into trouble. An auger in the combine's storage tank jams, and P.J. and a crew member climb into the tank to figure out the problem. They discover a broken part, which they don't have in stock. P.J. calls the dealership on the other side of the county. It's a busy time, and all their delivery trucks are out. The auger part won't be here until tomorrow. The combine is out of commission, and harvest of this field is stalled for at least a day.

Stymied, P.J. gets on the phone with his sprayer operator about 10 miles away. The plan is to spray a harvested soybean field with an herbicide that will stay in the ground to keep the weeds under control next spring. P.J. has hired a custom applicator to do this job. But he wants to make sure the job is done right. So he hops into his truck, and I follow.

The semi with a nurse trailer is already there when we arrive at the target field. On its flatbed is a huge tank of water and a couple of small tanks with herbicide. As we pull into the field, a self-propelled sprayer that looks like a praying mantis comes lumbering up with its signature bouncy gait. Its tires are nearly 6 feet tall to give the machine clearance of growing crops in the spring and summer. The tall tires and individual wheel suspension explain why this beast bounces as it runs on the road at up to 35 mph. This sprayer has arms that unfold to 60 feet, but some are as wide as 120 feet. Its product tank can hold up to 600 gallons of liquid. It's outfitted with precision sensors and mechanisms that let it vary application rates as needed. It also can automatically raise and lower the boom to keep it level even as the machine navigates bumps and slopes in the field. Sprayers like these are marvels of modern ag technology, which is why they can cost a quarter of a million dollars.

The sprayer pulls alongside the nurse trailer, and P.J. goes to meet the driver as he climbs down a ladder from the cab. The two confer briefly, then P.J. climbs onto the trailer to begin the process of transferring water and the right amount of chemical to the sprayer tank. This will take a while.

So while I hate to interrupt P.J., I remind him that I really need to get some family pictures, and it's getting late in the day. Are the kids home? His wife? Is Ricky available?

We'd talked about all this on the phone before my visit and while I photographed him today. I planned that we get the shoot finished in one day. But now P.J. throws me a curve. "I talked to Lisa [his wife] a little while ago," he says. "She's tied up at the clinic [she's an M.D.] and is not sure when she'll get home."

"I can come back first thing in the morning, if that works."

"I don't know. She leaves for work and the kids leave for school pretty early, and they're always running late." He says this last with a "what can I do" grin.

We discuss options. It's really important for the story that we show P.J. as not just a farmer. He is a family man, a father and husband, too.

As a compromise, we decide to try for photos of him with his sons Philip IV and Trevor, who are at the house now. Daughter, Colette, has some after-school activity and won't be home until well after dark. Maybe Ricky will be around.

He is. As I drive up to P.J.'s two-story white farmhouse, Ricky is in the front yard with his young grandsons, and he is in a better mood than when I saw him earlier. While P.J. goes inside with the boys to change into clean clothes, Ricky and I talk.

The man is proud of his family. Besides P.J., he has four daughters. One of them earned doctoral degrees; one is a physician; one is a physical therapist; and one does very well for herself in finance, thank you. Ricky jokes about P.J. as the one who "only" has a bachelor's degree. But I can hear his pride in that dynamo of a son I've struggled to keep up with all day.

P.J. described to Dan Miller the relationship he and Ricky share: "We love each other a hundred times a day. We may argue more than that. But I'm living my childhood dream. I'm working with my dad."

When P.J. and the boys return, we get to work, and I try to find a photo that portrays the family dynamic and says something about a successful farm. We move to the grand wraparound porch that frames the tall windows and black shutters of the impressive house. We try the matching rocking chairs on the porch. We try the stairs. It's not working, and I ask the four Haynie men to step into the yard with me. Maybe we can get that nearby field and the house in the same photo. Just then the sun breaks through the cloud layer that has dulled the light most of the day. Philip II has his arms wrapped around Philip IV, who stands in front of him. Philip III places his hands on Trevor's shoulders. Three generations of Haynies stand proud in front of their house, which the sunset has turned to gold.

I drive to the hotel that night thinking about that last photo of the day. It turned out just fine.

I return the next morning before sunrise. P.J. is correct: Lisa and the kids are rushing to get their day started. P.J. invites me inside for coffee while the rest of the family flies around in what I can only assume is their normal chaotic start to the day. When the last backpack if filled, we hurry outside into a gray morning with a sky only just beginning to lighten. These photos don't turn out as well as the sunset shots. But I'm glad I got to meet Lisa and daughter, Colette, even if it's only for a few frantic minutes.

Time for me to head to Richmond and my next assignment.

On the drive, I speculate about the Haynies. The family has fought racial discrimination for generations. And they seem to have won. After all, their farm and trucking businesses thrive, P.J.'s generation is filled with educated professionals, and their future looks bright. Yet as busy as P.J. is, he makes time to serve as an officer on the National Black Growers Council (NBGC), an organization devoted to minority farming issues. Why? Isn't that battle finished?

The hard fact is that many Black farmers, especially those that grew up in underfunded and de facto racially segregated rural areas, don't have the education a modern farmer needs for success in today's high-tech agriculture. NBGC helps undereducated Black farmers navigate bureaucratic mazes. It schools them on new farming technologies. And it gives them a social network that looks like them. It also lobbies for them in state legislatures and in Congress.

Another hard fact: Racism didn't disappear when the courts ruled in favor of Black farmers.

The Haynies remember both the distant and the recent past. They remember that when Phillip went bankrupt, it was because he could not get credit from banks. Yet those same banks gave credit to white farmers in much the same financial situations.

P.J. especially remembers, which might be why he has stayed politically active. As he told my friend Dan Miller: "My dad was determined not to be overcome. All he wanted was a fair shot. I saw him struggling. I was determined to help him out."

CHAPTER 12

COUNTRY SCHOOLS

If you want to start an argument in a rural community, suggest that two towns merge their schools. Nothing is more important to a small town's identity than its school, and anyone who fools with the school is asking for a fight.

I live in Clinton County, Missouri, where people—even those in their 80s and 90s—refer to themselves as Tigers or Mules or Bulldogs, indicating they attended school in Plattsburg, Lathrop or Gower. School pride and town pride are wound tightly together as twine around a bale of hay. This pride daily manifests itself in a bone-deep rivalry that pokes its nose into coffee shop conversations. It exhibits itself as envy about a rival town's new school building, sarcasm about how another school's new superintendent runs the district and, yes, outrage that one town's football team laid waste to ours on Friday night.

In my trips around rural America, I've relied on rural schools as a measure of a town's health. Strong schools indicate a community's willingness and ability to fund good education. Weak schools might mean community discord or economic fragility. When schools merge, it's usually because there is not enough money to support more than one school in a county. Or there are too few students to justify keeping the doors open.

In the spring of 2001, I read a wire service report about the town of Morland, Kansas, which was losing its high school. I decided to make the 350-mile drive to investigate, because I was curious to learn what had gone wrong there.

The farm town is in northwest Kansas, on the edge of the High Plains. It's a semiarid region sparsely inhabited by cattle ranches and wheat farms. Morland's population when I visited was listed at 164. Out my truck window on the way across Kansas, I saw scrubby land grazed by a few lonely cows. The south fork of the Solomon River weaved in and out of view behind a curtain of cottonwoods. Occasionally, I saw a center pivot sat idle, waiting for its owner to begin irrigating corn or soybeans. Spaced miles apart were farmsteads with modest houses, metal machine sheds and rusting grain-storage facilities.

State Highway 24 becomes Main Street as you arrive in Morland, and the speed limit drops from 55 to 30 miles per hour. If you travel five blocks without stopping, the road becomes Highway 24 again, and you speed up as you leave town.

Main Street is lined with mostly one-story brick storefronts, interspersed with metal buildings housing businesses such as a car mechanic and a beauty salon. There are gaps between several of the buildings representing buildings that burned or fell down and were not worth replacing. The town is about three blocks deep with small, neat homes north and south of Main Street. Morland also has its own low-rent district, which consists of a couple of blocks of neglected two-bedroom homes with paint-peeled siding and weed-strewn yards. A Methodist Church seems to be the only religious business in town.

Morland High School graduated its first class in 1917 with four students. By coincidence, that's the number of students in the school's last graduating class—the class of 2001. I was in Morland just weeks before Robbie Ellis, Michael Clayton, Cody Keith and Georgann Meier received their diplomas. Shortly after the graduation ceremony, the school closed its doors for the last time. The 15 underclassmen who would have attended Morland in the fall enrolled instead in various other schools, including the one in Hill City, 12 miles east on the state highway.

School closings long have been a fact of life in rural America. But the process seems to be gaining speed, especially in the Great Plains states. The culprit, of course, is out-migration. How are you going to keep school doors open if there aren't enough kids to attend or parents to pay the tax bills?

Census numbers from Graham County, where Morland sits, tell a familiar story. Population has declined for decades on the rolling expanse between the Rocky Mountains and the Corn Belt. In 1910, Graham County was home to 8,700 souls. That was the population peak. By 1930, the number of inhabitants had dropped to 7,772. After the Dust Bowl, it dropped again as families fled struggling farms to find paying jobs in the cities.

World War II and the promise of urban jobs it created sent more people down the road away from Graham County and toward cities near and far. Census takers found only 5,020 people in the county in 1950. About the same number were counted when Robbie Ellis' parents graduated from Morland High School in the 1960s. Senior classes then numbered in the teens. But the 1980s and 1990s saw even more departures from Graham County. By the 2000 census, the entirety of the county's population was a mere 2,946 people. Heck, there are high schools in Kansas City with more people than that.

For some, a declining population—and especially the closing of a town's high school—are signs of a tragic new era. Shelly Swayne, the last principal of Morland High School, told the Associated Press, "Some people are angry we had to close the school. Some people are sad. It's hard for us to see beyond our own boundaries. We might think this as a single phenomenon happening to us. But it's a lot bigger than we are."

To the Class of 2001, the school closing isn't a tragedy. These are teenagers, after all. Their vision is on the future, not on the past.

"It's not a big deal," Robbie Ellis tells me. She's an outgoing, take-charge kind of girl with plans of her own, and they don't include Morland.

The principal has gathered for me three of the four graduating seniors in the high school's empty gym. It's still decorated with Tiger mascots and victory pennants that boast the Morland Tigers won the Kansas State Class 1A basketball championships in both 1974 and 1975. The school was a basketball powerhouse. But recently, retired basketball hoops now are folded to the ceiling and hover like dusty memories. Still, the gym's wood floor is newly cleaned and polished. It looks ready for the next season—if there were going to be one.

Robbie tells me she plans to attend Colby College, 55 miles down the state highway in Colby, Kansas, for business and office tech classes. She's not sure exactly where a college education will take her. But she hopes for a career in some city.

Cody Keith is a skinny, self-assured guy in a wheelchair, who wears a wide smile and wire-rimmed glasses. Come fall, he plans to go to Kansas State University in Manhattan, 225 miles away. He'll be a mechanical engineer someday, he says.

Georgann Meir is a bright-eyed young woman with energy and wit to spare. She's headed to Kansas City and a technical training school. Maybe, she says with a winning smile, she'll become a cosmetologist. With her gift of gab, I suspect she'll do well.

Perhaps it's not surprising that all the graduates have plans for a future that will take them away from Morland. I ask if any of them will ever come back. They shrug in unison. Who knows?

Whatever the future, none of the Class of 2001 regrets the years they have had together. Georgann tells me that attending Morland High School has been "a total advantage. You know all the teachers really well, and they know you. With a class this small, everybody gets a chance to say what's on their mind."

"We've known each other for 13 years," Robbie says. "We're more like family than anything."

As if to prove it, she reaches down and ruffles Cody's hair. He snarls at her the way a brother snarls at his sister. And the whole Class of 2001 laughs.

LITTLE SCHOOLHOUSE ON THE PRAIRIE

While many rural school districts have closed or consolidated with neighbors, a school district in Platte, South Dakota, followed a different path in the 1990s. The Platte School District voted to maintain its four existing one-teacher rural schools when possible. One of those schools, LaRoche School, is a one-room schoolhouse 20 miles from Platte and not far from where the Missouri River bends and snakes its way through the wide-open spaces of southeast South Dakota's prairie lands. It's a region where cows and coyotes outnumber people, and neighbors might be miles apart. Despite the gaps, those neighbors form close bonds. They live the same hard-working lifestyles on adjoining farms and ranches that are healthy but not wealthy. Almost by necessity, neighbors help each other with the work, and they often help raise each other's children just as family members would.

In the fall of 1990, I contacted Karen Erickson, the LaRoche School's only teacher, and arranged to meet her on Tuesday of the following week. The Monday before our meeting, I made a five-hour drive from home to spend the night in Yankton, which left me a two-hour drive the next morning. Since I wanted to be there as school started, I left the motel before dawn on a two-lane highway headed west into the prairie lands.

The moon is setting as I leave the hotel, and its departure creates near-total darkness. I've driven the Great Plains at night many times, and it has always made me feel tiny and alien. There's an aloneness about it, a sense that my truck and I don't belong. In the daylight, the prairie is vast and primitive. But at least you can see the horizon and where you fit into the landscape. At night, the Great Plains is empty.

If you were to stop by the side of the road and look up, you'd see the naked, starry universe, stripped of the gauzy edges of city lights and all human activity except, perhaps, for the blinking lights of a solitary jetliner headed to some faraway airport.

Driving, you are in a moving bubble of light surrounded by immense blackness. I've looked down on those bubbles from the seat of a jetliner, and they look lonely and strange, like tiny luminescent sea creatures scuttling across an ocean floor.

On the Great Plains' two-lanes at night, all you see are your own headlights on pavement and on the yellow centerline stripes that zip past you monotonously. Occasionally in the distance are lights from scattered farmhouses isolated in the darkness. Every 30 miles or so, you see a pickup heading toward you as a speck of light in the blackness. Twin white headlights grow until they nearly blind you, whooshing by like a comet in the night that recedes into the distance, and all you see in your side mirror are two vanishing red taillights. You are alone again, slipping through the night. Even your truck's radio is scant company. One or two AM stations fade in and fade out, leaving you with a static buzz and a renewed sense of isolation.

Gradually, the glow of a new day appears in my rearview mirror. The pale light spreads upward gradually, and the sky in front me begins to turn from black to gray. A layer of clouds comes out of hiding, and through the side windows, the world starts to re-form. At first it is only shapes and shadows, but it soon becomes weedy ditches beside the road, then fencelines, then solitary stands of trees in the distance. The Great Plains has reappeared. I'm back in the real world.

As I turn off the highway and drive up the gravel road to the school, the dawning sun clears the horizon. It shoots rays of gold that illuminate the underside of a bank of clouds and turn them purple. The sunbeams bounce off the front windows of the little school ahead, and the panes seem to blink, as if suddenly awakened by a bright light.

The new day is gorgeous.

In the fresh light, the schoolhouse is a white clapboard building in a field adjacent to a grove of trees. It has a single dormer and a roof that slopes to the north so prairie winter winds can roll over it. It sports a brick chimney that suggests a wood stove inside. An enclosed porch juts from the building's main entrance and forms a vestibule to shield the main room from wind and cold when children open the door.

On the prairie this morning, the schoolhouse is aged and authentic. I can imagine the scene a hundred years ago as a farmwife and her children rode up the gravel road in horse and buggy.

As I exit the truck 100 yards from the schoolhouse to take in the view with my cameras, the front door opens, and a young girl with blond pigtails comes out. In her hands are the Stars and Stripes, which she hooks to a flagpole and hoists on a white rope. She sees me watching and waves shyly, then rushes back inside to tell her classmates the magazine guy is here.

Karen Erickson is a warm, motherly woman in her early 40s who greets me at the door with a strong handshake and a friendly smile. "Alright, alright," she says to the giggling kids behind her. "Settle down. This is Mr. Patrico. I told you he's going to spend the day with us. I expect each of you to be on your best behavior while he's here."

It'll take them awhile to get used to me. After all, a stranger doesn't often show up at this prairie school with cameras hanging from his neck and a reporter's notebook sticking from his back pocket. To make the situation more comfortable, Mrs. E (as they call her) instructs each of the kids to introduce themselves. It doesn't take long. There are only 12 children ranging from kindergarten to seventh grade. I learn that all but two are farm or ranch kids, and that Mrs. E is married to a farmer. When I tell them I drove all the way from my small-town home north of Kansas City, they seem impressed. When I tell them I have a 4-year-old daughter and a 6-year-old son, they give me credit for being a dad. And when I tell them I'm on assignment from a national magazine, they want to know if they will be famous.

"We'll see," I laugh. "But I have to tell you, the magazine wants me to get good pictures of you, and the only way I can do that is if you forget I'm here. Just have a regular school day. Pay attention to Mrs. E and not me. It'll be a good day."

Before long, the kids scatter to their desks and get on with the work—and play—of education in a one-room schoolhouse.

It's a 15 by 20 room with wide-plank wooden floors and a dropped ceiling. A green blackboard takes up most of one wall, and large windows fill the room with light. At the front of the room, Mrs. E's old-fashioned wooden desk is large and ponderous. Its drawers have wood pulls and brass keyholes. The swivel chair behind the desk is stained dark except for its arms, which are worn from years of use. The students' desks are newer: metal legs, a Formica top, a storage shelf below. Metal and plastic chairs slide underneath the desktop. The furnishings make me feel that I've been transported back to the 1960s.

The building itself dates to 1917. When it was built, kids arrived at school on horseback and in buggies. To travel much farther to a school in town was impractical for isolated farm kids. So schools such as LaRoche sprang up on the South Dakota prairies wherever there were enough farm and ranch families to share the cost of a teacher. In the old days, itinerant teachers agreed to stay a year or two at a prairie school. They were paid little. But room and board were provided by one of the families. It was a system that lasted well into the 20th century. It wasn't until main roads were paved and speedy motor vehicles became ubiquitous that parents were able to drive kids to town every day. Yellow and black buses also trundled down rural roads to pick up kids standing at the end of long driveways, sometimes waiting in tiny huts whose three sides sheltered them for prairie winds. As it became feasible to haul kids to town, prairie schoolhouses began to close.

LaRoche stayed open, in part because the state of South Dakota saw value in keeping farm kids closer to home. When I visited in 1991, there were 82 rural (one-teacher) schools in the state. By law, if five neighboring families wanted their kids to go to a rural school, the local district must find a way to make that happen.

LaRoche is part of the Platte School District, and Superintendent Jim Walker told me he liked the state's rural school policy. "We have five rural schools in our district, and the students do quite well. When they come to town for junior high and high school, they excel. Several of our recent valedictorians started in rural school programs."

Walker allowed that he might be biased in favor of rural schools. "I taught in rural schools myself," he says with pride.

Anne Nye also will vouch for rural schools, at least for LaRoche. When she and her family moved to the area from the big town of Mobridge, South Dakota (population 3,100) three years ago, she enrolled daughters Tali (fifth grade) and Sara (third grade) in LaRoche.

"When we arrived, we were impressed by how well the kids here were taught. We found out that our kids [from the big town] were actually a little behind the kids at LaRoche," she told me. "But they caught up because Mrs. E is able to spend more individual time with them."

Individual attention has a corollary. While one student is receiving personal lessons, the rest must fend for themselves. Rural school students are thus forced to be independent. That helps them develop good study habits, Superintendent Walker told me. "At a rural school, when the teacher is teaching the other grades in the room, students are expected to do a lot of work on their own. As a result, when they finally come to our town schools, they have more discipline and a greater ability to learn on their own."

There are, of course, disadvantages to rural schools. They don't have the technical resources town schools can afford. Nor can they offer specialized instruction for students who have learning disabilities. "At LaRoche," Walker says, "they have all the same teaching tools as our town schools—computers and TVs—and such. But they don't have as much physical education equipment. And they don't have access to a library." (This was in the days before Internet access became a necessary educational tool. Lack of broadband also would have been a liability for rural schools.)

Rural school kids can't participate in extracurriculars like band or sports. That's a key reason Walker thinks it's essential for rural school kids to come to town schools after the seventh grade. "They need the socialization that extracurriculars provide," he says.

Another potential problem for rural schools is finding personnel. When there is only one teacher, a lot depends on that person's abilities.

"It takes a special person to be a teacher in a rural school," Walker tells me. "I can't describe exactly what kind of person. But whenever I have had to select a new teacher for a rural school, I have relied on a feeling deep inside me that the person is right for the job."

Apparently, Karen Erickson fit whatever exceptional characteristics Walker's gut required.

When she started teaching at LaRoche five years ago, Mrs. E wasn't sure she'd like it. She had taught in Platte for several years and was comfortable in that kind of school. One teacher per classroom for one grade of students suited her just fine. Still, when Walker asked her to teach at LaRoche, she accepted.

School day. It's lunchtime at LaRoche now. Mrs. E has the students retrieve their lunch bags from a refrigerator in an alcove of the room where a microwave, stove and oven also reside. "You have to be a jack-of-all-trades here," she says to me over her shoulder as she puts a food tray into the microwave. "We obviously don't have a cafeteria, so I do everything from heating up lunches to cleaning toilets."

While the kids eat at a long table in a corner of the room, Mrs. E tells me that she quickly got over her hesitancy about teaching in a rural school, and it's been a fulfilling experience. "Now that I've been here, I think every teacher should work in a rural school for at least one year. I've learned a lot here." But it hasn't been easy. Unlike her colleagues in town, Mrs. E must prepare daily lesson plans for four different grades, which she teaches by moving from class to class, each in its own part of the room. And she must be able to juggle the emotional and educational needs of various age groups.

The reward? "You get much closer to your kids out here," she says.

The kids feel that, too.

When Tali and Sara moved to LaRoche, the rest of the students rejoiced. "They were excited to have new kids to play with," Mrs. E remembers.

But Tali was nervous that first day at LaRoche. She didn't know anyone and worried she wouldn't fit in. What if they were mean to her?

Although she now feels at home in LaRoche school, she misses some things about her former school. She tells me during recess that she liked having a lunchroom where she and her larger group of friends could meet and socialize. She misses having a gym for P.E. She misses, most of all, a music room. If only she could take music classes again.

"I also liked separate grades," she tells me frankly. "And there were so many more kids to play with. If you got mad at one, you could go and play with others. Here there aren't so many kids ... but I like them all."

Relationships that rural school kids develop last beyond their time at LaRoche, Mrs. E tells me. "Sometimes they fight like cats and dogs here. But when they go to school in town, they stick up for each other. Don't start a fight with one of my kids unless you want to fight them all."

Tali's mom, Anne, reinforced that theme. She tells me, "I'm really glad my girls have had the opportunity to go to this kind of school. It has been like getting to be part of another family."

Near the end of my day at LaRoche, the warm afternoon light has begun streaming through the large windows, bringing a drowsy quiet. All lessons are finished by now, and the kids are getting a head start on homework. Odie, the big black dog that adopted the school last year, is curled up in a corner napping and having a dog dream that sets his paws to twitching.

At her desk, Mrs. E is talking to fourth grader Melanie, who had trouble with her homework last night and wants help. Mrs. E's comforting words are too soft to hear from across the room. But I see Melanie lean against her, and I see Mrs. E slip an arm around her. Soon, the girl is touching her head to the teacher's forehead as they talk.

It's a simple gesture, a sign of trust and affection. It's not what you might expect in most student-teacher conversations. Here it seems natural.

Letters. I don't get a lot of feedback from story subjects. But a week after my story on LaRoche school appeared in mailboxes across the country, I received an envelope stuffed with several letters written with No. 2 yellow pencils in large, neat handwriting. Here are my favorites.

Dear Mr. Patrico,

Thank you for making us almost famous. All of us are very happy. Everyone is talking to Mrs. E about this. I am going to tell almost all my relatives about those pictures in the magazine. I wish Odie the school dog could write to you too.

Love,

Brandy

Dear Mr. Patrico,

Thank you for teaching me how to hold a camera. Thank you for the story. We liked the pictures too. It was fun to read about ourselves in a magazine.

Your friend,

Keith

Dear Mr. Patrico,

Thanks you for picking us to write about. Today we were going to dig fossils at our farm but it rained and we can't go.

Conrad

Dear Mr. Patrico,

We saw your article about us in the magazine. I read the part where you interviewed me, it was funny to read about what I said! We are kind of famous now! Could you send us copies of the magazine? We have a lot of requests for them.

Thanks for coming. It was very fun.

Your friend,

Tali

Dear Mr. Patrico,

I just want to add my note of thanks along with the kids. They were really excited about "their" article. One grandmother called first and a mom sent the magazine to school to show us. We soon had other calls. Now we've received letters and calls even from out of state. I'm glad school is nearly out so I can answer them properly.

To echo the kids … it is really neat to be a little famous. You made my sometimes difficult job sound so unique and special. There's one thing for sure, you made a memory that will last a lifetime.

Thank you!

Mrs. Erickson

I checked back with Platte School District in 2022 and learned that LaRoche school was no more. In 2003, the district had closed all its rural schools. Current Superintendent Joel Bailey told me that Platte School District itself had consolidated with a neighboring district to become Platte-Geddes School District. "It was just a matter of efficiencies," he told me of the closings. "There were not a lot of kids attending rural schools, and we had the expense of teachers and staff."

I suppose I wasn't surprised. Consolidations and closings inevitably happen when it makes financial sense to reduce the number of school buildings to save on upkeep and maintenance. Or when student populations drop to a level at which teacher salaries and small class sizes are not compatible. So LaRoche school's closing was probably preordained.

I did learn more of the history of South Dakota's rural schools. In 1917, when LaRoche school was built, South Dakota had more than 5,000 rural (one- or two-teacher) schools. Of course, the state also had many more farms and ranches in the early 20th century than it does now. The 100-acre row-crop and livestock farm that once supported a family is a thing of the past. On 1,000 acres where once 10 families thrived, now only one family can make a living—and a frugal one at that. Without those other nine families, there are fewer kids and no need for so many rural schools.

State Department of Education records indicate the number of South Dakota rural schools had dropped from 82 in 1990 (when I visited LaRoche) to 39 in the 2021–2022 school year. And of those 39, most (29) were Hutterite colony schools, which operate independently for religious and cultural reasons. Only 10 farm or tribal rural schools remained.

I find it sad that such an intimate form of education has all but disappeared. One-room schools like Mrs. E's were special, a part of rural America worth mourning.

CITY KIDS GO COUNTRY

A few months after I returned from my trip to South Dakota, I received a phone call from Kathryn Jackson, a rancher friend from Eureka, Kansas.

"Jim, we're hosting some elementary school kids from the city next week, and I thought you might be interested. I'm sure they wouldn't mind if you took some pictures," she said.

"I'll be there, Kathryn. When is it?"

I first met Kathryn and her husband, Happy (Harold, or Hap), a year earlier. They are both in their late 70s but still run a custom-grazing operation on several thousand acres of pasture in southeast Kansas. They met more than a half-century ago when she moved from the city to the Flint Hills to teach in a one-room schoolhouse near Happy's family ranch. During my first visit to the ranch, I mentioned that rural education was a special interest of mine. Kathryn, in turn, told me that she and Happy occasionally had busloads of city kids come to the ranch on field trips to learn about ranch life. She said she'd let me know next time that happened in case I wanted to take pictures and write a story.

A week after our phone call, I watch a big yellow school bus lumber up the gravel road to the Jackson ranch. When it stops, a veritable melting pot of kids pours out. There are black kids, yellow kids, white kids. They come swarming onto the Jacksons' front lawn, pull out their picnic lunches and immediately make themselves at home, eating, shouting and pointing at their unfamiliar surroundings.

These first- and second graders are from Washington Elementary School, in Wichita's inner city. Most have never been on a ranch, seen a cow up close or ridden a horse. But today they will. They will pick flowers growing near a pasture and see cattle grazing on the greenest grass in the world. They will try on chaps and smell fresh manure. And they will get an introduction to a world they had only read about in school.

That's exactly why Kathryn and Happy invited them to the ranch.

"We believe in educating children about country life," Kathryn tells me before the bus arrives. She's wearing a bright patterned blouse, loose slacks and opened-toed shoes. If it weren't for the cowboy hat floating on the grey curls on top of her head, she could be a teacher preparing for school. Happy is dressed in his customary denim jacket, jeans, and work boots. He's the image of a Flint Hills cowboy.

"We're crusaders," Kathryn tells me. "We think the only way we are going to preserve our country way of life is to get the next generation involved. These kids will go home and tell their parents and their friends about us. And maybe that will create a little understanding between city and rural folks."

Kathryn is proof that some teachers are never ex-teachers. Education is their passion, their reason for being.

The Jacksons have been on this educational crusade for more than a decade now. In that time, they have worked with the Kansas Farm Bureau, the Kansas Department of Agriculture and Kansas State University Extension to hook up with elementary school classes interested in rural life.

In addition to ranch tours, Kathryn carries on correspondence with elementary school classes she has "adopted" over the years. "I send them letters," she says. "And they send me letters in return. Some of them are real corkers."

Besides the elementary schoolers, the Jacksons also have hosted about 60 foreign exchange college students. They have had Japanese, Iraqi, Argentinian, Dutch and French young people live with them for weeks at a time. The Jacksons put them to work while teaching them how American ranchers turn green grass into beef. Hands-on, Kathryn says, is the best way to learn. One young Dutchman enjoyed ranch life so much, he stayed for a year, which was just fine with the Jacksons.

"We just like people," Kathryn says. "We educate them, and they educate us. It's amazing how much there is to learn about each other.

"For instance, we had one young man from Argentina who apparently thought all American ranchers were rich like his family. The first thing he wanted to know was where the servants stayed. I pointed to his bedroom and said, 'One stays there.' Then I pointed to our bedroom and said, 'Two more stay there.' He was shocked. But we put him to work anyway."

The kids from Wichita are finished with lunch now and surround the Jacksons' horse corral, peeking through the fence slats at the amazing animals inside. Two at a time, Hap and teacher Doug Poage bring the kids into the corral. They walk them to the two horses and introduce them. When the kids have patted the horses' necks and scratched their noses, the adults help them into the saddle for a slow ride around the corral.

Some of the kids are afraid of the horses and shake their heads "no" when invited to ride. But when their classmates make the trip around the corral without incident or injury, the timid kids build their courage and step forward tentatively for a turn. By the end, every kid has had a ride, sitting proud and brave far above the ground.

Another group follows Kathryn and teachers Shari Colaw and Jill Heberly to the old stone schoolhouse that sits at the head of the lane. Kathryn explains that she taught there many, many years ago and that her students from nearby ranches rode horses to class. The kids are awed by the idea of horses rather than buses. But they wrinkle their noses as they peer inside the dinky one-room school. "That's the whole school?" one asks.

As they return down the lane, some kids pick irises Kathryn planted in clumps years ago. They probably shouldn't do that without permission. But Kathryn doesn't mind, and she smiles when a second grader says, "I'm going to take these home to my mamma. She never gets flowers."

All too soon, the bus driver tells the teachers it's time to leave; it's a long drive back to the city. Some of the kids hug Kathryn and tell her they will miss her. They wave to Happy and the horses, then clamber aboard the bus. Kathryn and Happy stand in the gravel road to wave goodbye, and Happy slips his arm around his wife's waist.

When the bus disappears in the dust, Kathryn turns back toward me with a sad smile. "I always love when they come and hate when they leave," she says.

It seems the kids felt the same. Later, when I call teacher Shari Colaw to get a review, she says, "The kids loved it. They absolutely loved it. This is a memory they will have for the rest of their lives."

CHAPTER 13

CHURCHING THE COUNTRYSIDE

I grew up in a deeply religious family. My parents sacrificed much of Dad's modest civil service wages to send five children to Sacred Heart Catholic School and St. Thomas Aquinas High School. After he retired, Dad got up almost every morning, donned his duffer cap and drove his old Buick four blocks to church for 7 o'clock Mass. My older brother, Pat, the most truly religious person I know, probably would have become a priest if the Church allowed clergy to marry. But I am not a religious man. Despite my family background and the best efforts of 12 years of religion teachers like Sister Regina Claire and Father Palazzola, I developed no talent for religion. It just didn't "take" with me.

I do consider myself an ethical person—maybe even spiritual—and I try to treat my fellow humans in the manner Jesus preached. I can thank my parents and Catholic schools for that. They trained me to think critically about how my actions affect others and instilled in me a moral sensibility I might not have found elsewhere.

But the theatrics of church services always made me uneasy. And the hypocrisy I saw in organized religions' bombast on some moral issues and silence on others did not entice me to sit in a pew. I stopped going to Mass as a teenager, which I know caused my parents great pain. The Church's duck-and-cover strategy on priestly sexual abuse, which started coming to light in the 1980s and largely remains in effect today, did nothing to encourage me to return to the flock.

Outside of the Catholic Church, I also am offended by the many charlatans, grifters and predators who pose as God's spokesmen while fleecing their sheepish megachurch and televangelist congregations. I am astounded that so many naïfs write checks to support these frauds. Is the desire to believe in something higher stronger than the capacity to use good judgment?

In my college years, I enrolled in enough philosophy classes that I considered it my unofficial minor. And while I acquired a broader view of man's search for meaning, none of the philosophical explanations of the world pushed me either toward religion or away from it. I attended a few Quaker meetings thinking their pacifist views were preferable to Catholic doctrine, which preaches "Thou Shalt Not Kill" yet makes room for "just wars" and capital punishment. But the Religious Society of Friends didn't convert me either. I left myself open to non-Christian faiths but cannot honestly say that I pursued them or that they pursued me. I was adrift.

In the end, I've grown comfortable with a form of agnosticism that is probably another name for intellectual laziness. It is the best I care to do.

My own indifference toward religion aside, I've always been fascinated by faith's effect on other people. I avoid those whose beliefs seem only skin deep, and I am repelled by those who use religion as an excuse to exclude the rest of humanity from their tribe. Yet I find truly religious people to be admirable, especially when they act on their beliefs to improve the lives of others.

It follows that I've always been curious about the religiosity of the farmers and ranchers I have known over the years. Church is the center-piece of most rural communities. That's made obvious by the fact that church spires are the first things you see as you approach most any town on a two-lane road. Rural congregations are extended families or, at least, social networks in farming communities that would be pockets of isolation without them. "A friend of mine from church" is a common phrase I hear when farmers make introductions.

Through the years, I've held hands and bowed my head around farmhouse dinner tables as my hosts gave thanks for their food. I've listened as farmers described their work as "godly" because it provides sustenance for others. I've watched men with calloused hands gently cradle hymnals in church.

As pervasive as religion is in rural America, my travels have taken me to many shrinking towns whose churches need a new coat of paint but can't afford one. Religion sometimes struggles in the countryside. As farms consolidate and small towns get ever smaller, congregations dwindle. When there aren't many hands to feed the collection basket on Sunday, it's hard to keep the lights on. So I found myself wondering about the fate of churches, which are slowly disappearing in parts of rural America.

In 2001, I finally decided to research the topic and began making phone calls.

To my surprise, I learned that, at least in parts of Missouri, rural churches were having something of a revival. Jere Gilles, University of Missouri rural sociologist, told me: "People think rural churches are dying. But in our most recent sample (415 churches in 99 Missouri townships from 1982 to 1999), that doesn't appear to be necessarily true."

Gilles told me 80% of rural congregations in his study held their own or actually grew during that time span. Of course, that meant 20% of congregations were contracting; but Gilles emphasized the positive. He explained that the reasons for some congregations' growth varied case by case. But one important factor was the influx of new families that had fled chaotic cities to find tranquility in rural America.

To prove his point, Gilles directed me to the Central Christian Church (Disciples of Christ), in Callaway County, Missouri. It had the good fortune to be located in a geographic triangle of cities, farmland and highways that had become a haven for urban escapees. To the east is Fulton, a college town of about 12,000 souls. To the south, Jefferson City is the state capital, with a population of 40,000. And to the west is Columbia, home to the University of Missouri and a population of more than 120,000 year-round citizens whose numbers have exploded in recent decades. Former inhabitants of those three cities had spilled into the country to build their rural dream homes, and many of them were within a short Sunday drive of Central Christian Church.

Thus, the church's congregation had grown over the last 10 years. So much so that it finally could afford a full-time pastor, something it had not had for many years

Growth meant more people in the pews, more pots at the potluck dinners and more money for the treasurer to count every week. Growth meant more people to volunteer for committees and to help with maintenance work at the building. Importantly, growth also literally meant fresh blood. Church is not only a place to meet new friends; it is also a place for young adults to meet a potential spouse, a place to raise children.

All of which had Pastor Bill Nigus in an optimistic mood when I called. He had been pastor at Central Christian for about a year. "Our longtime members are excited and open-minded about the potential of growth," he told me with pride. "They want it and encourage it." He invited me to a Sunday service and to stay afterward to partake in the fellowship dinner: "I'll introduce you to people when you get here."

So on a warm, mid-November Sunday, I drive from a Fulton motel in search of Central Christian: out of town, out of the suburbs and into the country. I find the white clapboard church floating between a narrow blacktop road and a harvested soybean field. It has a grassy parking area filled with dusty cars and pickups. Kids run across the lawn, releasing some preservice energy while getting their Sunday best a little wrinkled and stained. Adults wander among the vehicles and gab with neighbors before rounding up the kids and filing through the open church door. The pews inside are nearly full on this sabbath with a diverse group of worshippers. There are young families seated next to grandparents. Sunday dresses blend with blouses and slacks. And suit jackets rub elbows with flannel shirts tucked into blue jeans.

Pastor Nigus greets me at the door. He is in his late 30s, a young man with a goatee, wire rims and a buzz cut. He looks like—and has the enthusiasm of—a high school band teacher. After we shake hands, he calls the congregation's attention to the journalist with the camera in the back of the church. "He's here to watch us pray," he jokes. I wave as the Christians twist in their seats and nod at me in welcome.

The service commences. The crowd sings Protestant hymns with great earnestness. Both the minister and laymen take turns at the pulpit and read aloud from the Scripture. Youngsters gather at the altar for a lively children's sermon, complete with a well-disguised parable. Then Pastor Nigus delivers the main sermon with a slow, loud voice that even the older churchgoers can hear. Forty-five minutes after it starts, the service segues to the fellowship dinner, perhaps the most important part of a rural Sunday service.

Like almost every other church potluck I've attended, this one is in a basement room with half windows and a low ceiling that ricochets conversations until they are an indistinct buzz. Serving lines form at the foot of the stairs, and ladies in bright aprons and hair buns spoon food onto outstretched plastic plates. Families gather at long tables and sit on metal folding chairs. News (and gossip) of the week passes among congregants. There is laughter and lots of warm smiles. Everyone seems at home.

"We started to see a lot of new people moving into the area 10 to 15 years ago," Raymond Miller tells me as we sit together eating. He has been a member at Central Christian for more than 60 years. "Everybody who went to our church back then was part of a full-time farm family. Now you can count the farmers on your fingers. The rest all work in town."

Middle-aged Chuck and Annie Bowman are among the newer members. They moved here two years ago from Jefferson City, where they had been active in an urban church. "In the city, congregations are not as close-knit as they are here," Chuck tells me. "When they have functions here at Central Christian, almost everybody attends."

Having many social functions is part of Pastor Nigus' strategy for recruiting and retaining members. "Nothing attracts a crowd like a good carry-in meal," he tells me with a wink.

In the 1990s, about 70 Central Christian members showed up for services and potluck. Ten years later, it is a disappointment if 100 do not attend Sunday services. This is a rural church success story.

Times change. But not all rural churches have benefited from urban spillover, especially after 2008. The Great Recession plugged up the outflow of people from the cities, because folks could no longer afford a dream home and 20 acres in the country, and gasoline prices made commuting prohibitively expensive. Demographic tides had turned. It occurred to me that God might be eternal, but the fate of rural churches ebbs and flows.

My 2001 story about rural churches was appropriate for the times. But the intervening years were difficult for farm communities I visited. The shrinkage I observed had intensified during the Great Recession, and I wondered once again what was in store for small-town congregations. In 2018, I decided to revisit the subject. Almost miraculously, my friend Del Deterling sent me a lead that brought me back to church.

Del is an agricultural journalism legend whose work brightened the pages of Progressive Farmer for more than 35 years. A Texas German with Lutheran roots, Del is a consummate professional. He can turn a mundane subject into lively, informative copy. He always keeps his antennae tuned for new ideas and is on top of trends before they become so. But as he has slowed down, and travel has become less appealing to him, he bequeaths story ideas now and then to some of his friends. One came to me in the form of a clipping from a Lutheran newsletter. The story idea Del sent me was about an Iowa farmer whose second job was as a Lutheran minister who shepherded two rural congregations.

The idea looked like gem to me. I thanked Del, tracked down Pastor Steve Struecker and gave him a call. I was only a five-hour drive away, I told Steve as I asked if I could come visit. He was busy with harvest but said he was willing to have me come if I was willing to ride in his combine while we talked. It was a deal. We set a day and time, with a meeting's exact location to follow.

Steve's hometown of Whittemore is in north-central Iowa, about 120 miles north of Des Moines. The closest town of any size is Fort Dodge, 50 miles away with a population of about 25,000. Unlike what I'd seen in Callaway County, Missouri, there hadn't been much urban spillover in Humboldt County, no infusion of financially secure city folks looking for a country home and a church to attend on Sundays.

Some of the towns I drive through on my way to the Struecker farm that November day are hollow shells of what they once had been. Such rural towns often have a busy Casey's convenience store and maybe a grain elevator on the outskirts, but Main Street has withered. It has a business or two flanked by empty shops with cracked windows. On either side of the street are brick and frame buildings with ghost signs of nearly forgotten businesses and vacant windows waiting for a new owner to take interest. An old brick school building is boarded up and home to pigeons that fly through gaps in the plywood.

The drive north of Fort Dodge is on good Iowa highways with wide shoulders where winter snows can be pushed out of the way by huge plows. Set back from the highways are flat and gently rolling hills covered with corn plants turning a dingey yellow-brown and ready for harvest. Soybean fields are losing their leaves and are—or soon will be—ready to combine.

Here and there are groves of trees that sheltered farmhouses in bygone eras but now serve only as spots to park a few round hay bales or unused and rusting pieces of farm machinery. Occupied houses are few and far between.

Corn harvest. Getting directions from farmers has changed greatly since I started in ag journalism. Early on, farms had rural route numbers, not physical addresses. Local postmen knew how to find them, of course. But farmers gave strangers directions based on landmarks rather than mailbox numbers. "Turn east on Guyer Road for about three-quarters of a mile. You'll see a white barn and two silos. Go past that until you come to the intersection where the old schoolhouse used to be. Turn north there. We're the first place on the west side of the road."

Fortunately, rural homes have become part of the 911 emergency system, and everyone has a street address. That make directions easier to follow. And when GPS arrived on the scene, getting lost was next to impossible.

Steve had instructed me to call when I got close to his farm and he'd "drop a pin" by text to me. That pin would give me GPS coordinates to the field Steve was harvesting. This is so much easier than looking for "where the old schoolhouse used to be."

I learned long ago that, once you got close, the best way to find a farmer working in the field is to slow your vehicle and roll down your window. You can't always see a machine in the field, but you can hear it a long way off, especially combines. They are factories on wheels with chains clanking, belts humming and a diesel engine roaring.

I hear Steve's combine long before I see it and pull off the gravel road, cross a ditch and drive into an opening in a partially harvested cornfield. A semi with a grain trailer attached is parked in the field near the road waiting for Steve to make his next appearance over a small rise. An older man standing by the semi waves as I park my pickup out of the way on the edge of the field.

"Howdy," I say. "Steve here?"

"Yep. He'll make his way here in about 10 minutes."

The man's name is Ted, and like many a harvest helper, he is retired from a job in town. He grew up on a farm, though, and loved the work. So he's eager to help Steve at harvest by hauling grain from the field to the storage elevator in town. He works in tandem with another driver who now is on his way to the elevator.

Harvest is a choreographed dance. Combine fills semi. Semi goes to town or to on-farm grain storage. Another semi shows up, and the combine begins to fill it at the end of the field. Sometimes a tractor with an attached grain cart is part of the dance. They drive alongside the combine as its hopper fills and, in the middle of the field, the combine swings out an augur and unloads into the grain cart while bouncing along at 4 m.p.h. Tractor and grain cart take their fresh load to the semi waiting at the edge of the field, and the dance continues.

"Been workin' with Steve for 10 to 12 years now," Ted tells me. "I love being back on the farm."

Ted and I chat about the usual menu of farm topics: weather, quality of the crop, how hard it is to make a living as a farmer these days. We have just started on the subject of commodity prices when the sound of a combine approaching gets louder and louder, and we can talk no more.

A corn combine coming through the crop is an impressive sight. Steve's is a 12-row, John Deere S780—a newer, midsized model. The top of the combine's cab appears first above the 7-foot-high cornstalks that form a curtain between us and the machine. As it chews its way toward me, it suddenly emerges from the corn like an elephant coming out of the tall grass. For a moment, it comes to a halt and shivers as if deciding where to go next. It's a magnificent machine, a marvel of mechanical engineering.

At its front is the header, which has horizontal, cone-shaped fiberglass row units that slide between rows of corn as the machine bulls its way forward. The row units funnel stalks to rotating knives and gathering chains that cut the stalks and pull them into the header's maw. The same mechanism strips the ears from the stalks. As the ears fall onto a conveyor, an augur draws them into the feeder house, which propels the ears inside the body of the combine. A thresher squeezes the ears to separate kernels from cobs. A series of internal screens and fans removes dust, cob and chaff. They blow debris back into the field. Meanwhile, harvested kernels are lifted by a conveyor elevator into a grain tank.

It's a noisy, dusty process that can collect about 6,000 or more bushels an hour. Larger combines can collect more than 90,000 bushels of corn in a 12-hour day.

By the time he gets to the end of the row, Steve's combine grain tank is full. So he eases the behemoth alongside the semi's trailer and unfolds a delivery augur. More chains clank as corn feeds from the grain tank, through the augur's spout and into the grain trailer. The corn flows in a long, golden stream into the trailer, sending clouds of dust and corn fines upward. It takes only a couple of minutes to unload 400 bushels.

The augur stops screaming and shudders to silence, and Steve steps out of the combine cab onto a platform and climbs down a ladder to the ground. He is tall and thin, with a stained grey Carhart hoodie and a faded green John Deere cap with a grease thumb print on the underside of the bill. His wire-rimmed glasses are speckled with corn fines, and he has a friendly, toothy smile. "You must be Jim," he says, and he shakes my hand.

We stand in the chaff and stalks to chat for a few minutes. But it is obvious Steve is a busy man who is kindly making time for me during peak season. "I have about 20 more acres to do in this field," Steve says. "Want to hop in with me, and we can talk while I combine?"

A modern combine cab is an air-conditioned control room on wheels that rides high above the crop. The command seat's armrest is outfitted with control buttons and knobs. A couple of computer monitors are mounted on a cab post to keep track of machine functions. One of the monitors displays in real time the quantity and quality of the grain flowing past sensors in the beast's belly. Wrap-around tinted windows give an almost unobstructed view of the factory floor outside. A second, smaller seat (called a jump seat) is for passengers or the occasional journalist. Tucked under it is a cooler for lunch or maybe even a small refrigerator. A combine driver needs nourishment for the long hours he pilots the machine.

Years ago, those long hours were more strenuous than they are today. Keeping the combine between the rows required fatiguing concentration. At the end of a day, a combine driver could be mentally exhausted. Today, combines can steer themselves, and that eases the work and also makes it more accurate. GPS and autosteer keep the row units precisely positioned between rows of corn. All the driver has to do is align the machine and press a button; the machine takes over from there.

This field is a half-mile long, so after Steve presses that button, he only need glance at monitors to check how the machine is operating. That leaves him free to turn at least part of his attention to me.

Interviews in combines cabs are nothing new to me. I used to try to write in my reporter's notebook. But those rolling giants bounce and shake through uneven fields, and my already barely legible handwriting disintegrated into gibberish. So now I use my iPhone as a recorder. This not only makes for better notes, it frees my hands so I can unpack my camera to take pictures while we interview.

As Steve and I start down the field, I tell him a little bit about me because I feel that sharing something about my life with my subjects makes me more relatable. In this case, it seems to work, and Steve reciprocates, which is the whole point of the interview.

Steve and his son, Andy, 30, and business partner, Bill Lindgren, run a corn and soybean operation spread over a 50-mile radius. Their farm is a few thousand acres, which is typical for Iowa. Steve didn't want to tell me exactly how many acres he farms. Envy among neighbors is a common vice in rural communities.

From his earliest memories, Steve wanted to farm. Like so many farmers I've met, he yearned to follow the boot prints of his grandfather and father, who farmed some of this same land. Theirs was a much smaller farm—240 acres—and included livestock as well as crops. That was typical in those days: Raise cattle and hogs; plant corn and hay to feed them. Steve developed a more contemporary vision of Iowa farming. He eliminated the livestock component years ago to concentrate on crops because he could grow and sell enough crops to cover the revenue he lost from not having livestock. Besides, crop work is seasonal, while livestock is 24/7.

Under his management, the farm has tried and tested various modern cropping techniques to improve profitability. He also is careful to protect the soil and water on his land. Strip-tillage is his latest experiment. It's a method for tilling only the strips of soil into which he plants. The rest of the soil is left undisturbed to reduce both soil and water erosion. This contrasts with more traditional farming techniques that plow the whole field and spread fertilizer and chemical over much more soil. The older methods often damaged the soil, wasted fuel and spread far more chemical than was necessary.

Environmentally friendly strip-till was impossible in Steve's father's day because it requires special equipment and GPS accuracy, which allows a farmer to plant in the same rows year after year. That, in turn, will allow him to place costly fertilizers (potential pollutants) such as anhydrous ammonia in exactly the same spot every year, reducing the total amount necessary for high yields. "We try to fertilize only the crop and not the soil in between the rows," Steve explains.

I can tell he is proud of his cutting-edge methods. They make him feel good about his own accomplishments and his stewardship of the land. Farming is, as they say, in his blood.

But being a pastor? That's a career choice that involved some evolution.

An omniscient observer might have predicted it. Steve had always been religious, and he expressed his piety in community mindedness. Better, he acted on his civic inclinations. For instance, he spent 20 years in the county sheriff's reserve to provide civilian support to law enforcement. Not because crime was rampant in his part of Iowa but because he wanted to serve the community and help during emergencies. Looking back on that experience, he tells me, "It made me understand there are two sides to every story. It helped me become more patient and not jump to conclusions about people."

Then came a turning point. Six years earlier, his cousin, Jeff, who was a close friend of the same age, died of a rare blood disease. The death hit Steve hard. Among the things he had admired about Jeff was his involvement in church. The unexpected death started Steve thinking about his own commitment to his faith. "That was a pivotal moment in my life," he says.

Steve had always been active in the church. But now he wanted to do more. As he neared 50, he made a midlife decision to become a lay deacon. That was Step 1 of a spiritual journey, and it got him involved in the day-to-day life of his Lutheran church in Whittemore.

Step 2 came quickly when the Lutheran pastor who served two neighboring communities of Livermore (population 380) and Lu Verne (population 300) became ill, and two temporary replacement pastors were called in to help. Newly minted Deacon Steve volunteered to assist them.

"People asked me why I cared about two congregations 30 miles from me. I had no connection with them at all. But I knew that farming would allow me to volunteer, because I can usually arrange my own schedule. I could farm to make a living and still be able help these two churches. It's easy to say, 'Let somebody else do it.' But I believed God was calling me to those churches."

Eventually, the temporary pastors had to move on, which created something of a local crisis. Without those pastors, it seemed likely both churches would close. Something in Deacon Steve's soul revolted against that probability: "I could not let the doors close on those two churches."

Step 3 began when a pastor friend suggested to Deacon Steve that he think about becoming an ordained minister. This was the biggest step of all. But after talking it over with his wife, Kathy, he took it. Deacon Steve decided to become Pastor Steve, even though that process required four years of distance learning courses and two annual trips to a Lutheran seminary in St. Louis, nearly 500 miles from home. It was "like getting a master's degree" and "the hardest four years of my life," he tells me. But he persevered and was ordained in 2015.

Livermore and Lu Verne became his congregations. "And here I am serving their needs."

I listen closely as Pastor Steve relates his story. I am, after all, skeptical of religions, churches and the clergy. But I detect in Pastor Steve no false notes, no pretenses of sanctity. By the look in his eye, the catch in his voice, I judge he is who he seems to be: a deeply religious man committed not only to his beliefs but to his community and to his neighbors.

I am relieved. This will be an easier story for me to write than if Pastor Steve had been less genuine.

Family affair. The decision to enter the ministry, of course, radically affected the Struecker family's life. Kathy Struecker had married a farmer and thought her dual roles as a farmer's wife and a full-time employee of an insurance company were hectic enough. Now she understood, she would have a third job as a pastor's wife.

Raised Catholic, Kathy was unfamiliar with her new role as the wife of a cleric. She told me in a phone conversation that she quickly realized as a Lutheran pastor's wife in a rural congregation, she was part of a package deal. She would be a full-time partner with all the duties and responsibilities that came with the job. She'd be there with her husband on Sundays, help with paperwork, coordinate with church committees, teach bible school. Who knows what all she'd have to do?

When she and Pastor Steve considered this new career, they thought of son, Andy, whose life was about to change with or without a pastor father. He was finishing studies at Iowa State University, where he would earn an agronomy degree. His parents were thankful when he assured them he wanted to return to the farm. That meant he could take over some of the farm chores that had been Kathy's for years. In the end, Kathy told me, the opportunity for ministry "came at a good time for us as a family."

A typical Sunday for Pastor Steve and Kathy now goes something like this: They leave the house about 7:30 in the morning to prepare for the 8:30 service in Livermore, a half hour from home. After the service, they enjoy social time with congregants then drive 10 miles to Lu Verne for a 10 o'clock service. After that fellowship hour, the couple runs home for a few hours of rest and an abbreviated Sunday dinner. Then they hustle back to Lu Verne for evening bible classes.

Sunday is no day of rest for the Strueckers.

Nor are most other days. Husband and wife each teach children's bible classes on Wednesday evenings, and the vacation bible school Pastor Steve and Kathy started has become a drawing card for area kids—both for those who regularly attend church and those who are "unchurched."

The list of pastoral chores also includes funerals, visits to shut-ins and emergencies of all sorts that tend to pop up at the busiest times. All of this in addition to farming, a job that waits for no man or pastor.

The workload can be too much, even for Pastor Steve. "There are times when I've said, 'I give up. I can't do this anymore.' Without Kathy, this would not have been impossible; she has helped me through it. I'm lucky to have her."

Fortunately, too, Pastor Steve is physically and emotionally equipped for both his farming and his clerical professions. After spending even a short amount of time with him, I conclude that he is energy and spirituality clothed in farmer's cap and jeans one day, a white alb and seasonal stole the next.

Sometimes his two jobs cross paths. For instance, harvest is so busy on the farm, and the days are so long, Pastor Steve sometimes doesn't have time to sit in an office and write his Sunday sermon. That's when autosteer helps in ways that agricultural engineers didn't foresee. During those field straightaways when the combine is driving itself, Pastor Steve makes notes about his next sermon.

Changing landscape. The notion of a Lutheran farmer/pastor probably goes back to the founding of the faith. Followers of Martin Luther became clergy while also holding day jobs such as farmer, blacksmith or shopkeeper. Centuries later, Pastor Steve is something of an anomaly for the modern Lutheran Church of Missouri Synod, which not that many years ago frowned on the idea that pastors could have simultaneous lay careers. A shortage of clerics has loosened the modern rules, says Steve Turner, a pastor and the Synod's president for the Western District of Iowa. He is the friend who encouraged Pastor Steve to consider ordination.

"The opportunity came along at just the right time," Turner tells me during a phone conversation. "Because if we didn't have Steve serving Livermore and Lu Verne, I believe those congregations would be closed today, and we would have lost our footprint in both those communities."

The fact that Pastor Steve is a full-time farmer doesn't bother Turner.

"I joke with Steve that he gets to do exactly as I wanted to do," says Turner, who grew up on a North Dakota sunflower and wheat farm. "I would have loved to have been able to farm and be a pastor. But that option wasn't available when I was a young man."

A shortage of pastors changed that.

It's an issue for many denominations in much of rural America, Turner says. It seems especially obvious in parts of the Midwest where 150-year-old rural villages have three or four church buildings, many of them without pastors and some now vacant. Turner's district has lost three congregations in the last three years.

"It's one of the biggest challenges I face as a district president," Turner says. "But it's the hand we've been dealt. Our communities have been growing smaller and our congregations are also growing older."

Some of those older congregants have trouble adapting to new realities, Turner admits. "People in small towns say, 'We want it to be like it was when we were growing up and when our kids were young.' But it's a different world now, and there's no going back."

Turner sees rural school consolidation as a parallel story to what is happening with small-town churches. As baby boom kids made their appearance in the 1950s and 1960s, many rural communities went on school-building binges. When that generation graduated and moved away, student enrollment began to shrink. Neighboring villages sometimes chose to consolidate school districts rather than to operate expensive separate schools for an ever-smaller number of students. As a result, Iowa's small towns today are littered with empty schoolhouses. One school complex might serve an entire county that once had a dozen schools. School bus rides of an hour or more are common for rural students.

"Churches are in the same boat but 20 to 30 years behind the trend of abandoning schools," Turner tells me. "The trend is finally catching up to churches, too."

Congregations inexorably have grown older and smaller. Now the critical mass—and financial means—to keep churches open is disappearing. More and more stained-glass windows are boarded up in steepled buildings that sit empty.

At the same time, the rural Midwest also is struggling to welcome a new demographic, Turner continues. Diverse people now move to small towns because of the low cost of housing. They commute to jobs at businesses and meatpacking plants 30 to 40 miles away. Many are on the lower end of the economic spectrum and are ethnically different from their neighbors. Hispanics, Asians, African Americans and immigrants of all sorts call rural Iowa home now, and the old guard of North European descent is not always eager to welcome newcomers.

Such a clash of cultures can create real challenges, Turner says. "We have to help our people see this diversity not as a negative but as an opportunity to maintain and grow our congregations. Steve is one of those guys who does see it as an opportunity."

God willing, diverse newcomers will be the saviors of rural churches, Turner adds.

Another of Turner's hopes for the future is to find more clergy who are willing to serve multiple "partner" congregations, which split the meager salary of a pastor and share his services. Meanwhile, each church congregation retains its own identity without consolidating with a neighboring village's.

"I also wish we had more guys like Steve who could be bi-vocational," Turner explains. "He has a heart of gold and wants to reach people with the good news of Jesus Christ."

Part of the trend. While we ride together in the combine cab, Pastor Steve tells me he is aware of the demographics: "Back in the day, you had four or five families living on every section (240 acres). We don't have that anymore." He watched large farms buy out small farms and saw families move away. To survive as a businessman, he also bought neighboring farmland and, as a result, witnessed families he had known for years leave the community. Today Farmer Steve acknowledges some survivor's guilt. But guilt is tempered by the fact that his farm supports three families plus several seasonal employees at planting and harvest.

I come to understand that Pastor Steve's gospel message is a traditional one. He watches from a distance as modern megachurches explode near the cities, and he concludes: "The practice of Christianity is a changing landscape, and I don't like some of what I see. What do people want out of church today? Some want entertainment for an hour. They don't want to be told they are a sinner. They want to hear they are doing a good job. Unfortunately, that is not what church is all about. They don't always want to hear it, but I tell people: We are all sinners. We are in need of forgiveness."

Despite the stresses of his pastoral work, Pastor Steve finds it fulfilling, even when dealing with death. "Being with people at the end of life. Being there for them as they are dying. It may sound morbid, but I enjoy doing funerals. It is an opportunity to connect with a person and the life that they lived."

Even more than ministering to those at the end of life, Pastor Steve enjoys ministering to the young. "The most rewarding thing about being a pastor is sharing the gospel, especially with children."

Pastor Steve has reconciled his two professions. "It's so easy to relate farming to religion," he tells me. "As farmers, we care for the land. We fertilize it and try to understand its needs. In return, it gives us food. As a pastor, I tend to the congregation's spiritual needs. I deliver the gospel's message weekly, and it gives us food for the soul."

Our conversation lasts four or five more rounds of the field before he brings the combine to a halt near the semis, and we join the rest of the harvest crew for a quick dinner brought to the field by Ruth Lindgren, wife of Pastor Steve's partner. Son Andy, who was driving a second combine, is there, along with Ted and two other helpers. Also, there is Carter Nath, a serious young man from the neighborhood who drives trucks at harvest and plays the organ at Pastor Steve's services in Lu Verne. I look at him and see a future farmer/pastor in the making.

The day started warm for November in Iowa, but as the sun dips lower in the sky, the evening air is cool. Dinner is served on paper plates and in plastic cups from the back of Ruth's SUV. The diners don't take time to sit because they have hours of work yet to do. They stand in the debris of shredded corn leaves and talk about the day's work. Pastor Steve draws Andy aside for a short private talk. I watch them nod together and see Pastor Steve place his hand on Andy's shoulder for a second. Then they do a quick inspection of both combines to be sure the gathering chains aren't clogged and the chaff spreaders are clear.

Dinner is over in a few quick minutes, and the crew prepares to go back to work, waving thanks to Ruth as they walk to their separate vehicles.

I have a few more minutes with Pastor Steve before he jumps back into the combine. He will work until well after dark and be back in the command seat as soon as the dew is off the standing corn the next morning. I ask if I can return after harvest to follow him as he goes about his pastoral duties. He agrees that I should see that side of his life, too, and we say our goodbyes.

Then I head for a motel in Fort Dodge to transcribe my interview recordings and to process my photos.

Going to church. I return to Humboldt County one Sunday morning a few weeks after my harvest visit. It is getting close to Christmas, and Zion Lutheran Church is decorated for the season. Potted chrysanthemums glow red and green in the sanctuary, and a ribbon across the front of the altar proclaims, "Gloria!"

I arrive well before the services so I can meet Kathy, who I had not met on my first trip, and to take pictures of Steve preparing for his pastoral role. I also meet Andy's wife, Brittany, their toddler, Jackson, and his 4-year-old sister, Anna.

The vestibule where we chat is lit by colored sunlight filtering through tall stained-glass windows—a spot of red here, a streak of gold there. The vaulted body of the church echoes with the clip-clop of hard Sunday soles on children's shoes and the low hum of adults greeting one another. The air has the faint, dusty smell of rural churches. They are occupied only once or twice a week, and most of the time, no one disturbs the quiet or stirs the air. Today the place is alive with about 30 congregants. Some young families. Some older couples. One or two widowers who have come alone.

I follow Pastor Steve into the sacristy to photograph him donning his clean and starched clerical robes and to ask a few more questions. Outwardly, he looks to be an entirely different man from the one I had met in a cornfield. His clothes are clean and pressed, his face clean-shaven. But he maintains the same demeanor he had in that cornfield. He is once again doing work he cherishes.

It is a relaxed service. Everyone knows everyone else; there are no strangers other than me. After everybody settles in their accustomed spots, Pastor Steve comes down from the altar and ranges into the polished wood pews of the nave. He greets several congregants then stoops to pick up granddaughter, Anna, and carry her around with him. He has made her a part of the service and has shed some of his clerical veneer. He's just another proud granddad. The churchgoers are engaged. They laugh at his witticisms and nod when he is serious.

As he does most Sundays, Pastor Steve calls the children to the altar for a brief sermon. Grandson Jackson crawls into his lap as Pastor Steve sits on the carpeted steps. Anna sits straight and proud beside her granddad. He jokes with the nine kids and asks each of them a question. Then they all hold hands, and he prays with them.

As he stands, Pastor Steve faces the rest of the congregation and says earnestly: "Let's thank the Lord for the children. They are the future of the church."

CHAPTER 14

MISSOURI MULES

Pity the poor mule. He's been maligned for eons as dim-witted, unyielding and cantankerous. Listen to people slander by insinuation this cursed crossbreed. "Muleheaded," "stubborn as a mule" and "ornery as a mule," they say.

You hear other slurs about this noble animal. "Unnatural," people say. They are an infertile, ugly cross between the majestic horse and the laughable donkey. And maybe the ultimate sniggering line: "If God had wanted us to have mules, he'd have invented them himself."

Missourians beg to differ. They hold mules in high regard. So much so, they anointed mules Missouri's state animal. Missourians understand the mule is an animal of extraordinary strength and stamina. His dam (usually a Belgian or a Percheron horse) endows him with size and muscle. His sire (usually a Mammoth donkey) gives him an unshakable self-confidence that makes him less skittish than a horse and more likely to persevere in the face of loud noises or owner stupidity.

Not long ago, the mule's defining characteristics made him virtually indispensable on some Missouri farms. From the 1820s into the mid-20th century, he pulled the plows and the wagons that kept farms working. It wasn't until the gas-powered tractor arrived huffing, clanking and coughing smoke that the mule's place on the rural scene faded like an old photograph.

In the early 1980s, I met a Missourian whose relationship with mules was still intense. Gene Chipman, whose farm was in northeast Missouri near Perry, greeted me on the farm in a gray Stetson and dark sunglasses. The leathery man in his 70s had a cigarette in his mouth, which he replaced with another as soon as the first's glow died. He wore a big belt buckle with a mule's head on it, had a raspy voice and exuded a certainty about himself that is reminiscent of the mules he bred.

As we walk to a wire fence corral, Gene tells me that mules have been a major part of his years on Earth. He says he always introduces himself to strangers as a mule trader, because that's who he is. He earns his living breeding and selling mules, and he has won "14 or 15" world championships at the Missouri State Fair, the be-all and end-all of mule shows. Without mules, Gene allows, he would be a stranger to himself.

"When did I first own mules? I can't tell you when I first had outright ownership of one. But I've been around them since I could walk to the barn," Gene says with a laugh and a cough.

His first barn and the mules it held were in Henry County, in western Missouri, where Gene was born and where his father farmed. As a young man in 1938, Gene bought 200 acres of better ground in Ralls County, where he now lives, and moved his mules there. The next year, he bought 160 acres more. Until he purchased his first tractor during World War II, Gene and two hired men used 15 mules to plow, plant and harvest those 360 acres of corn, oats and wheat.

Even after he bought his first tractor, Gene still worked his mules. Although their role in the cropping operation diminished over time, Gene's mules earned their keep as draft animals until he retired from farming a few years ago and left the business to his son, John Roy.

Gene didn't retire from his mules, however. They were steadfastly part of his identity.

MULISH HISTORY

Who knows whether the first mule was an amorous animal accident or the result of an experiment by some Bronze Age genetic tinkerer. Pictures of mules date to the Egyptian pharaohs, and the Old Testament calls mules the "Royal Beast" and "the riding animal of princes." My how the mule's image has deteriorated over the millennia.

The American Mule Museum can guide you along a time line that shows Christopher Columbus brought donkeys and horses to the New World in 1495, and conquistadores soon used mules to explore and conquer New Spain. Up north in Britain's former colonies, mules were a favorite of farmer George Washington, who bartered with King Charles of Spain for good-quality breeding stock. At one point, the father of our country reportedly had 58 mules working at Mount Vernon.

The first mules came to Missouri in the 1820s from the new nation of Mexico, which had just been granted independence by Spain. The mules (and plenty of burros) were backhauling items for the first traders who left Franklin, Missouri, for Mexico in 1821 on what became known as the Santa Fe Trail. The Missouri traders started their journey with draft horses pulling wagons filled with goods to sell in the Mexican territory. On their return trip, they hauled Mexican crafts and silver in the wagons, and they also led pack animals—including mules—loaded with goods. On later trips out west, Missourians replaced draft horses with mules.

William Becknell, known in history books as "The Father of the Santa Fe Trail," led that first trip in 1821 and figured the sturdy Mexican mules he brought back to Missouri would be highly tradable to Missouri farmers. These were not the large animals we think of today. They had been bred by crossing a variety of smallish mares with randy donkeys. The result was short equines who weren't much to look at but had a great capacity for carrying heavy loads.

Mexican mules were welcomed on Missouri farms as useful animals. But it wasn't long before breeders in Kentucky, Missouri and Tennessee determined that if small mules were good workers, larger mules would be even better workers and could pull heavier equipment and shorten the workday. Breeders began enticing plus-size draft horse mares to mate with donkeys. The result was larger mules.

If bigger is better for the dam, why not for the sire? Breeders since George Washington's time had crossbred European donkeys like the Maltese and the Andalusian to create larger donkeys. Ultimately, they produced the American Mammoth Jackstock, which, as the name implies, is massive. Males stand at least 14 hands high (56 inches) at the shoulder, only slightly shorter than a 16-hand Belgian horse. When bred with draft horses (made easier by their extra height and, umm, reach), Mammoths gave their mule offspring an additional size jolt.

Hybrid vigor plays a part in mules' characteristics. Mule people will tell you that mules get their stamina, robust health and sure-footedness from their donkey side. Horses give them size and speed. Mule people, who often ridicule horses as inferior specimens, will tell you that the stubbornness of mules is really a sign of intelligence. Tell a horse to do something—say cross a swift stream—and with enough encouragement, he will do it. Tell a mule to do the same thing, and he will look over his shoulder at you and seem to ask why he'd want to do such a silly thing. You somehow must persuade him it's in his own interest. If you want a mule to do something that is obviously dangerous, the mule will refuse. He will say, in effect, "Go to hell." And that will be that. No gentle persuasion, no amount of kicking, spurring or cursing will make the mule budge. Once I heard a mule trainer (yes, there are such people) describe it like this: "You can get a horse to do about anything. You can lead one up to the edge of a cliff and, with enough motivation—whether it's yellin' or whippin'or whatever—you can get him to jump off. Not a mule. You lead a mule to the edge of a cliff, and you can't pull him over with a freight train. A mule is too smart."

I know a little about mules, donkeys and such having lived for 30-plus years about seven miles from Lathrop, Missouri, which has for more than 100 years vociferously proclaimed itself the Mule Capital of the World. Most "Capital of the World" claims are part vanity and part fact. Lathrop's claim is mostly fact.

In the 1880s, cousins J.D. Guyton and W.R. Harrington started a mule-breeding and trading business in Lathrop. They were good at what they did and soon became the largest mule dealership in the world. They kept three enormous barns in Lathrop to house about 1,000 mules at a time. As their customer base grew, they expanded to facilities in Kansas City and East St. Louis, and produced so many mules, it took a troop of about 500 buyers to service burgeoning markets.

At the turn of the 20th century, things were going extremely well for Guyton and Harrington's company. So they explored international markets for mules and landed a lucrative contract with the British Army to provide mules for its Boer War campaign. War was good business for mules and Guyton and Harrington. In 1900, armies and their artillery pieces were getting larger, and mules were up to the task of keeping supply lines flowing. See, mules are not as skittish as horses; they don't run away at the first cannon shot. They can survive on rougher rations and are more sure-footed, meaning they are adept at pulling heavy loads through cratered frontline landscapes—all handy traits to have in the chaos of war.

When World War I descended on Europe, Guyton and Harrington Mule Co. saw orders for its mules multiply. It now needed 18 buildings and more than 100 stable hands to care for its breeding stock. Many of its Missouri mules went to U.S. government buyers. But the British Army remained a loyal customer and bought more than 180,000 Missouri mules from Guyton and Harrington during the war.

World War I was the zenith for mule sales. (That's about the only good thing you can say about it.) Along with peace came the ascendance of motorized vehicles, and army mules were replaced by freight trucks. On the farm, tractors inexorably edged out mules, which became an artifact of a bygone agricultural era between the end of the War to End All Wars and the beginning 20 years later of the next world war.

Still, mules persisted, especially in Missouri. They became novelty items for gentlemen farmers; they were nostalgic reminders of simpler times on the farm; they even became athletes competing in jumping mule contests. For evidence of the mule's place in Missouri culture, consider that the majestic mule is the mascot for Lathrop High School, and the University of Central Missouri proudly calls its athletes Mules and Jennies. Meanwhile, mule traders such as Gene Chipman still have a solid market niche for themselves and their mules.

MISSOURI MULE MEN

A tan mule with a gray muzzle nuzzles Gene's arm as he leans against a fencepost and tells me that for most of his 60-odd farming years, he viewed mules as either working animals or animals he could trade. But in 1950, he found a way to make those beasts of burden earn real money. That's the year he took his first string of mules to the Missouri State Fair and discovered his mules were special; they could win championships. Suddenly, Chipman mules were a valued brand; they had cachet in mule circles and brought top dollar.

Selling prize mules isn't like selling prize racehorses. Racehorse buyers likely are looking to the future. They value the prestige of owning a winning horse. But what they really want is the horse's genetics, so they can pass them on to a new generation of—even more valuable—prize winners. Buyers can't do that with mules, because mules are sterile. A horse and a donkey have a different number of chromosomes (64 and 62 respectively), so their mule offspring can't reproduce. In the mule-trading world, buyers aren't looking far into the future. They just want a particular mule, a purple-ribbon winner that is a prize unto itself. Just as often, they want an animal that will do real work for them.

After his first few show wins, Gene discovered that his line of Belgian/donkey-crossed mules were a new, more profitable revenue stream. And soon, he had two groups of mules: one for work and one for show.

"You can't show mules and work them too," he tells me. "That would be like going to church in your work clothes."

To maximize his new business model, Gene knew he had to get his "Sunday clothes" mules into show shape. That's when he acquired a mule-showing partner, Richard Kohl, of Vandalia, Missouri. "He is the best mule barber that ever lived," Gene tells me through a puff of cigarette smoke. "He is an artist. The best I've ever seen."

Gene and Kohl have spent the past 30 years showing mules at county fairs and state fairs. It's been both enjoyable and exhausting. In recent years, the partners have cut back on the number of shows they attend, and Gene tells me one day soon they may have to give up all shows, including the granddaddy of them all, the Missouri State Fair, home of the world championship.

Kohl is now 76 and making noises about being too old to keep up the work. Gene lowers his voice to say, "When Richard Kohl stops going to the fair, so will I."

In all those years of sweating in summertime show tents and arenas, napping in stalls and eating concession stand food, Gene tells me he has learned to recognize at a glance a winning mule.

"The best mule we ever had was a mare we found standing in somebody's farmyard. My wife, Elsa Mae, didn't want me to spend money on it. But I bet her that mare would win the first show we entered her in." Not only did that mare win the first show, she won her first 17 shows.

"Seventeen shows, 17 sets of judges, 17 purple ribbons," Gene says with a kind of reverence in his voice. It's as if he was describing royalty.

Gene never traded that honored mule. She died happy of graceful old age in his pasture. That big belt buckle he wears? It has her picture on it.

That mule was the exception to Gene's rule to trade a mule when it's on top. "The glory you win in the arena is gone as soon as you get back to the barn," he tells me. Don't bask in it; use it to make a little more on your mule investment.

Besides, with the cost of transportation and of going to fairs, he says he can't afford to keep mules just for the meager prize money they win. When they get back to the farm, you still have to feed them and pay veterinary bills for them. So he trades often. "If you have mules, you've got to trade them. It's just a fact. If you can't trade them for money, trade them for whatever you can get."

Traders market. Leaning into the conversation, Gene let me in on some mule-trading secrets. First and foremost, to be a successful trader, you must understand a changing market. In the old days, Missouri farmers bred jacks to Percheron mares to produce the familiar black working mules of local lore. But tastes changed, and in 1980, more jacks are humping Belgians, because that's how to get those honey-colored mules that are strutting away with purple ribbons these days, Gene tells me. That's why his broodmares are now Belgians and not Percherons.

Some folks want a riding mule rather than a draft animal or a show animal. Westerners, for instance, take riding mules for wilderness trips through regions that are too rugged for most horses. If that's what you want, you need Appaloosa Quarter Horses or Tennessee Walking horses as broodmares. "Riding mules are real popular now," Gene says with what looks like a smirk. "Kind of like boats and travel trailers, and other such luxuries."

What about jumping mules? Missourians lead the world in jumping mule competitions. When horses jump in competition, they get a running start and leap stylishly through the air. Not so for mules. In competition, they must start from a standing position, take a couple of steps and fling themselves over a bar. It's not as elegant a sight as a steeplechase jumper clearing a hurdle and a water hazard. But a jumping mule is unquestionably an athlete. The world record for mule jumping is an astonishing 72 inches over a bar.

It's obvious Gene thinks riding mules and jumping mules are a perversion of the draft animals he's loved for so long. But he's willing to make money from breeding riding mules. He also makes money from sales of jacks and jennies—jennies being female donkeys. Some folks, for their own reasons, will breed a jenny with stud horse. The result is a hinny, which is generally smaller than a mule, has rounder ears and looks more like its father the horse. Hinnies, unfortunately, do not generally get the hybrid vigor that makes mules sure-footed, intelligent and perceptive. Hinnies are, for better or worse, more like horses.

About this time in our conversation, Gene's son John Roy wanders up. From his face and body type, he will be his father's doppelgänger in 30 years. Right now, he is in his mid-30s, friendly and talkative. He's also proud of the family's business and especially holds in high esteem donkeys that are facile and prolific breeders. "You would not believe how much money I have made off the first jenny I bought for $50. They [the farm's dozen or so donkeys] produce as much income as any livestock here."

John Roy is one of a new generation of Missouri mule owners who finds himself immersed in mule culture. Another is Ronald Jump, of Bolivar, Missouri. Also in his mid-30s, Ronald tells me on the phone that he has owned the ingredients for mule-making—donkeys and Percherons—for eight years. He's had some success with his breeding stock, showing the grand champion jack at the Tennessee State Fair and the junior grand champion stud jack at the Missouri State Fair.

Ronald tells me he is fascinated by the nature of mules. Even though he is too young to remember when mules were primarily farming implements, he used a team to plant pasture grass just for the fun of it. And if there is a nearby town festival that wants a team of mules to pull a wagon in a parade, Ronald is there.

Besides the joy of working with them, Ronald tells me, he just plain likes mules. Their personalities do not conform to mulish stereotypes. "Mules won't hurt themselves like horses do," he tells me. "They won't eat too much, and they won't get spooked and go charging off and break a leg in a ditch. They're easy to keep. And if they're in a barn, they will only mess one corner of the stall."

Mules are not the stubborn, ornery critters folktales would paint them to be. Neither are they stupid. "Hell, they're a lot smarter than horses," Ronald tells me.

Gene Chipman, who has lived in the mule world much longer than Ronald, says it's a mistake to stereotype mules. They're individuals, he says: "Sure, some of them are smart. But some of them are just plain dumb. They forget overnight more than you can teach them in a day.

"What the hell, though. You know a lot of people like that too, don't you? Just plain stupid. But you wouldn't say all people are stupid, would you?"

CHAPTER 15

RIVER STORIES

I was raised a few miles from the confluence of two of America's greatest rivers: the Mississippi and the Missouri. They were always just beyond the horizon during my childhood in the north St. Louis County suburb of Florissant. I could almost feel their presence.

As a teenager in search of solace from a newly lost love or whatever adolescent drama I was experiencing at the time, I pedaled my bike out of our suburban neighborhood and into farmland that bordered the Missouri River. I'd pump away until I found the forested bluffs overlooking the river and then park the bike and make my way down the slope, through the ancient trees that hid the "Big Muddy" from view. There weren't trails to the riverbank at that time like there are now. The river's edge was still primitive and its access still hidden. But I would scramble down the bluffs until I reached the mud on the bank. Driftwood branches and whole trees lay on the edge and were fine spots to sit and watch the mesmerizing flow: eddies that swirled with whitecaps in midstream; flotsam from who knows how far upstream; if I was lucky, bald eagles hunting for fish, making slow circles in the sky or perched in tall branches. The river never failed to calm me with its immenseness, its power, its eternal nature. My turmoils seemed petty beside it.

If I was particularly ambitious, I could bike to Pelican Island, which sits in a bend in the Missouri as it steers south to meet the Mississippi. Farther east, Sioux Passage Park lies in deep woods. Beyond that is the Columbia Bottoms Conservation Area and, finally, the magical Confluence Point State Park. It's a primeval landscape of forests, mud and mystery where the 2,300-mile journey of the Missouri ends and a rejuvenated Mississippi gains strength for its voyage to the Gulf of Mexico. The two rivers have met and married there forever.

French Jesuit and explorer Pierre François Xavier de Charlevoix in 1721 wrote of this spot: "I believe this is the finest confluence in the world. The two rivers are much the same breadth, each about half a league; but the Missouri is by far the most rapid and seems to enter the Mississippi like a conqueror, through which it carries its white waters to the opposite shore without mixing them, afterwards, it gives its [muddy brown] color to the Mississippi which never loses it again but carries it quite down to the sea ... ."

I am not as poetic about the rivers as the adventuresome Jesuit priest. But they have always been part of me. Growing up, our family took riverboat rides on The Admiral, an idiosyncratic aluminum-hulled riverboat that docked on the Mississippi levee in St. Louis. And we stood in the thin shadow of the Gateway Arch to watch barges bound for New Orleans churn past. Grandpa Navin came from up near Hannibal, Missouri, and we'd sometimes make journeys upriver to see our country cousins. Side trips included visits to the Mississippi riverfront in that scruffy little river town. Sam Clemens, of course, grew up in Hannibal, but as Mark Twain he renamed it St. Petersburg for his Tom Sawyer and Huck Finn tales.

No matter the town's name. The river is still the Mississippi, and it still rolls south toward the Gulf. It is the "Father of Waters" and full of might and majesty, as is its skinnier, wilder mate the Big Muddy Missouri.

As I grew older and moved about the country, I carried my fascination for rivers with me and met other rivers—all smaller but equally intriguing. In the mid-1970s, for instance, I found myself working for a newspaper in New Ulm, Minnesota, a rural community perched on hills above the Minnesota River. It was my first river community outside of Missouri, and it taught me that river towns—large and small—share a keen kinship with the river that birthed them.

The Minnesota River starts at Big Stone Lake near the Minnesota and South Dakota borders, and flows southeast past New Ulm. Then it makes a turn north at Mankato and joins the Mississippi at the Twin Cities. The river, of course, was the reason New Ulm was founded in an 1850s rush of white settlers into Sioux territory. The Sioux didn't much appreciate the new neighbors and, in 1862, burned much of the town, sparing (local legend has it) the town's multiple breweries.

Over the years, the rebuilt New Ulm moved up the southern bluffs of the river and maintained a scenic view of the waterway. In Minnesota winters, the river freezes and becomes a playground for townsfolk. They strap on skates and skim over glassy ice. They turn pirouettes and charge through sprint races. They drag out nets made of PVC pipe, and hockey games break out. Bundled up mothers come and sit on riverbank benches to watch their children glide on the ice.

On weekends, a crazier crowd roars onto the river in old cars. They spin in circles and shoot snow in fantails into the crisp winter air. They hold drag races on ice 2 feet thick. One winter, town entrepreneurs held a lottery. One of them volunteered to leave his car on the ice until the river thawed enough that the clunker fell into the water. The lottery winner was the luck person who correctly predicted the day and time the vehicle sank.

Perhaps less crazy are the hardy souls who crouch over holes they drill in the river ice in search of walleye. Arctic winds turn mustaches white with icicles, and breath becomes clouds that shine in the sun. There is something ancient and audacious about these sorts of ice fishermen.

Other ice fishermen prefer more comfort. They use pickups to tow small houses on skids onto the frozen surface. In those houses, men of otherwise good repute pretend to fish for walleye while drinking beer and whiskey. Ice fishing houses vary in size and sophistication. But most resemble backyard toolsheds. Some have fancy woodwork around the windows. Some have no windows at all.

One January day when the thermometer tried its best to achieve zero and a bright but thin sun gave little comfort, I trudged onto the ice, my boots crunching a dusting of snow atop the frozen river. I wanted to find out what goes on inside an ice fishing house and chose one of the fancier ones in the makeshift village in the middle of the river as my target. I knocked on the door.

"Come on in!"

I opened the door to see three bearded men sitting in aluminum lawn chairs around a rectangular hole in the ice. Each held a bottle of beer. None had fishing poles in hand, but I saw several stacked against the far wall.

I introduced myself and explained I was with the newspaper.

"Oh, gawd," one of the men said pointing to my cameras. "You're welcome to come in. But please don't take any pictures. We don't want our wives to know what we do in here."

That set off a round of boisterous laughter, hoots and hollers.

"Want a drink?" the jokester asked, tilting his beer bottle toward an open case of beer.

"Nah, I'm working. Maybe later," I said and silently thought, "It's 10 o'clock in the morning."

"Have a seat anyhow and watch us fish." Another round of laughter.

The friends resumed their chatter as if I wasn't there. I looked around and was amazed how cozy and warm the house was because of a portable heater vented through the roof. An eerie light reflected up from the hole and lit the faces of the men. They had pulled down the tops of their insulated bib overalls and shed their coats, leaving them in flannel shirts with rolled-up sleeves that revealed thick cotton undershirts. Heavy boots still protected their feet, which rested on the naked ice. Behind the men on a wall shelf, piles of potato chips and other snacks lay next to bottles of whiskey, brandy and schnapps.

"Sure you wouldn't like a beer, at least?"

"No. I really have to get going soon. I was just curious about what the inside of one of these houses look like."

"What!! You've never been ice fishing?"

"No. I grew up in Missouri. Our rivers don't often freeze solid."

"Isn't that strange? Do you fish?"

"A little."

"What kind of fish?"

"Oh, crappie mostly. And catfish sometimes."

"What? Catfish? You don't eat that shit, do you?"

"Well sure. If you bread it and fry it, it's pretty good."

"Aah. I don't believe it. It tastes like mud. You know what we do here if we catch a flathead? We hit in the head with a hammer and throw it back."

Hilarity ensued again. When it died down, the fisherman nearest me said, "Now if you want good eatin' fish, you can't beat walleye or northern pike. That's what we got here. That's what we're fishin' for now."

"Caught any today?" I asked, nodding to their unused poles and grinning.

More laughter.

By the time I left, the three anglers had convinced me to have a beer. And if I had a beer, I might as well chase it down with a shot of schnapps. After all, it was cold outside, and it was a long walk to the riverbank.

Boat ride. One August day in 1978, after the ice had melted and the Minnesota River had begun to saunter past town in its relaxed summer fashion, the newspaper's editor, Bill Macklin, surprised and delighted me with an assignment. He wanted me to write and photograph grain barges on the river. Seems the paper was planning its annual "Salute to Agriculture" edition and needed a lead story. Bill explained that the river was a key part of New Ulm's and southern Minnesota's agriculture. Barges that traveled on it carried local grain to export markets, where it brings higher prices for wheat, corn and soybeans.

I had no idea the Minnesota River was large enough to carry barges. But apparently, as it nears the Twin Cities, it widens, deepens and makes itself useful as it prepares to enter the Mississippi. Excited about an excuse to ride on a working riverboat, I made some calls and arranged passage on a barge towboat departing Port Cargill, a grain terminal in Savage, Minnesota. The plan was to hop aboard and experience for a few hours a riverman's life on barges that carried Minnesota grain to New Orleans. It sounded to me like a real-life Tom Sawyer adventure.

Weeks later, as I wait on the Savage grain terminal docks for the towboat Viking, a barge pokes its head around a river bend. It's a rusty red steel box pushing waves of brown Minnesota River water ahead of it. Lashed to its side is another barge just as big: 200 feet long, 26 feet wide and about 15 feet deep. Behind it, I see two more barges tied tightly to the stern of the first two.

Finally, the Viking appears, an unlikely-looking river queen. Her bow is square to better "face up" to the blunt-ended barges. Her wheelhouse is set high on hydraulic shafts, which can raise it for a good look down the river or lower it to squeeze under a bridge. Behind the wheelhouse is an engine room (always deafeningly loud, I learn), the galley and mess (also noisy when the crew gathers there), sleeping quarters (you get used to the noise, I'm told) and a laundry to serve a crew of seven.

The tow swings wide around the point, coming straight down the river now and revealing its full size: more than 470 feet long. It can carry as much as 6,400 tons of grain. Viking, I learn, is a short-haul towboat meant strictly for work on the Minnesota River. It has two jobs today. The first is to wrangle empty barges and bring them to the grain terminal. That's what it is doing now. Then, when the barges are filled with grain, it will gather four and move them to the Northstar Fleet, a gathering of barges just south of St. Paul. There, Viking's tow (the term for a block of barges) will merge with others to become a tow five barges long and three barges wide.

Imagine more than 767,000 bushels of grain in a 1,000-foot-long string of steel boxes headed on a weeklong voyage down the Mississippi to New Orleans, where it will be loaded onto oceangoing ships. Those behemoths, in turn, will haul more than 2 million bushels of grain to points beyond the Gulf of Mexico into the Atlantic or through the Panama Canal to the Pacific.

To make that happen, the Viking crew has preliminary work to do. The towboat pulls into the wharf and, after much maneuvering, comes to a halt. Captain Mike "Peewee" McReynolds steps out of the wheelhouse and hops onto the wharf. He's in his mid-20s—very young for a captain—has wild, kinky black hair, bushy sideburns and '70s-style oversized glasses. He is, as his name suggests, short. My escort from the towboat company has been in radio contact with Captain Mike (I can't bring myself to call him Peewee) and introduces us. Captain Mike gives me a welcoming handshake, and I'm immediately impressed and relieved. Not all story subjects welcome intruders into their workspaces. Until I feel a friendly handshake, I'm always wary that I will be treated as a nuisance at best and a pain in the ass at worse. But Captain Mike seems amiable, even eager to have me shadow him for a few hours. He invites me onboard and introduces me to a few of his scruffy crew members, who nod and return to their chores at the bustling port.

Port Cargill's loading dock is in a narrow river channel just off the main Minnesota River channel. Onshore crews are busy moving grain—in this case, soybeans—from giant storage elevators up the hill to the barges. The process involves a system of wide noisy augers and conveyor belts several hundred yards long that stretch from the elevators downhill to the wharf. The barges are so massive, it can take as long as three hours to fill each of them. Crews position barges under a grain chute and then pry open the massive lids on hinges that screech, metal on metal. When lids flop open onto the barge tops, I hear an empty echo, like thunder, in a deep canyon.

While barges are filling, Viking disconnects its original tow, which are empty vessels it brought from moorings upriver. Now it can begin its wrangling work: repositioning several other barges from slips and wharfs along a five-mile stretch of the river. Some of the barges recently arrived from New Orleans and are full of salt, fertilizer or long metal pipes. Viking moves them to wharves where they can be unloaded. That will free up their holds for grain, which will make the trip south on the Mississippi.

For Viking's crew, this is the part of the day where they really earn their living. The crew is young and strong, and they work bare-chested in the hot summer sun, sweat trickling over muscles strained taut. They pit their backs and arms against the weight of both the barges and the river current as they tug on cables to swing barges into position to make a tow. Mechanized winches do much of this work. But some spaces are too narrow or awkward for machines. So muscular young men must fight the battle. As I watch, two crew members tug with all their might on a cable tied to the front of a barge. They use a mooring pier for leverage as they pull the cable to swing around the front of the barge. Suddenly, the cable springs loose and whips through the air. It cuts a gash in a crewman's forehead. An inch lower and he would have lost an eye. His partner grabs the cable and holds on while the crewman wipes blood from his face. They laugh—as young men do when frightened—and continue the battle.

When they have finished making that tow, the men climb back aboard Viking, which putters into the river and pulls up to a tow of four barges already tied two across on the bank. Captain Mike has no use for two of the barges, but radioed instructions tell him Viking must move one of the empty barges upstream for loading. As luck would have it, the one the crew must move is against the bank, blocked by the other three.

Captain Mike maneuvers Viking to a position perpendicular to both the river's current and the barges' sides. She butts her prow against the outmost barge, and two crewmen leap from Viking to the barge. They tie it to Viking, which pulls it out, her broadside against the current, her straining engine wheezing oily black smoke.

The boat moves that barge to the end of the pack of four. The crewmen secure it with rope and hurriedly jump from barge to barge until they reach the target barge just in time to meet Viking as she returns. They now lash the target barge to Viking so they can push it upstream to where it will be filled. After four hours of this game of dominoes, Viking is ready to gather four barges full of grain and push the tow downstream to the Northstar Fleet.

Now the barge handlers can relax. Their heavy work is finished until they reach St. Paul six hours later. Life on the river is like that: hours of feverish, backbreaking work followed by hours of downtime and boredom. For me, this downtime is a chance to talk to the crew and learn more about a riverman's life.

Viking's crew stays onboard 24 hours a day, seven days a week, 30 days at a time. They work six-hour shifts: six hours on, six hours off. In the crew of seven, there are two pilots including the captain, two deck teams of two each and one cook. If they choose, the men can work 30 days and have 30 days off. Most of Viking's crew prefer to take less time off than they are entitled because the lure of extra pay is stronger than the lure of attractions on the land.

"It's a great life for a single man," crewman Fred tells me. He has a scraggly red beard and long strawberry blond hair that he keeps out of his eyes with a headband. He just turned 30, is single and has been on the river five years. The life suits him. "All you gotta do is work hard and live.

You ain't got rent to pay. They feed you great, and there's good people on the river."

Fred makes about $300 a week, and his only expense while on the river is one carton of cigarettes a week.

He's a Southerner whose accent is Arkansas-bred and sounds out of place in Minnesota. After a short stint in the military, he drifted for a while before settling into life on the river. "One day I just heard about this job on a towboat, and I thought I'd give it a try. I was hungry when I started. But hell, they fed me like a king. So I decided to stay. I loved it. Still do."

Fred's shipmates on the Viking come from a variety of backgrounds. Two others, like Fred, climbed onboard after military duty. Two came from the forests of northern Minnesota and wanted to see more of the world. Two are the sons of rivermen; they inherited the lifestyle. The hodgepodge of young men gets along well with their shipmates. They joke. They roughhouse. They tell tall tales. Life on the river is good. "Hell," says one, "if you didn't like it, you wouldn't last long." Living in close quarters, if a riverman didn't get along with his mates, he'd soon find himself on land, maybe not by choice.

Captain Mike is the only married man on the Viking. That gives him a different perspective on a riverman's life. The crewmen admit he is not the grey-haired, pipe-smoking veteran they might have envisioned when they signed onto the Viking. But they tell me he's earned their respect and obedience, both necessities when working in an environment that can turn dangerous at any time.

I'm on the bridge with Captain Mike as the sun sets at 9:30 after a long Minnesota summer day. Lights from buildings shine along the shoreline, and lights from other river traffic dance on the water's surface. A small bulb illuminates the controls in the cramped cabin, and Captain Mike keeps his head on a swivel so he can observe the river both ahead and side to side. Though navigating the lower Minnesota is not easy, especially at night, this is the quiet part of the trip. And Captain Mike indulges my questions. I think, secretly, he enjoys the fact that he has company and a stranger to talk to.

He tells me that he spent his first six months on the river as a deckhand on a towboat. He decided he liked the life and the money. But he had ambitions beyond deckhand and set his sights on captain. This was six or seven years ago. He learned the trade by watching other pilots and occasionally handling the boat himself. "I learned by the seat of my pants and had some good men teach me to pilot," he tells me. Of course, there were some formal studies, and the licensing test was rigorous. But he passed the test three years ago and has not looked back.

Captain Mike clearly loves life on the river. He talks fondly of rivermen he has known and the stories they shared with him. As we cruise in the night, he tells me that one of America's most favorite rivermen is also one of his favorites. "When I become captain, my mother gave me a collection of the complete works of Samuel Clemens bound in leather. Just beautiful." Both the books and their contents, he meant.

River life has changed since young Sam Clemens watched riverboats from the bluffs near his Hannibal, Missouri, home and vowed to earn his own pilot's license to steer steamboats up and down the Mississippi. In Clemens' day, pilots were celebrities; they were princes of the river because what they did was incredibly dangerous and difficult. "They didn't have river charts or radios," Captain Mike marvels. "They steered entirely by memory. It was just crazy."

Other things about river life have not changed. The slow pace. The sometimes comforting, sometimes unpredictable flow of the river. The rivermen's rough, free lifestyle. "There's a lot to be said for this life," Captain Mike allows.

His original towboat job was supposed to be a temporary summer job while he studied social science at the University of Minnesota.

But working the towboats gave him a sense of excitement and freedom he couldn't find "on the bank."

"Hell, if I'd have stuck with what I was studying, I would be sitting behind a desk instead of steering this boat. I can't imagine that now," he says.

Out of the dark, a crackling radio voice tells Captain Mike that another towboat is heading upstream toward the Viking. He and the other pilot begin radio chatter that is part gossip, part business. They must plan how they are going to safely pass each other in the narrow channel. Captain Mike probes with his powerful searchlight, watching the other boat and the shore at the same time. Eventually, the other boat eases to the north side and toward a slip. The two captains wish each other a good night.

Now that he can relax again, Captain Mike tells me that he has not been home to International Falls for more than two months. "That's too long," he admits. "I knew it was too long when I called home yesterday and my 3-year-old daughter wouldn't even talk to me. My wife wasn't happy either." He shakes his head and continues: "That's why when I'm on the river, I try not to call home very much. Talking to my wife makes me want to go home."

Ahead, the Minnesota and the Mississippi converge. Not far into the Mississippi, a light rain begins to fall, and the wind picks up.

As the river surface begins to get rougher, Captain Mike's shift ends, and pilot Mike Toomey takes the helm. It will be his job to steer Viking into the bright lights of the Twin Cities channel and toward the Northstar Fleet. Once there, Viking will drop off its barges before heading back up the Minnesota. Larger towboats will form tows and push grain barges down the Mississippi all the way to New Orleans.

Deckhands Steve and Fred stick their heads into the cabin to report to Pilot Toomey. They are dressed in yellow slickers, and all three men curse the fact that a thunderstorm has descended, and a heavy rain has begun pound the boat. Winds pick up, and waves roll the boat side to side.

A new tension fills the air, and I'm not eager to find out what life is like on a towboat in the middle of a summer storm. I can sense the rivermen share my anxiety. But the deckhands leave the bridge and find shelter until the Viking and its barges reach the fleet.

Fortunately, by the time we pull up to the fleet, the frighteningly close lightning has moved off, the rain has turned to a light drizzle, and the river has calmed. The crew scrambles onto the darkened barges preparing to tie them up with the rest of the fleet, which lies secure against the bank.

It's wet and slippery on the metal barges, and I watch as the men use flashlights to find their way. In 15 minutes of hard work, Viking has shed her tow and moved toward an open spot in the wharf. This is where I shake hands with Pilot Toomey, wave to the crew and disembark. I turn and watch the Viking head upstream in the rain. She's hunting barges to push back into the Minnesota and upstream to Port Cargill. In the night, her lights bob and weave among the other lights shining on the Mississippi. Soon, she disappears.

FATHER OF WATERS

"S-t-e-a-m-b-o-a-t's a-comin'!" It was a cry that turned Sam Clemens' boyhood hometown on the banks of Mississippi River upside down. Mark Twain later wrote: "A drunkard stirs, the clerks wake up, a furious clatter of drays follows, every house and store pours out a human contribution, and all in a twinkling the dead town is alive and moving."

And this from Twain, too: "The great Mississippi, the majestic, the magnificent Mississippi, rolling its mile-wide tide along, shining in the sun; the dense forest away on the other side; the point above the town, the point below, round the river-glimpse and turning it into a sort of sea, withal a very still and brilliant and lonely one."

Twain's love of the river was infectious. Growing up near both the Mississippi and the Missouri, I shared the romance, the thrill. It's perhaps not surprising then that I gravitated toward river stories during my career. And there have been a lot.

I've explored the Shenandoah, the Willamette and the Rio Grande. I've traversed the Susquehanna, the Delaware and the St. Lawrence. I've met the Colorado, the Columbia and the Snake. In river valleys across the continent, I've discovered that the nature of a river shapes the culture of the farming communities that live beside it. The Platte River, for instance, is shallow and broad. It's not fit for barge traffic, but it spreads its waters wide beneath the surface and makes it possible to irrigate crops from shallow wells. As a result, the valley is home to some of the best corn farmers in the country. Similarly, the Willamette River Valley and the microclimates that surround it makes for a glorious variety of both crops and the people who grow them. I made multiple visits there because I found the valley's culture fascinating.

But it's the Mississippi that first captured my imagination, and I've pursued stories along its banks from where it meets with the Minnesota to where it merges with the Gulf of Mexico. There are plenty of reasons a farm journalist would concentrate on the Mississippi. Chief among them is its economic importance to farmers and the nation. The river helps give Midwest farmers global market reach and makes the United States wealthier by the grains they sell abroad.

The Mississippi River System, which includes the Missouri, the Illinois, the Ohio, the Arkansas, the Red and dozens of lesser rivers, forms the backbone and ribs of American agriculture's grain export business. Corn, soybeans and wheat are barged down those rivers to the Mississippi and then to the Port of New Orleans, where grains elevators line up to receive harvests from Ohio farms and Kansas farms, Iowa farms and Tennessee farms. Chutes from those elevators then funnel grain into the bellies of oceangoing vessels bound for Africa, Europe, South America and even Asia. Without the river system, which is so much more cost-effective than rail or truck transportation, markets for America's midcontinent farmers would be humbler. The entire nature and history of the rural Midwest would be altered.

I first wrote about the Mississippi and its importance to farmers in the late 1970s. The issue at the time was Lock and Dam No. 26, in Alton, Illinois, just north of St. Louis. It was the smallest in a series of locks on the Mississippi River System and had become a pinch point for barge movement. Its small capacity slowed traffic to a crawl. As we all know, time is money. The barge industry and agriculture were not happy about delays at No. 26. And in the 1970s, they pleaded with Congress and the U.S. Army Corps of Engineers to replace No. 26 with a new set of locks. The negotiations that followed were the basis of my reporting.

The locks and dams that serve the Mississippi start in Minneapolis and are strung like links in a chain along the great river as it flows south. Locks and dams are crucial to river navigation because channel depths vary according to terrain and rock formations in the riverbed. If the channel is less than 9 feet deep because of rocks or other impediments, loaded barges can't clear. Locks serve as stairsteps so vessels going either upstream or downstream have enough draft to pass to deeper water.

Going downstream, a boat enters on the high side of a lock chamber filled with water. Once the boat is in the chamber, huge gates close behind it to seal off the chamber, isolating it from upstream water. Ports in the downstream gate then drain the water in the lock, lowering the boat to the level of water on the other side. When water levels on both sides of the gate are equal, the downstream gate opens and the boat eases into the stream and cruises on its way downriver. Reversing the process raises boats traveling upstream.

Lock and Dam No. 26 was long enough at 600 feet to handle a tow of up to three barges long. Problem was, since it was built in 1938, the length of barge tows on the Mississippi had grown to more than 1,000 feet. To pass through Lock and Dam No. 26, tows must "double lock" to continue down the river. That is, the towboat's crew must break its tow in half to navigate through the locks. First one half then the other would navigate the locks. That doubles the time needed to clear the area.

When I visited Lock and Dam No. 26 in the summer of 1978, I climbed the levee on the Illinois shore to see for myself as towboats pushed their 15 barges (five long and three wide) to the bank, dropped half of them on the back and pushed the remainder into the locks. On the other side, the barges were attached to a system of electric winches that pulled them to the bank to await the rest of the tow. The second half—towboat and barges—then passed through the locks. They recoupled with the original half and sailed downstream. The process, I was told, took up to 10 hours.

No wonder shippers were frustrated.

In the 1970s, more than 28.6 million tons of grain passed through the locks at Alton every year. Another 58 million tons of petroleum, coal, fertilizer, iron and steel also went through. In both directions. All of which represented $5 billion in products held up by No. 26.

Once past St. Louis, the Mississippi—engorged first by the Missouri and later by the Ohio—becomes a superhighway with no locks or dams all the way to New Orleans. The number of barges in a tow can grow exponentially. The largest tow on record on the lower Mississippi was nine barges wide and eight barges long. It covered almost 13 acres.

Yet 1970s shippers were stuck just north of St. Louis with measly tows of 15 barges slowly squeezing through a set of locks that was built during the Depression.

A coalition of industry lobbyists descended on Washington to urge Congress to build a new lock and dam. That's where I picked up the story.

As far back as 1974, the Corps had drawn up tentative plans for a new set of locks and a dam three miles downstream from the existing set. Cost was estimated at about $421 million. Not cheap. But not out of reach for a federal project of such economic importance.

Nothing is ever that simple.

The Sierra Club and the Izaak Walton League filed suit to stop the project because they feared larger tows would lead to more dredging on the Mississippi, and more dredging would destroy natural habitats. The environmentalists were joined in their opposition by the railroad industry. It seems the railroads deemed it unfair that the federal government would foot the bill for a project that would benefit their transportation competitors. The railroad industry, they claimed disingenuously, received no such government help.

The courts got involved. The project stalled. Lock and Dam No. 26 remained a bottleneck. It's a story I followed for years. Eventually, the environmentalists dropped their suit because the Corps convinced them it did not plan to deepen the channel beyond the 9-foot depth already needed for barges. That would minimize the extra dredging environmentalists dreaded. For the rail industry, Congress crafted a compromise that imposed fuel taxes on towboats to offset some building costs.

Construction finally began in 1979 and was completed in 1994, and the new Melvin Price Lock and Dam No. 26 was opened for business. It's eight stories tall and 4,000 feet wide. Its main lock is 1,200 feet long and 110 feet wide to accommodate 15-barge tows. It can raise or lower those massive tows as much as 19 feet in less than an hour. Cost: more than $1 billion. I wrote my last story about Melvin Price in the 2000s. It was about—you guessed it—delays on the Mississippi River System. Barge tows had gotten even larger.

DOWN RIVER TO THE BOOTHEEL

I wasn't done with the Mississippi. In the summer of 1991, I did a piece for Top Producer magazine about the unique agricultural nature of the Bootheel of Missouri that lies in the southeast corner of the state, where seven counties hug the Mississippi. Yes, it does kind of look like the heel of a boot.

To get to there, I drive south from St. Louis on Interstate 55, which parallels the Mississippi. For the first 120 miles are so, I pass through rolling hills that are the rounded backsides of river bluffs on the east. On the west, the hills are the beginnings of the Ozark Mountains. Just past Cape Girardeau, I climb one last hill, and as I crest it, I'm atop Crowley's Ridge. I pull over because I'm astounded every time I see the vista. Below me lies a broad plain of farm fields interrupted only by farmsteads and windbreaks. The plain is so flat, the highway doesn't disappear over some distant hill; it vanishes as its four lanes converge into a single point on the horizon.

Welcome to the Bootheel—the beginnings of the Delta. From here to the Gulf of Mexico, the land on the west side of the river seems to know no hills. It's as if a giant bulldozer came down from the sky and scraped away all the lumps and imperfections most landscapes possess. It's as if God said, "Want to see flat? I'll show you flat."

Actually, the Gulf of Mexico, the Mississippi River and the Ohio River can claim some credit for this preternatural flatness. Sixty million years ago, the Gulf lapped up against what is now Crowley's ridge. The ancient Ozark Mountains formed the Gulf's western shoreline. As the Gulf receded, it left behind a rich patchwork of alluvial soils in places 40 feet deep. Over the eons, the Mississippi and the Ohio, which converge just north of Charleston, Missouri, contributed their own gifts of flood-borne organic matter, sand and gumbo soils.

In the Bootheel, this rich variety of soils partially explains the lush diversity of crops grown there. Rice is planted on the heaviest soils; cotton, corn and soybeans grow on the ridges; and fruits and vegetables of almost every description—from watermelons to potatoes—prosper on sandy soils.

"You want to know what really makes the Bootheel special? You gotta see this," says Sonny Martin, a 50ish farmer with a camouflage farmer's cap and a plaid short-sleeved shirt with a reading glasses case in its pocket. We're standing beside one of his rice fields, its deep green plants about ankle high. An irrigation pump is throbbing in the distance, and water is bubbling out of holes in 6-inch metal pipes to land in ditches surrounding and nourishing the crop.

He bends down and wrenches the top off a well casing. "Look it down here," Sonny says in an excited Southern accent as he points down the hole like a boy showing off his favorite toy.

Glistening not more than 10 feet below is water—water for Sonny's rice, water for his corn, water for his cotton, water for his vegetable crops.

"We've got more damned water than we know what to do with. But we're working on it," he says, a sly smile sneaking through his salt-and-pepper beard.

Combine that wondrously high water table with some of the best soils on the planet, and it's little wonder that Sonny is smiling. Add a long growing season and a collection of aggressive farmers, and you begin to understand why the Bootheel is one of the most productive and diverse farming regions in the country.

On only 10% of Missouri's total cropland, the Bootheel's seven counties produce 25% of the state's total farm revenue. In 1990, the Bootheel produced 31 million bushels of soybeans, 28 million bushels of corn, 314,000 bales of cotton and almost 5 million pounds of rice. Side by side are thousands of acres for melons, root crops and vegetables. As the locals say: If a crop doesn't grow well in the Bootheel, it's probably not worth growing.

Despite its modern-day equivalence to the Garden of Eden, the first white settlers to arrive in the Bootheel weren't looking for farmland. They were French traders and trappers who hit the region in the late 18th and early 19th centuries. The area now known as the Bootheel was nothing but swampland and primordial forests. Good for trapping beaver and other fur-bearing mammals, but certainly not ideal for farming. Nonetheless, a trickle of farmers took a shot at farming the few dry ridges in the region, just as President Thomas Jefferson and Napoleon Bonaparte in 1803 completed a deal that transferred ownership of the Louisiana Territory—of which the region was a part—from France to the infant United States. About 820,000 square miles for about $15 million. Not a bad deal, Tom. Of course, Napoleon needed the cash to fight his impending war with Britain.

About 200 of the Bootheel's first farmers settled around New Madrid, a town on the Mississippi planned by one of George Washington's former officers as a center of commerce. Of course, the officer didn't know that his town sat atop a major seismic fault. In 1811, that fault shifted and produced an earthquake that sets the standard for strength in North America to this day. The land literally rolled in waves. The Mississippi River rose up, turned and flowed north instead of south. Bells in church towers as far away as Washington D.C. rang because of the shock. What was left of the little town of New Madrid woke up to find itself on the Kentucky side of the river. And by one newspaper account, "All but two families moved away."

They didn't move far. A new New Madrid today sits on the Missouri side of the Mississippi. It boasts a museum that schools tourists on the great earthquake. It has a thriving business district and a levee at the end of Main Street that looks high enough to keep out King Kong but is meant to tame the Mississippi's floods.

It wasn't until the 1830s that immigrants from Kentucky, Tennessee and Virginia made a real attempt to farm the Bootheel. And it was a formidable task.

The flatland that lay between the few ridges were covered with nearly impenetrable swamps. For 70 years, hopeful farmers had to content themselves with working the ridges. Even then, periodic flooding—from creeks that backed up when the Mississippi had seasonal swells—made farming risky at best.

But in 1907, locals conceived the Little River Drainage Project. At its planning, it was the largest drainage project in the world, designed to convert 1.2 million acres from swamp to farmland. It took 25 years for crews to carve 1,000 miles of ditches and build 300 miles of levees. They moved more than 1 million cubic yards of earth, an amount greater than that moved to create the Panama Canal. When they were finished, waters that once formed swamps now flowed into the Mississippi, and land in seven counties became prime farm ground. The project made possible large-scale farming in the Bootheel.

A SOUTHERN VIBE

Take away his zip code, and a Bootheel farmer has more in common with an Arkansan than another Missourian. The accent is Southern; so is the attitude.

"We are part of the South," Johnny Boyd Thompson Jr. tells me. Johnny Boyd is a gentleman in his late 70s who wears a straw fedora and white shirt, fashion that would be right at home on an Arkansas front porch. Johnny Boyd grows cotton. "We have never been nor ever will be truly part of Missouri," he tells me with pride.

The fact that the seven Bootheel counties are officially part of Missouri can be credited to (or blamed on if you so choose) a few politicians and influence peddlers. Shortly before Missouri achieved statehood in 1821, a small group of men with power and vision decided that the future looked rosier if their landholdings were in the state of Missouri rather than the territory of Arkansas. So they persuaded the Missouri legislature to annex the Bootheel counties, which hang like an ungainly appendage from the southeast fringes of Missouri. Some Bootheel natives have never forgiven them.

"We are so far removed from Jefferson City [Missouri's state capitol] that we might as well not be in the state for all the attention they pay to us. Besides, the hill people don't like plains folk like us," Johnny Boyd tells me with a smirk. "So we developed a southward looking mentality. When we talk about going to the city, we are talking about Memphis, not St. Louis, even though they are about the same distance from here. And when we talk about farming, we think about how things are done in the Delta, not how they are done in the rest of Missouri."

It's not surprising, then, that when the lands dried, the first major crop Bootheel farmers planted was cotton. The growing season is just long enough for cotton, especially some early-season varieties. What's more, the Bootheel has some advantages over much of the Cotton Belt. On average, its soils are much more fertile, and its winters are cold enough to kill off some of the pests that plague cotton growers in the South.

But even with those advantages, cotton gave way to corn and soybeans in the boom years of the mid-1970s.

"When prices for corn and soybeans peaked, we saw a lot of cotton ground go to soybeans," George Paul Harris tells me. He is middle-aged and has the paunch to prove it. His neat hairstyle and just-pressed shirt indicate he is persnickety about his appearance and his business. His business is ginning cotton, and we are standing in an oddly quiet gin in the town of Senath. If this were harvest season, the gin would be so loud we couldn't hear each other talk. Large metal machines would be blowing hot air to dry the fibers, separating the fibers from seeds and foreign matter, cleaning the fiber and forming it into bales for delivery to end processors who make shirts like the one George Paul wears.

George Paul has seen the industry ebb and flow in the Bootheel. "Cotton is hard, hard work," he says. And when you see that you can make more money for less work growing something else like corn, you'll likely do it."

Following that logic in the late '70s and early '80s, Bootheel cotton farmers in droves switched to soybeans. As is always true in agriculture, things changed. Soybean and corn prices dropped, cotton prices improved, and farmers planted more cotton. Rice gained popularity in the '80s, and by the time I visited in 1991, it claimed more than 80,000 acres, including 600 acres planted by Sonny Martin.

"Of all the crops I've grown, I think I like rice best," he told me. "Once you get water on, it's easy to grow, and we get a good price for it. It's kind of ideal for the Bootheel because it gives us more flexibility and diversity."

Sonny knows about diversity. Besides rice, he has acres planted to corn, soybeans, cabbage, broccoli, green beans and other vegetables. "We are so diverse, it just wears me out," he says with another sly smile through his beard.

That diversity has helped make Bootheel farmers among the most prosperous in Missouri.

Wealth is obvious as I drive the flat country roads. Set back from two lanes or nestled on the outskirts of town are sizable brick ranch-style homes with circular drives, manicured lawns and swimming pools behind tall fences. They have three- and four-car garages that shelter fancy bass boats. They have luxury SUVs and shiny pickups that never get muddy. These are the Southern version of well-to-do farmhouses. The homes of many Bootheel farmers look like homes of bankers and businessmen. That speaks to local farming culture, where many of the largest farmers live far from the land they manage and close to town. They hire others to drive tractors and combines. Rich Bootheel farmers interact more with entrepreneurs and capitalists than with other farmers.

The farming wealth here and in the rest of the Delta is deep but not wide. The state of Mississippi endures the highest poverty rate in the nation, followed closely by Louisiana and Arkansas—all Delta states. And the Bootheel counties are no different. They consistently rank among the poorest in the state, with Pemiscot County at the nadir with a poverty rate of almost 30% in the 2020 census. As in the rest of the Delta, much of the burden of poverty falls on descendants of slaves, African Americans who make up more than a quarter of the population in Pemiscot County. But whites are not immune. They share with Blacks high unemployment and slim prospects for advancement.

Driving through the Bootheel, I see a tar paper shack surrounded by weeds and squatting desolately in a field far from any other dwellings as if shunned by its neighbors. I see a house tucked in a scraggly copse of trees with a rusting car in the front yard, its hood open to the sky like the naked mouth of a skull. I see Black children playing in the dusty front yard of a shotgun house with a blue tarp patch on its roof to keep out the many rains.

Bootheel towns reinforce the reality of poverty existing side by side with wealth. They remind me of farm towns I've seen in the Delta where one segment of the population lives in neat neighborhoods, while another segment literally lives on the other side of the railroad tracks, the side reserved for those who survive on minimum-wage jobs or welfare checks. All parts of the country—urban and rural—have pockets of poverty that lie near wealthy neighborhoods. But the near and visible contrast between rich and poor in the Bootheel is jarring.

HEADING HOME

On my last night in a hotel in Sikeston, I went over my notes and photos to assess my trip. I felt it had gone well. I'd secured some good interviews and gained some insights to add to my pretrip research. I was pleased with my reporting work. The only downside was that there hadn't been any of the unexpected incidents that sometimes add spice to my trips. I hadn't had any wild adventures to make the trip memorable. No accidents. No injuries. No crazy stories to tell friends when I got home.

As is my habit, I had kept a list of photo "needs" and photo "haves" during the trip. I keep the list to help me discover if I missed photos necessary to tell the story. My list that night showed I had no photos of the Mississippi as it flows past the Bootheel. That seemed like a conspicuous omission since the river lay behind every aspect of the story. But the Mississippi is really an unseen actor in the Bootheel, hidden as it is by imposing levees. I realized I had not yet found a vantage point where the river and farmland could be captured in the same frame. A levee was always in the way. An airplane would be the perfect vantage point, but I didn't have time now to track down a plane and pilot. If I couldn't juxtapose the river and farm fields from the air, next best thing was to find an elevated spot where I could see over the levee and show both the river and some agricultural activity, say, loading a grain barge in port. Fortunately, I had seen a river terminal with tall grain bins just north of Caruthersville. Just the spot to shoot over the river. At dawn the next morning, I headed in that direction.

Dawn in the Delta is different from dawn elsewhere. The heavy humidity that hangs in the air dulls the sun, and it rises as a scarlet globe. It casts a red hue over landscapes, which can be wonderful for photographs. That was my hope as I drove near Caruthersville on Port Road, which runs in the shadow of a levee hiding the river to its east.

It was impossible to miss the river terminal. Seven huge, corrugated metal grain bins sat a hundred yards from the levee, connected by gigantic conveyor belts encased in sheet metal tubes through which grain flowed toward the levee. Once the tubes topped the levee, they descended to a metal structure with its feet in the river. Tubes attached to the structure would shift to fill the holds of barges moored on the river.

Atop the levee was a control tower where operators direct the flow of grain to barges. I reasoned if I could get to the control tower, I'd be able to shoot down on the river and the barges I hoped were there, and I could include in the frame farmland on the Tennessee side of the river. A solid storytelling photo complete with geometric lines formed by the pipes, depth from the change in heights and color from the rising sun. When I drove into the parking lot at the base of the control tower, I saw only one parked car. More good news. I figured I would only have to convince one man—whoever had driven the car to work—to let me into the control tower. My guess was that he was the controller on duty.

I peered up at the control tower and saw that its cabin had glass on three sides. Even better, it appeared that there were sliding windows, which meant I might be able to open them and shoot with no glass between my lens and the scene. This was looking good. Now if only there is a barge or two moored below the levee, I'd have my photo.

It was a long way to the top, probably five or six stories of expanded metal steps with several landings. Seeing no gate between me and the steps, I started up. I was in good physical shape and used to long walks. Still, the weight of my cameras and the steepness of the climb forced me to stop at a landing and catch my breath. At the second to the last landing—maybe 30 feet below the control tower cabin—I could hear country music blaring from a radio. Whoever was in the tower had the volume cranked up so loud, he probably wouldn't hear me approaching.

I made it to the top landing and the door to the control room. Rather than open the door or knock on it, I leaned over and looked through its window. A solitary young man with straw-colored hair and a thin beard was sitting in the controller's chair. His head was tilted back, and beneath his ratty farmer's cap, I could see his eyes were closed and his mouth was open as if it was moaning. My gaze traveled down to his lap where a newspaper was spread like a painter's drop cloth to catch spills. In his right hand, he gripped his rigid penis, which he was stroking with enthusiasm.

Now there's something you don't see every day: A young man masturbating on a red sun morning in a tower 100 feet above the Mississippi with a view of Tennessee on the other side while Patsy Cline sings "Crazy" on the radio.

I pulled back my head and leaned against the wall, out of sight from the cabin. What the hell! I hurried down those stairs, jumped in my car and pulled away. In a few miles I found Interstate 55 and headed north. It was a long drive home, and I thought about that lonely young man. Was this a regular routine for him? What did he imagine as he spread that newspaper and reached inside his jeans? What if the music hadn't been so loud and—mid-stroke—he'd heard me coming up the stairs? What would have happened had he opened his eyes and seen me see him?

I'd found a crazy Bootheel story after all.

CHAPTER 16

COWBOYS AND GRASS FARMERS

Like a lot of kids in the 1950s and 1960s, I grew up a cowboy. Or at least I had cowboy hats and a pair of six shooters in a plastic holster. Cowboys in my youthful world drove dogies on cattle drives, fended off Injun attacks and went to saloons to wash the trail dust from their parched throats. There were good cowboys and bad cowboys on the black and white TV, and they fought each other over frontier justice and pretty women.

Even when I got older and understood that what I saw on television was fiction, I continued to be enamored with cowboy culture. Still am today, although now I can relate it to the dozens of actual ranchers and cattlemen I've known over the years.

Real cowboy culture has some of the same elements of the fantasy Wild West culture I saw on television. Real ranchers are every bit as self-reliant and resilient as the TV sort. They battle the elements, the markets and the vagaries of modern America.

Real ranchers—both men and women—can be as tough and cantankerous as any fictional cowboys, which tells me that stereotypes have some basis in reality. Western ranchers, especially, share space with civilian landowners and government agencies in ways that often lead to conflict. For example, Wyoming coal mine owners and ranchers clash over property rights. Environmentalists, who travel from the cities to occasionally commune with Nature, try to tell ranchers who live on the land how to best take care of Nature. And the U.S. Bureau of Land Management, which leases grazing rights on hundreds of thousands of acres of public land, often fights with cattlemen about what those leases entail and who, exactly, should control the land. Such conflicts are sometimes bitter, and justifiably or not, ranchers feel outgunned and persecuted. But they persevere because they make their living the way their fathers and grandmothers made their living, and it's the only way they can countenance.

A sense of history and place is especially important to today's ranchers. Most can tell tales of ancestors long buried in the church cemetery. They look across their pastures and see vistas of Nature at her most beautiful. They take pride in their ability to accept Nature even when she betrays them with sudden storms, grass fires and droughts. In the coldest winters and the hottest summers, they still chore; they still feed and water and use winches to pull calves from mama cows who have trouble birthing. Because that's what ranchers do.

That's part of why I admire ranch culture. It accepts that the world is both wonderous and harsh, and that the cowboy's role is to enjoy and to endure. It's not a coincidence that some of the most solid people I've ever met had cow manure on their work boots.

TEXAS

When I visited the Rightmer Ranches, near the tiny town of Muldoon, Texas, a two-year drought was testing the family's devotion to ranching. Streams dried up in 2010, pastures turned to dust, and cows bawled their discomfort. It was so bad, Clay Rightmer had one of his employees cut the lower branches of trees so the cows would at least have something green to eat.

273

"I'll be honest," Clay told me standing outside his ranch house, "it has been rough."

So rough that he'd liquidate his herds? Not a chance. It would take a lot more than two years of no rain to get Clay Rightmer to consider that. He is a cattleman to his bones. Tall, thin and with a nervous energy that makes it hard for him to stay stationary for long, the 51-year-old loves the activity and the challenge of ranching.

He is the fourth generation of Rightmers to run cattle in Fayette County, 65 miles southeast of Austin. If you count all the branches of his family tree, his forebears have ranched here since the mid-1800s: through the Civil War, through the Dirty Thirties, through the inflationary 1980s. His father, Harrell, taught him the cattle business and instilled in him a love for ranching.

"You cannot find a better life no matter how hard you look," says Harrell, who, at 77 years old, gives testimony to his love of the life by continuing to work side by side with Clay.

He Everywhere you look in Fayette County you see evidence that the Rightmers live among kindred ranching spirits. Heavy-duty pickups with gooseneck attachments for cattle trailers cruise up and down the two-lane roads. Pipes that once were parts for nearby oil field rigs are scavenged and used for railings in cattle pens, which sprout from the landscape like hardscrabble vegetation. And cattle beyond counting graze the pastures, as much a part of the landscape as the live oaks and bluebonnets that take up all the space that isn't grass.

With an annual average precipitation of only about 32 inches, thin soils and summer heat that would wilt most crops, cattle are about all this flatland is good for. Even cattle are not a cinch, especially in drought years. But the Rightmers and their neighbors not only persist, they thrive—at least in normal times.

These central Texans are a stubborn, tight-fisted lot. Clay tells me that frugality is a survival tool. As evidence, he mentions his recent choice of cottonseed rather than corn as a supplemental feed for his cattle. "Corn prices got crazy for a while," and cottonseed was a fraction of the price of corn. "The cows love it," he says. And it's easier on his balance sheet. He's also proud of the vintage U.S. Army truck he bought for practically nothing. He welded arms onto it and created a machine to haul big round hay bales.

The Rightmer ranch—about 500 mama cows on about 4,700 acres—is built on simplicity. Clay and Harrell have a real estate and appraisal business to augment their ranching addiction. So the simpler the ranch chores, the better.

The drought messed with that simplicity. "It changed everything," Clay says. His cows' reproductive cycles were skewed, and calving became chaos rather than a planned event. Weeds invaded where they had never been, and other weeds emerged at different times, so spraying schedules had to be scrapped. The cost of hay skyrocketed.

The Rightmers hope rains will help put everything back on schedule. But Texas being Texas, the family has long prepared for drought. They bred their cattle for it.

The family started using Brahman seedstock in the early 1970s because of the breed's ability to tolerate heat. They experimented mixing other breeds with the Brahmans (which originated in India) looking for the perfect genetics to produce both gentility and hardiness. Those other breeds have included Black Angus, Red Angus, Limousin and Charolais.

"Our cows are bred and socialized to be easy to work," Clay tells me with an air of satisfaction. "We can work 100 cows in 45 minutes, because they come when we call them, and we don't have to force them into the pens."

I observe that tameness later in the day when, on foot, Clay whistles cattle from a pasture into a pen. Amazingly—at least to me—they file peaceably into a pen and then into a working chute where they get a squirt of a liquid that repels nasty biting flies that are a bane of cattle on pasture.

Twenty years ago, Clay added to the human gene pool at the Rightmer ranch. He met a pretty, red-haired young woman at a cattle show in Houston, wooed her and made her his wife. Jennifer, who was a city girl through and through before she met Clay, says it took her only about a year to get used to ranch life. Now she will never go back to the city. "No, no, no," she laughs. "This is the good life."

The couple added daughter, Lane, now 17, and son, Reed, now 14, to the ranch. Haying and hay handling are among their ranch chores. I watch Reed operate a front loader with a spear attachment as he picks up 1-ton bales and loads them onto a truck, which Lane drives to a storage area. In the heat of a Texas July, it's hot, wearying labor. But their father insists that hard work and responsibilities are important for all kids. He believes that doing chores gives ranch kids an advantage over their city cousins. If he babied his kids, they would not be as strong as they need to be. Clay tells me: "Kids that don't bleed and sweat on the land will not stay on the land."

I've heard variations of that a lot in my travels. Farmers and ranchers believe their children have a better shot at successful lives than city kids because chores they do give them a sense of responsibility. They immediately see the consequences of shirking a duty: If cows don't get fed, they don't gain weight, and they might even die. I saw some pretty tough city kids while growing up, and I always thought a city kid could easily take a country kid in a fight. I'm not so sure today. Kids who grow up choring seven days a week no matter what the weather or what their own mood have a determination and a confidence built into them that might make the difference in a fist fight or a job interview.

Clay and Jennifer Rightmer don't want their teenagers to be focused solely on the ranch. Both kids are also busy at school with enough activities to keep the road between the ranch and town humming as Jennifer ferries kids in her SUV. During my two-day visit, I watched Lane fill dinner plates at a benefit dinner and Reed play in a baseball game. This was after they had done their chores. The Rightmer kids are busy from dawn to nighttime.

Jennifer is chief traffic cop for the ranch family and volunteer extraordinaire. Her schedule is busier than the other family members because she coordinates all their activities with her own multiple responsibilities. One morning, she chairs a meeting at school; that afternoon, she coordinates a covered dish fundraiser for the high school color guard; then she zooms to the next town down the highway to watch Reed at his evening baseball game.

The life of a ranch wife may be "the good life." But it's also a hectic life.

As a role model, Jennifer says she owes a debt of gratitude to her mother-in-law, Billie, who worked side by side with Harrell all those years. When her outside work was done, Billie would go inside and work some more to provide meals for the men.

"When I came here, I didn't know anything about cooking other than something like Hamburger Helper," Jennifer laughs. "Billie taught me to cook."

In the office Clay and Harrell share, I'm greeted by Ben, Clay's beloved Weimaraner, who does his dog duty and sniffs me carefully from foot to crotch. When I pass the scent test, Ben does that little circle all dogs do before reclining full length on the floor.

Mounted high on the wall behind the two desks is a 10-point buck, and on one of its antlers Clay now hangs his white cowboy hat. This is the first time I see Clay without his hat, and I realize he is mostly bald. Also on that wall are two large plat maps of Fayette County and the surrounding area. On the ledge near the large front window is a black-and-white studio portrait mounted in a frame. It shows four serious-looking Texan gentlemen in dark suit jackets with handkerchiefs tucked neatly in the breast pockets. They have on four styles of cowboy hats, which indicate the way hat styles changed over four generations. The youngest of the cowboys is 7-year-old Clay, who is standing on a box to bring him up to height with the others. He wears a bow tie. Beside him are his father, Harrell, and grandfather Charles, both in string ties. Great-grandfather Will wears a bow tie like Clay.

The relationship of his family to the land is an emotional subject for Clay.

He is deeply appreciative of the fact that he is the beneficiary of his ancestors' toils that converted an inhospitable environment of cactus, heat and snakes into a land where food—in the form of beef—grows plentifully. He is aware that his grandfather died of a heart attack during a particularly stressful time for the ranch. He counts himself lucky that he has a chance to work with his own father. "We often disagree about the best way to do a job. But we work well together nonetheless," Clay says. And he is aware that what he does on his watch will shape his children's lives.

So he does his best to take care of the land and has invested much time and money into conservation projects such as building ponds. "Water begets wildlife," he tells me as he guides his pickup down a dirt path, and terrain turns from pasture into scrub growth. He is proud that turkey, deer, fish and other species have thrived because of the many ponds we pass. "I could make a lot of money with hunting leases if I chose," he explains, and maybe one day he will. But for the moment, the headaches and liabilities of dealing with hunters do not appeal to him. For now, the game and fish are banked resources for his family and friends.

Clay does not know if Lane or Reed will want to continue the family's ranching heritage. "That is entirely up to them," he says. But if they do, he wants them to start with good land, sturdy cattle and an appreciation for the way of ranch life.

For himself, Clay says, there may be one more expansion in acreage before he is ready to let go. That might mean trading some improved acres for a larger number of rough acres—more work, more building the ranch's quality and value. After that, he says, "Jennifer and I love to travel. We'll have to depend on someone else to run the ranch occasionally. But we'll always be here. Ranching is in my blood."

WYOMING

Three hours north of Denver, I take an exit off Interstate 80 and follow Highway 13 a few miles north in search of the town of McFadden, Wyoming, where I am supposed to meet rancher Shanon Sims of Sims Cattle Co.

McFadden is the name of the town on the address Shanon sent me, but darned if I see a town as I turn off the highway. There is a wide spot in the road and a cluster of mailboxes. And I do see a small white building that looks as if it was—or is—a post office. There are other buildings or remnants of buildings here and there on what appear to be abandoned streets.

I call Shanon to tell him I am in McFadden as he requested. "I'll be right there," he says, and a few minutes later he drives up in his pickup. "Yeah, I guess I should have told you there isn't much to McFadden anymore," he laughs.

Turns out, McFadden is a ghost town. As with many towns in rural America, when society and the economy changed, the existence of McFadden was no longer required. It was largely abandoned decades ago by Ohio Oil Co. (now Marathon Oil Co.), which built it in the 1920s as an oil camp and then pulled out half a century ago. The company had built tarpaper shacks for workers, set up a few stores and a community center, and erected a couple of schoolhouses. The graying skeletons of those remain, along with a few newer houses. Somehow McFadden, which is now officially "a populated place" rather than a town, has retained the zip code

82083. The U.S. Postal Service says that zip code covers almost 500 square miles with a population density of about one person per square mile.

That should tell you something about the remoteness of the territory Sims Cattle Co. calls home.

I follow Shanon's red, heavy-duty GMC pickup out of McFadden, down a gravel road and across a small bridge over a rocky creek. The creek's narrow valley is lined with cottonwoods and other opportunistic tree species, which have found water in a dry land and cling close to it. Meadows of waist-high, dark green grasses spread among the trees and reach the edge of the hills. The grass on the hills is shorter and is a pale green-blue because moisture is scarce, and the soil is poor. The air is dry and fragrant with a hint of sage.

We're about 7,300 feet above sea level in a land of endless vistas spread under a blue dome. Flattop hills lay along the horizon like dunes on the edge of a green sea, and if you swivel your head, you can see line upon line of tall white sticks rotating in the wind as turbines capture energy from the air and pump it into underground powerlines.

A century and a half ago, there would have been herds of buffalo on those hills trailed by nomadic tribes of hunters on foot and on horseback. There would have been temporary villages with teepees and camp smoke. There would have been another civilization.

Shanon's truck pulls into the yard in front of ranch headquarters, which is a small, white house encircled by a low decorative fence and festooned with flower beds blooming in the July sun. Melinda, Shanon's wife, comes out of the front door to greet us. She's dressed in blue jeans, a sleeveless purple tank top and a welcoming smile. The two of them are a handsome couple in their late 30s. He is tall and lanky with thick black eyebrows, grey eyes and salt-and-pepper hair showing itself below his ivory-colored cowboy hat. She is tanned and pretty with three studs in each ear, a gold nose ring and blonde hair pulled into a practical ponytail.

I'm here to spend a couple of days photographing Shanon and Melinda for a story in Progressive Farmer magazine. They are one of five young farm and ranch owners the magazine will honor for the excellence of their operations. Senior editor (and my friend) Dan Miller has already visited the ranch and will write the story. My job is to capture images of the Sims family as they work. We timed my visit so that tomorrow I can watch as they round up and work more than a hundred cattle.

First they show me around the homestead.

Without the newer truck and an SUV parked in the yard, this might be an earlier era on a Wyoming ranch. Melinda explains that they like to live close to the land, so she keeps chickens and a milk cow. She has a large vegetable garden and freezers full of beef and venison to feed Shanon, herself and their two children: son, Kagan, 14, and daughter, Jentry, 11.

I get a walking tour of the place, which includes several wood-framed buildings covered in red metal siding. There's a small barn where Melinda milks Rosie the cow and a large barn with a hay loft accessed from the ground with a pulley. Riding harnesses and lariats hang among horse stalls, and a neat office in the barn contains two no-frills metal desks and a couple of file cabinets. Other outbuildings sit nearby for storage and for chickens.

When Melinda excuses herself to start dinner, Shanon and I climb into his pickup for a trip around a small part of the 25,000-acre ranch. A little history comes with the tour.

Shanon is the fourth generation of Sims to ranch in the Rock River Valley. His great-grandfather and great-grandmother were hardy settlers who put down roots in one of the nearby creek valleys more than 100 years ago and managed to scrounge a living out of a harsh environment. Much as Melinda does today, they grew gardens in the bottomland and raised chickens and maybe a hog or two. They grazed cattle, too, some in the valleys, some on the hills. Over time, the cattle side of the operation became larger and more profitable, and the Sims family stopped being homesteaders and started being ranchers. Ranching has come a long way since then.

The Sims Cattle Co. of today is comprised of Shanon and Melinda, and Shanon's parents, Scott and April. They have a more sophisticated philosophy than their forebears had about the business of ranching.

"We are in the business of harvesting sunlight," Shanon tells me. The animals are simply a means to convert an otherwise unusable protein source (forage grasses grown with sunlight) into meat that humans can consume. In what Shanon describes as a holistic process, the Simses work in cooperation with Nature, which shapes the way they interact with their surroundings. I can't imagine the 1920s Sims speaking in such elegant terms.

To make our discussion less ethereal and more substantive, Shanon stops the truck in the middle of a hilltop pasture, and we walk among the thin grasses and sandy brown soils. The grasses don't look like much to my untrained eye, but Shanon is proud of the several new species he and his father have introduced in recent years, including blue grama grass, Indian ricegrass and blue bunch wheatgrass. In the prairie highlands, the new species help hold the thin soil in place and help it to absorb the meager 16 inches of precipitation that falls each year. In lowland meadows, the Simses irrigate from creeks to produce a bounty of hay to supplement the cattle's grazing diet.

In the same highland pasture, Shanon shows off a pond he and Scott dug in conjunction with the Wyoming Game and Fish Department. The pond provides water they can pump to watering tanks for the cattle. But it also attracts antelope and waterfowl, kind of a thank-you gift to Nature.

The takeaway from my tour with Shanon is something he summarizes in a single word: sustainability. "We want this place to be here for our kids and grandkids," he says.

By the time we return to the homestead, dinner is ready. I meet Kagan and Jentry around the table, and chat with Melinda about the virtues of Instant Pot cooking. I've only just graduated to hard-boiling eggs and making rice in my pressure cooker, but Melinda makes main dishes, beef roasts and the chili we now enjoy. She can start a meal and leave to do chores while the pot finishes the work.

Before my visit, I had asked for a recommendation for a nearby motel. But this being the wide-open spaces of Wyoming, Shanon had told me a long drive to a motel would be silly. So he had invited me to spend the night in the unoccupied bunkhouse, which is a short walk from the family home. With dinner done and conversation slowed—and with the roundup scheduled to start before dawn the next morning scheduled—I say my goodnights and head in the direction of the bunkhouse. But it is still twilight, so I wander a little with my cameras into the trees near the creek. I find a footbridge and listen to the water splashing over the rocks. Down the stream, I spy a deer and her fawn who tiptoe out of the woods and warily sip a drink of cool water. I hear what sounds like ducks splashing in a pool down the creek. By the time I walk out from the trees' canopy, the encompassing sky has turned black velvet, and more stars than I believed possible fill the heavens. It is a gorgeous evening that reaffirms to me why people like the Simses love their ranch lifestyle.

When my alarm goes off at 5 a.m., I walk through the heavily dewed grass to the house. In gray predawn light, I see that the family is already up and leading horses from the corral to the horse trailers. They are throwing saddles onto the horses' backs and cinching them in place. Scott and April have driven over from their house a mile or so away and are putting hay and water in the trailers. There isn't much conversation, because the family has done this many times before; it's a well-accustomed habit.

I meet Scott and April for the first time, and we shake hands and smile like new neighbors. We'll talk more later. But now, they are too busy for conversation.

When the last horse is trailered, and the two cow dogs are in truck cabs, I go to my pickup to follow the caravan out to the pastures. "I have breakfast for you," Melinda says as she hands me a warm aluminum foil packet which contains an egg and sausage sandwich. "And here's some coffee." This is in a stainless thermos.

We are off to round up cows. Our headlights pick the way as we wind over gravel county roads until we come to the same pastures I had visited yesterday with Shanon. Through the barbed wire gate, the Simses park their trucks just as the sun breaks the horizon and turns the steel sides of the horse trailers a glowing gold.

Out come the horses one by one. Double-check the cinches. Adjust the harnesses. Lead the horses away from the trailers through one more fence gate and mount. All the family is here. Shanon and Scott pair up and move off due west where we can see cattle on the sides of the hills. Cowboys will get behind them and shout and wave their arms to get the animals moving north toward the working pens. Melinda, April, Kagan and Jentry will get on either side of the flowing herd to keep them pointed in the right direction.

Back at the ranch, they had offered me a horse to ride. But I declined the offer, telling them I'm clumsy at best on a horse, and my heavy camera gear beats the hell out of me at a trot. Besides, I don't want to spook the cattle. Instead, I'll follow in my truck.

It was a good decision. I find that they are working close to the road, and I can follow at a distance, taking photos in a glorious dawn light that is the stuff of a photographer's dream. At my back is a cluster of those white stick giants capturing wind. Their slowly turning blades glisten at the edges, and I'm close enough to hear their gentle whir. It's a perfect morning.

It takes only an hour for the cowboys and cowgirls to move the cattle the mile or so to the working pens. Generations of practice mean the Simses are good at what they do, and the more than 100 cattle are cooperative today. Those recalcitrant few that aren't interested in following the herd inevitably must deal with the cow dogs, who show them who is boss with a nip here and there around the hooves until the wayward cows fall into line.

All in all, it is an ideal roundup. From my outsider's vantage point, it looks easy, maybe even fun.

Soon, the real work of the day begins. Working cattle (in this case vaccinating and prepping for artificial insemination) is not fun. This bunch of cows bawls and kicks as they find themselves trapped in a corral. They bawl and kick some more as they are forced into the working chutes. And they bawl and kick once their shots are finished, and they are let out to mill around in a holding pen.

The process takes hours and includes a lunch break with canvas chairs set up beside Melinda's pickup, which is as well-stocked as an urban food truck. Over sandwiches and homemade cookies, I get to talk to Scott and April for the first time. I find him to be friendly and intelligent, but not keen on small talk. April, on the other hand, showers me with good conversation and jokes. We are best friends in a matter of minutes, and she doesn't mind my questions about life on a high-plains ranch.

When the crew goes back to work, I follow with my cameras and climb into the pickup bed for a better angle. Around 2 in the afternoon, with the cows still protesting their lot in life and the Simses still doing their jobs, a Toyota pickup pulls into the pasture and parks not far from my vantage point. My day is about to take another enjoyable turn.

Don Sims is the Toyota driver. At 88, he is the family patriarch. Father of Scott, grandfather of Shanon and great-grandfather to Kagan and Jentry, Don Sims is a character. He wears a battered white cowboy hat and equally battered blue jeans held low on his hips by leather suspenders. He has a neat mustache, dark sunglasses and a huge smile. He doesn't look a day over 75. He leans on a wooden walking stick and toddles over to the pickup, whose bed I am using as a shooting platform to get a better angle on the action in the pen. I'm pretty sure he says something like: "Hey, young fella. Whatcha doin'?"

I jump out of the pickup bed and extend my hand to greet him. It doesn't take long before he is my newest best friend. Don can talk. If Will Rogers never met a man he didn't like, Don Sims never met a man to whom he couldn't tell a story.

Don and I soon decide the rest of the family would be working cattle for quite some time yet, and it wouldn't hurt me to sightsee some other parts of the ranch. Besides, Don wants to give me some local history.

Off we go in his Toyota truck over the hills and into the past.

Don's first story occurs to him as we pass a pond. "You know how they used to make ice? Once a beaver pond was frozen solid, they'd score the ice with a plow that had a sharp tip on it. They'd pull the plow across the ice with horses that had cleats they'd screw onto their horseshoes. Then they'd use ice saws to cut out 50-pound blocks. They'd load those onto wagons to haul to buildings in town, and they would cover the ice with sawdust so it would last through the summer. We made ice cream all summer with that ice and cream from our own milk cows."

Don says all this in about a minute and a half as he drives like a bat out of hell down a rutted dirt road. He has a destination in mind that would help illustrate his next story, and he can't wait to get to it. He brings the truck to a halt on a road overlooking a ditch.

"You know anything about Butch Cassidy?"

"Just what I saw in the movie."

"OK, I'm gonna tell you a story. My dad's first cousin Mary Calvert married Elzy Lay, and Elzy Lay was Butch Cassidy's right-hand man. OK. Ever heard of the Wilcox robbery?"

"No."

"Well, the town of Wilcox was right down the line here on the trans-continental railroad. And Butch and Elzy and their gang held up a train as it left town. Once they got it stopped, they disconnected the locomotive and the express car from the rest of the train, and moved 'em across a bridge, which they then blew up the bridge to keep the Pinkertons from getting after them.

"Well, those boys had a wagon waiting for them, and they loaded the safe out of the express car into the wagon. They come this way, while some of the others decoyed the Pinkertons to Hole in the Wall, which was their hideout up north of here.

"And so, they got right here where we're settin', and they had the safe in the back of the wagon, which they dropped off into the ditch here and blew the door off the safe, which had 1892 engraved in it. This was in 1899 or so when this all happened. Well, years later, my dad bought this land and was cleaning out that ditch and rooted that safe right outta there. They put that safe in the territorial museum in Laramie along with a picture of my dad."

"Wow. That's a good story." (I meant it. It was a good story. But being a skeptical journalist, I later checked out Don's tale. To my astonishment, he had it correct, right down to the details of the blown-up bridge and the safe in the wagon, which was later found empty in a ditch. The gang got away with about $36,000, a great heist in those days.)

Don isn't finished.

"Butch Cassidy was quite a character, no doubt about it. He and another cousin of my dad's was boyfriend and girlfriend. When he come back from Bolivia, she told the story that Butch and her and some others would go fishin' around here. But he'd disappear for a while. And she knew darned good and well that he was goin' and lookin' for a cache of gold. Because they got to talkin', and he told her that when you did a holdup, you had these bags of gold, and you were on horseback when you were making their getaway. So you probably cached it somewhere because you couldn't carry it or go into town and spend it. So it kinda made sense he'd hide it somewhere."

I start to interrupt to say the movie had Butch Cassidy dying in Bolivia not coming back home. But I think better of it because Don is still talking, and I sense another great story is just around the bend. (Research later informed me that there is some controversy about whether Butch Cassidy really died in Bolivia or whether he escaped and returned home to live a long life incognito. So it is with outlaw legends.)

"My great-grandmother, whose maiden name was Shepherd, come from New York, and they floated down the Ohio River et cetera, et cetera, and took off from Council Bluffs in 1847. They belonged to the Mormon Church. She was just 13 and comin' through on the Oregon Trail, and she was on the next wagon train behind Brigham Young's when they landed in Salt Lake. Then in 1851, they sent a group of Mormons to California because the church had bought a large ranch down there, and they was to colonize it. But in 1857, they called that group back because the federal government was going to take back Utah because Brigham Young wanted to separate it from the United States and have a country of his own.

"In the meantime, they had what they called the Mountain Meadows Massacre. What happened was, they had a group of people who come through from Arkansas that the Mormons didn't want to settle there, and they assassinated everyone in this wagon train except for a handful of kids 6 years old and younger. They was the only survivors out of a hundred and some people. The Mormons had dressed up like Indians and did this. My great-grandmother who had set up in Santa Clair just outside of St. George in Utah, she found out about this and, boy, that's when she quit the church.

"So then, they went to raisin' horses in the desert this side of Colton. This was in 1876, and they had about 400 head of horses, and they was comin' right through this country and going to Denver, which had miner's gold at that time. They got as far as Rawlins when winter hit 'em, and they got into backcountry, and that was where my grandmother was born, right there under a wagon. Later she gave birth to 22 kids and had four sets of twins. My mother was the only twin that survived. One of the older girls about 14 or 15, she kinda fell in love with the deputy sheriff there in Rawlins. Well, the family was supposed to go on to Denver. But this girl, she jumped off the wagon and married that ol' boy. She was the mother of this girl who took up with Butch Cassidy."

(Yes, I researched the Mountain Meadows Massacre, and something very much like Don's version did happen, although the motives, details and results are up for interpretation, depending on who is telling the tale.)

By now we are driving again, and Don is still talking.

"You want to see this old saloon I bought? It's full of history."

"You bet. Let's go." I want to hear more Wild West tales from this old cowboy.

NEW ZEALAND

Cattlemen are cattlemen around the world. Their job is to convert sunlight to grass and grass to edible protein (beef) via the multiple stomach compartments of bovines. (No, cows don't really have four stomachs, only four compartments in one stomach.) In my travels, I have discovered that accomplishing that task most efficiently is the difference between a cattleman who prospers and one who takes a job in town. I also have discovered that in New Zealand, cattlemen are not cowboys; they call themselves grass farmers. Because that is how they see themselves. With a fierce concentration on grass, they have earned the reputation as some of the most efficient and innovative farmers of their kind.

A couple of decades ago, I began to hear about rotational grazing, a technique invented by the Kiwis and brought to North America by advocates of the practice whose enthusiasm for it is reminiscent of gospel slingers at a revival. Rotational grazing involves moving animals frequently, using movable—usually electric—fences. The frequent moves ensure healthier pastures, more efficient use of grass and faster-growing cows. If cows were smart, they might stop roaming pastures and move about them intentionally to accomplish the same goals. But as any cattleman will tell you, cows are not smart. They might be admirable; they might be predictable; they might even be lovable. But they are not smart.

It is not surprising that it was the Kiwis who came up with a more efficient way to graze cattle and sheep. New Zealand's economy depends on making the most of a small amount of land, and grass farming dominates the country's agriculture. Grass farmers make the most of each acre.

So it was with some anticipation that I drove to meet Jack Brice at his farm near a New Zealand town appropriately named Bulls.

Fifth-generation New Zealand farmer Brice is graying and friendly. His fair skin bespeaks a British Isles ancestry, and his smile would be familiar in any country pub in England, Ireland or Scotland. Jack has always been an early adopter of technology, and it has paid off for him. The 63-year-old grass farmer first adopted what he calls the TechnoGrazing system in 1998. It's a set of rotational-grazing techniques developed a couple of years earlier by his grass-farming neighbor Harry Wier. Now TechnoGrazing—or variations of it—are among the dominant philosophies with his countrymen in a land known for its expertise in finishing livestock on grass alone.

"With very good utilization of the grass, we generally carry double the stock per hectare over a conventionally run farm," Jack says proudly.

He farms on the southern edge of New Zealand's north island, where temperatures are moderate and an average of 32 inches of rain annually falls—a great place to grow grass. Every year, Jack raises as many as 550 crossbred bulls for beef, much of which goes to the U.S. He also produces about 1,000 market lambs and 500 purebred Poll Dorset sheep. A final piece of his farming puzzle is a few dairy heifers for export to China. "They are tough customers, very particular," Jack says of the Chinese.

Jack does all of this on about 400 acres of grass. Tall fescue, ryegrass, orchardgrass, white clover and other temperate forages make a home in his pastures. He also grows chicory and plantain as rotational crops. Jack uses no nitrogen fertilizer but does use lime "with a trace mineral blend with animal health in mind." He sprays for weeds only rarely. With that regime, the grass stays productive for years without reseeding.

The secret to his program, of course, is how he grazes his land.

Jack has nine permanent paddocks ranging in size from 19 to 54 acres. He used GPS instruments to divide paddocks into parallel lanes, which average 2,600 by 160 feet. The lanes, in turn, are divided into temporary "breaks," smaller sections that run perpendicular to the lanes and vary in size according to time of year, quality of forage and number of animals feeding there.

Electric fences powered by solar collectors separate paddocks, lanes and breaks.

Into each break Jack rotates "mobs" of cattle. Mobs vary in size, but 12 to 16 animals are a typical mob. The animals stay in each break for about two days, then Jack moves them and the fence to an adjacent area to create the next break. Over the course of 32 to 96 days, the cattle eat their way from one end of a lane to the next as Jack moves the breaks. As the cattle move, forage plants in the breaks they already grazed have time to recover. Nothing is grazed too long or too hard.

"This pasture system is more sustainable [than conventional systems] … pastures don't need renewing [reseeding] as frequently. It works so well, we don't use any supplementary feed," Jack says.

Of course, all that cattle movement creates a lot of work for a grass farmer. Jack adapts by adopting innovative electric-fencing technologies.

Neighbor Wier is a genius in that arena. I had just come from his impressive, well-appointed farmhouse and had taken an armchair lesson in the grazing techniques he had pioneered. But mostly our conversation was about the gadgets he manufactures and sell. The Wier family runs Kiwitech International Ltd., which creates and sells tools for electric fencing. The company has direct sales in Australia, Europe and South America. Kiwitech plans to sell in North America but doesn't have a distribution network here yet.

The day I visit Jack, Laura Wier, Harry's auburn-haired twentysomething beauty of a daughter, joins us. We ride in a pickup together to one of Jack's lush green pastures, while Jack leads us on a tricked-out ATV (he calls it a "bike."). While we park and walk into the pasture, Laura narrates for me as Jack demonstrates the tricks his bike can perform. First, Laura indicates the pipes that project from the front of the vehicle and extend in a V shape about 3 feet over the driver's seat. Jack drives straight into a single-wire fence, and the pipes lift the strand and carry it over him so he can drive "through" a live fence without stopping. Next, Laura describes how another metal bar structure—this one on the side of Jack's ATV—draws a fiberglass fencepost toward the vehicle and simultaneously plucks it from the ground while the vehicle continues rolling through the pasture. Jack grabs the post and puts it into a rack that looks like a quiver of arrows mounted near the vehicle's hood. With the spools of wire stored on the bike, he now has the material to form a new lane or break.

If you have a lot of fence to move, you don't have time to stop and get on and off your bike, Laura says.

When Jack and the ATV get to the end of the lane, Laura demonstrates a "release hook" her father developed. With a series of sharp tugs no animal is likely to perform, she unhooks a locking mechanism, and the strand of wire flies toward her. Once the wire is free, Jack winds it onto a reel, which is powered by an electric motor running off the ATV's battery.

For those without an ATV, Kiwitech sells a handheld version of the system, which is light enough for a person to carry on foot when setting a new fence. One version of that product can handle three strands of wire at a time.

To demonstrate how to sort cattle into a new break, Laura now pulls from the ATV a device that looks like a fishing rod and reel. On the reel are yards of flexible electric wire; on the end of the wire is a weighted metal hook. She flings the wire over the heads of the cattle in the break and onto the wire at the far end of the same break. When the hook makes contact, her "fishing line" is now live (electrified), and she can use it to encourage the cattle to move where she wants them. The cattle have learned from experience to respect the wire, and Laura uses it to guide them down the lane to new grass in a new break. Once the cattle are in position, she secures them with a live wire across the lane and lets them enjoy lunch in their new break.

After we drive back to Jack's farmhouse, Laura waves goodbye. Jack and I continue our conversation about life as a New Zealand grass farmer. Like any farmer or rancher, Jack tells me, he has his good years and bad years. In a typical year, he estimates his forage production at about 7.5 tons per acre. The best year he remembers was in 2004, when great weather made the grass grow fast and the cattle fatten easily. By happy coincidence, prices were good that year, too.

As cattlemen the world over would be, Jack was satisfied to have made some money that year in a profession that is always hard but not always profitable. "It was an exceptional year for us," he says with a large smile. I've seen that same smile on American cowboys when markets are good, grass in plentiful and mama cows and calves are well-fed, healthy and content.

CHAPTER 17

PHILOSOPHERS, PROPHETS AND POPULISTS

"There was once a town in the heart of America where all life seemed to live in harmony with its surroundings. The town lay in the midst of a checkerboard of prosperous farms, with fields of grain and hillsides of orchards where, in spring, white clouds of bloom drifted above the green fields .... Then a strange blight crept over the area and everything began to change. Some evil spell had settled on the community: mysterious maladies swept the flocks of chickens, the cattle and sheep sickened and died. Everywhere was a shadow of death .... On the mornings that had once throbbed with the dawn chorus of robins, catbirds, doves, jays, wrens, and scores of other bird voices, there was now no sound; only silence lay over the fields and woods and marshes."

This "Fable for Tomorrow" is how Rachel Carson begins her masterpiece, "Silent Spring," a book that awoke an environmental movement and turned agriculture on its head. Prior to "Silent Spring," talk of the dangers of pesticides was confined to science conferences and laboratories. Carson gave a vivid, poetic voice to the topic and made it a part of mainstream conversations in rural coffee shops, urban boardrooms and government offices.

"Silent Spring" was published in 1962, and its impact was immediate. Suddenly, the way farmers grew the nation's food was controversial, even dangerous. Consumers revolted and demanded changes in the way farmers put food on the nation's tables. Government agencies began their own research, and politicians threatened new regulations.

Some farmers reacted to all with anger and denial. "To think those ingrates in the cities would question the purity of our purpose and the safety of our products! They would starve without us!" Other farmers were perplexed and wondered if they could survive economically while farming in some new, as yet undetermined way that was "environmentally friendly."

The consternation and debate were almost two decades old by the time I entered ag journalism. But social and political temperatures had not yet cooled.

Other factors roiled the farming world. The 1980s also were financially devastating for American farmers. As I relate elsewhere in this book, several economic issues popped the balloon that had floated farmers' fortunes for much of the 1970s. Inflation, cratering commodity prices and soaring fuel and fertilizer prices killed the dreams of thousands of farm families. At one point, about 250 farmers declared bankruptcy every day. Dozens committed suicide rather than face a future off the farm.

As defeated farmers left the fields and moved to town, surviving farmers and outside investors bought their land and turned multiple small farms into one large farm. Families were displaced, and the farming towns and villages that relied on their trade began to shrink. Storefronts went vacant. Schools consolidated. Roads went unrepaired for lack of tax dollars.

The combination of environmental awareness and economic upheaval posed an existential threat to rural America. "Silent Spring" erased a sense of innocence among farmers, and the diminution of small farm numbers meant the loss of rural culture and its unique brand of humanity. For some observers, the country seemed to have strayed from a righteous agricultural path and was headed down an unsustainable dead end.

My job as a farm journalist in those days often brought me into contact with corporations pushing the latest large machinery and the most potent chemicals. The farmers I visited were their satisfied customers, and the magazines that employed me depended on corporate advertising dollars to pay my salary. I was part of the system changing the very nature of agriculture in ways that I didn't understand or condone.

That bothered me. So I occasionally deviated from my job description as a member of the trade press. I was a journalist, after all, and journalists are—or should be—curious about different points of view. I made it a priority to meet messengers of an alternative agriculture.

WENDELL BERRY

Wendell Berry is a farmer, professor of English, philosopher and author of profound yet humble prose about the current condition of farming's soul. His was—and is—one of the most influential voices in the alternative agriculture movement. I met him in 1989.

The University of Kentucky in Lexington, where Berry taught English for six years, features a leafy campus with tall trees shading sidewalks and instilling a sense of history. Some of the buildings look as if they could have been here since the institution was founded in 1865 as the Agricultural and Mechanical College of Kentucky.

However, when I find the building where Wendell Berry inhabits an office, it is a 20-story-tall, drab concrete construction devoid of tradition. Having read Berry's gentle, graceful prose, I wonder how uncomfortable he might be in such a confining edifice. I ride up the elevator to the 13th floor where Berry's nameplate is affixed to the door of a nondescript, cramped office.

The man himself is anything but cramped. At 55, he presents me an open face and a shy smile as he extends a hand in greeting and welcomes me to his academic workspace. It's a teacher's simple office with adjustable shelves bolted to a wall, a Formica and metal desk with a swivel chair, and a couple of plastic chairs where visiting students perch while talking to the professor.

Berry waves me to one of those chairs and, after some pleasantries about my trip and the balmy weather, we begin our interview. He speaks in soft Kentucky tones, broad and comforting. As he makes his points, he fixes generous gray-blue eyes on me as if to make sure I understand and to reassure me that I can ask for clarifications if his explanations aren't clear or if my understanding wavers.

As Wendell Berry sees it, American agriculture has traded its soul for promises of high production and big bucks. It has not been a good trade, he says.

"We accepted the destruction of the farm community as a reasonable price to pay for high production. But if you have lost your neighbors and your schools and the whole local economic structure, what good has high production done you?"

It's the kind of question Berry has posed for decades in essays, poems, novels, short stories and lectures. When he is not writing or lecturing, Berry runs what he calls "a hill farm" in Henry County, Kentucky. It's "125 acres of marginal ground, some sheep, two cows and a few acres of corn" he tells me with an engaging mixture of pride and humility.

On first meeting, it is easier to imagine this man as a farmer than as a philosopher/English professor. He looks uncomfortable in an office environment. His hands are oversized and strong, and his lanky form would be at home striding across fields and pastures. But he is as eloquent and earnest as a poet, and as he warms to his subject, I sense a philosopher's eye for the ironies and subtleties of this world.

"One of the ambitions of industrial farming has been to imitate factory methods," he says, pausing to make sure I'm following him. "That is, substitute machines and chemicals for people."

He pauses again, paws his balding head, and looks down to the floor as if gathering his thoughts. "But that idea makes people expendable, and to me, the loss of people from farming is nothing short of disastrous. When you have an industry that is systematically eliminating the children of its participants, what becomes of the future?"

Big is bad in Berry's view. He has no use for large farms. He says they are bad for communities and bad for farmers. He says large farmers cannot possibly care for their land as well as small farmers can.

By dint of their methods, large farmers are more responsible for soil erosion and water pollution than their smaller neighbors, Berry says. They also are partly to blame for the sweeping changes in the rural socioeconomic structure, for the hollowing out of towns and villages in farm country, for the demise of agricultural traditions.

"Does one large farmer do as much for his community as several small farmers? Of course not. He can't." He can't replace all those dislodged farmers on school boards, city councils and church committees. He doesn't buy as many groceries or hardware store items. He's likely to do business with out-of-town farm suppliers. His large equipment takes jobs from multiple farm owners and their employees.

But large farmers are victims themselves, Berry wrote a few years prior to our interview: "They [large farmers] have long ago lost control of their destinies. They are no longer 'independent farmers'... but are agents of their creditors and of the market. They are 'units of production' who ... must perform 'efficiently'—regardless of what they get out of it either as investors or as human beings."

Who or what is to blame for all of this? "The things that are now wrong with agriculture all come from human willingness to manipulate

Nature," Berry says. "Scientists have found more and more ways to manipulate Nature, and those ways have been used by industrialists to convert health to wealth."

If this all sounds a little ill-tempered, Berry will admit to the charge. His poem, "The Contrariness of the Mad Farmer," is a kind of an in-your-face acknowledgement that he doesn't value politeness as much as he values truth-telling. "I am done with apologies. If contrariness is my inheritance and my destiny, so be it. If my mission is to go in at exits and out at entrances, so be it. I have planted by the stars in defiance of the experts, and tilled somewhat by incantation and singing, and reaped, as I knew, by luck and Heaven's favor, in spite of the best advice."

Berry tells me he has been in love with farming all his life. His father was a Kentucky attorney who owned farms, and young Wendell used to ride with him and his business partner to visit their farms. "I always sat in the backseat of the car so I could get out and open the gates," Berry remembers.

He remembers, too, listening from the backseat as the two men in front discussed each farm and what was right and wrong with it. The conversation inevitably came down to the tenant farmer, the man who was doing the actual farming. And that fellow came in for some close scrutiny.

"I learned a lot about farming sitting in that backseat," Berry tells me.

Despite his interest in agriculture, Berry never became a full-time farmer. As a young man, he won a prestigious writing fellowship that set him on a career course of writing and teaching.

But he always came back to farming. For the two decades before our interview and since, Berry owned and operated a small farm where he uses draft horses instead of tractors. The horses are, one suspects, both a badge of honor and a ticket of admission into the club of "traditional" farmers. Their presence on the farm seems to say, "Wendell Berry knows the essential, true nature of farming because he has seen it from behind a horse."

That image helps Berry connect with one segment of his farming audience, those who cherish the old ways as the best ways. But it estranges him from another segment of farmers. It is hard for a man who owns several 300-horsepower tractors to take seriously the farming philosophy of a man who plows with two horses. The fellow with the tractors understandably dismisses Berry as a romantic, a thinker whose time has come and gone. Or worse, he dismisses Berry as a fundamentalist missionary, a man with the moral arrogance to tell prosperous large farmers that their ways are unacceptable, even evil.

And that dismissal is unfortunate. Because contemplations that come into Wendell Berry's mind and find their way onto paper are worth studying. They edge around agriculture's nuts and bolts, and peer into its heart. They hold up a mirror and dare farmers to look at it. Sometimes the mirror seems to distort reality. But just as often it reflects a startling image that can cause a "modern" farmer to wonder: "Is that how I really look? Is that who I am?"

Self-questioning—not providing answers—is what Wendell Berry is all about. I ask him how a large farmer can scale back to an "acceptable" size and still give his family the lifestyle they are accustomed to having. Berry's answer is vague, necessarily so, he says. "I don't think there is a single solution. But before you do anything at all, you must change the standards by which you judge farming. It's more complex than just production."

It's a philosopher's response, not a missionary's. A missionary would preach pat answers found in a book.

"My purpose," Berry says, "has always been to enlarge the boundaries of discussion as much as I can, to talk about long-term effects of modern agricultural practices, not only its physical effects, but its social and cultural effects, as well. I have always tried to tell the truth as best I can."

Some critics claim that Berry traffics in nostalgia, that he yearns for a world that was not as ideal as his memory makes it. I didn't ask him about that charge. But I sense he would admit it has some truth.

In 2006, he published the novel, "Andy Catlett," which is part of his fictional series of books about a small farming community in Kentucky that seems remarkably like Berry's ancestral Henry County. The main character is 9-year-old Andy, and the narrator is the boy grown to adulthood who is the same age as Berry is now and whose voice on the page sounds remarkably to my ear like Berry's in his office.

It's 1943, and Andy has traveled by himself from the town where he lives with his lawyer father and his nurturing mother to the Port William farm maintained by his elderly paternal grandparents. The story is deeply nostalgic. It portrays his loving grandparents and their neighbors as salt-of-the-earth people, whose determination and strength of character have built an enviably simple life. But it's a life that is fading into a new world, where tractors are replacing draft horses, and a generation of farmers is wending its way to country cemeteries. It grieves Berry to watch that world vanish, and he won't let it go without a fight.

"Increasingly over the last maybe 40 years," the narrator says, "the thought has come to me that the old world in which our people lived by the work of their hands, close to weather and earth, plants and animals, was the true world; and that the new world of cheap energy and ever cheaper money, honored greed, and dreams of liberation from every restraint, is mostly theater. And I fear, I believe I know, that the doom of the older world I knew as a boy will finally afflict the new one that replaced it."

That might be simple nostalgia. It might be a desire to protect memories. It might be a warning that the new world is just as transitory as the old, so don't be surprised if it, too, vanishes and leaves you yearning for yesterday. Above all, it says, don't disrespect the past. It shaped who you are today.

Our talk ends, and I ask if I might take his photo. Berry tells me he is awkward in front of a camera but agrees to look toward the window as I ask so the light filtering in will fall full on his face. That is the simple approach, an uncomplicated way to make a portrait. But it's not satisfying in this case. After a few unsuccessful attempts at a better image, I ask him to relax for a moment, and he swivels his desk chair so he faces away from the window. He looks slightly downward rather than at me, and his face collects itself into an instinctively patient expression. Slanting light from the partially open window blinds paints faint stripes on the back of his graying and balding head. Behind him on the shelves are books of poetry and philosophy. He comfortably crosses his arms and waits for instructions. I have none to give him because I like what I see. It is an unconventional portrait that has a contemplative feel. To my eye, it captures the complexity and the gentleness of its subject.

WES JACKSON AND THE LAND INSTITUTE

Wes Jackson wants to save us. Like an Old Testament prophet, like a voice crying in the wilderness, Jackson tells anyone who will listen that modern agriculture is killing the planet Earth. If farmers don't change their ways, their children will face a bleak future of famine, environmental poisonings and energy shortages.

That was Jackson's disturbing message when I first met him just west of the Flint Hills in the mid-1980s. It still is today.

Jackson is one of the most colorful and influential figures of the alternative agriculture movement in the last four decades. In 1990, Jackson was named a Pew Scholar in Conservation and the Environment. Two years later, he received a MacArthur Fellowship (sometimes call a "genius grant"), and in 2005, he was among the Smithsonian's 35 people "Who Made a Difference."

The attention and accolades have come in part because of Jackson's tent revival-style advocacy of sustainable agriculture. He's a hard man to ignore once he takes the podium. His renown also flowed from The Land Institute, which he founded in 1976 near Salina, Kansas, as a working farm/laboratory focused on changing modern agriculture from the familiar to something almost unrecognizable. Jackson's main contention is for the last 10,000 years of agriculture, man has relied on the flawed concept that planting fields to one kind of annual crop is the most efficient and sustainable way to grow food. Jackson preaches there is a better way.

To find that better way, The Land Institute investigates and invents farming methods that rely on perennial crops rather than annuals. The Institute intends to end monoculture and replace it with polyculture, multiple perennial crops planted in one field. The goal is to cut reliance on weed killers and insecticides, and to reduce dependence on petroleum by minimizing fertilizer applications and limiting the number of tractor trips. Such game-changing ideas for more sustainable food production enticed coverage of Jackson and The Land Institute from major national media including The Atlantic Monthly, The Wall Street Journal, the Los Angeles Times, Audubon and National Public Radio.

The uniqueness of Jackson's agricultural ideas has made many in mainstream farming circles label him a kook. But much of his message has a ring of truth to it. For instance, he rightly points out that modern agriculture's dependence on petroleum for fuels, fertilizer and pesticides is unsustainable in the long term. What, he asks, will farmers do when the world's petroleum barrel runs dry or when efforts to mitigate climate change shut down oil fields?

Jackson also notes that ag chemicals increasingly show up in our water and food supplies. What will farmers do with the nonagricultural world shouts "Enough!"?

Finally, Jackson examines the boom-and-bust cycles in agriculture and asks: If modern agriculture is so great, why are so many farmers unable to survive?

Good questions, all. They are the basis for Jackson's decision to establish The Land Institute, which he envisioned as a combination think tank and research farm where he and a handful of disciples could contemplate the future of farming and write new epistles about how it can change the world.

The Land Institute is also a training ground for subversives. Jackson hopes his disciples—all of whom hold degrees—will return to land-grant colleges for graduate degrees and, in the process, spread a new testament of farming to the next generation of doctoral candidates. That would lead to larger, well-funded research projects based on Jackson's vision of the future. The academic impact would be substantial.

Perhaps most importantly, though, The Land Institute serves as a pulpit for Jackson to spread the word.

I first visited his training grounds on a warm summer Kansas day in 1986. I got there by driving west on Interstate 70 from Kansas City through the lush green Flint Hills and turning south into Salina, halfway across the state. From the south side of town, I took the first gravel road east for a few miles, crossed a bridge over the Smoky Hill River, then proceeded up a hill where I found The Land Institute's compound. It was a modest facility at the time with a few small, sparse buildings and a plain house where Jackson and his wife, Dana, lived.

Jackson, who was in his early 50s, greeted me with both curiosity and skepticism displayed in his eyes. He had entertained many journalists, and I'm sure he wondered into what category I fell. Was I, like the general press, naive about agriculture but eager to absorb and disseminate his ideas? Was I, as a member of the establishment farm press, there to dismiss his ideas as radical hokum? Time would tell.

He led me into a classroom complete with chalkboard, school desks and library shelves filled with books on genetics, agronomy and soil science. I felt I had traveled through time to my college days and was about hear a science lecture.

It turned out to be more like a sermon.

Wes Jackson preaches with a fervor and righteousness one might expect from a missionary in a pagan land. His flexible, loose-skinned face changes quickly as he speaks. His hands fly about. He looks upward for guidance, and when he looks back down, his solemn blue eyes fix on me as if to ask, "Are you getting all of this? Do you believe yet?"

I soon realize that Jackson is much more than an evangelical preacher. Sophisticated in thought but rumpled in appearance, modest in lifestyle but brimming with intellectual pride, Jackson is complex. To hear him speak is to hear a philosopher, a scientist, an ecologist wrapped in the same energetic body. His ideas twirl and intertwine, and sometimes tangle in one another. They are sometimes infuriating, sometimes innocent, sometimes charming. But he presents them with professorial skill and self-assurance. This would be a fun interview—if I could get a word in edgewise.

When I finally succeed in slowing him down, Jackson gives me some biographical history. He grew up on a Kansas farm with dreams of attending college and eventually teaching agriculture. He earned a bachelor's degree in biology from Kansas Wesleyan University, a master's in botany from the University of Kansas and a doctorate in genetics from North Carolina State University. He later established and served as chair of one of the United States' first environmental studies programs at California State University, Sacramento.

"I like to flash my credentials," he tells me, "so that people don't think I'm some kind of weenie outsider yapping about things he doesn't know."

Though not an agricultural outsider, Jackson was born skeptical about the status quo, and at some juncture in his academic career, he began to doubt that modern agriculture was on the right path. It had strayed, he decided, had left Nature's way and was now wandering aimlessly down a dead-end road of man's creation.

To save it, Jackson left the safe, tenured world of academia, and with his wife, Dana, bought 188 acres of Kansas prairie. Together with a few benefactors, they founded The Land Institute, which is "devoted to sustainable agriculture and stewardship of the Earth."

In 10 years, he and a rotating band of young academicians have striven to find new cropping methods that avoid soil erosion and eschew petroleum products. In so doing, they studied the crop potential of at least 4,300 plant species, and they departed almost entirely from conventional agricultural thought.

For instance, Jackson and his followers believe that while monocultures depend on chemicals and mechanized tillage to defeat weeds and insect pests, polycultures can naturally reduce crop damage by creating a stronger growing environment, which stifles invaders. They also believe that planting annuals every year is a tremendous drain on soil and energy supplies. Fields of compatible perennials would address those issues.

On the surface, of course, these are marvelous ideas. Who can argue against the notion of a field in which diversity of crops alone inhibits pests? And who really likes to plant every year?

The difficulties come when you begin to ask about the practicality of raising several perennial crops in the same field. For example, how do you harvest a field in which mature and immature crops stand side by side, by hand? Or how to you breed a perennial to produce abundant seeds when perennials, by nature, use energy from the sun and soil to produce large root systems, not large quantities of seeds, which are the grains we humans eat?

Have faith, Jackson tells me. All those questions have answers; we just must look for them.

In the past, he argues, ag scientists brought biases to farming issues and looked in the wrong places for answers. He also implies that greed and laziness had something to do with the oversight, especially on the part of USDA and land-grant colleges. "It should not be taken too lightly when someone charges [they] ... have become subsidiaries of the petroleum-chemical companies," he wrote in his book, "New Roots for Agriculture."

Jackson is not as harsh or as haughty when he describes conventional farmers' individual failings. He calls them "beloved enemies" and tells me they farm the way they do because of a lack of alternatives, not a lack of concern. He intends to provide them those alternatives, even if it takes 50 or 100 years. After all, it took 10,000 years to get in this predicament. What's another century or so?

His vision of farming Utopia looks something like this: Large farms are a bitter memory of past failures. A typical Kansas farm is about 160 acres. Farms in areas of more rainfall are even smaller. Farm homes are partially underground and use solar and wind power as their energy sources. On fertile bottomland, people plant annual crops like wheat, corn, rye, barley and oats. In most of the other fields are mixtures of perennials like Canada wild rye and lespedeza stuevei. The machinery to plant and harvest the crops is powered by methyl alcohol produced on-farm from woodlots and perennial crops. Draft animals are a key power source. Fertilizer comes from both human and animal waste spread on fields. The animal waste comes from horses, chickens, hog and bovines, all raised on the same. Green manure crops also help fertility levels. International grain merchants and "the poison peddler" chemical companies are part of a closed chapter in agricultural history.

To my ears, Jackson's Utopia sounds like a simplistic step backward rather than a future paradise. After all, didn't modern technology free farmers from following teams of workhorses and feeding backyard flocks of chickens? How can farms that rely on old methods produce enough food for an expanding population? Don't we need more production capability, not less?

I'm missing the point, Jackson tells me, with a look that says he has heard these questions before and is disappointed—but not surprised—that I am no smarter than the last journalist who asked them. "We have no choice but to change directions," he says. Modern agriculture inevitably will collapse; we need a new agriculture.

And don't bet on new technology to cure agriculture's disease, he continues. Technology is what got us into this mess in the first place. Instead of technology, we should depend on learning Nature's secrets. "The philosophical beginning point should be that the future of the human race depends more on the discovery of knowledge about Nature than on invention," he declares.

Invention, Jackson says, creates commercialism, and we will never buy our way to Utopia.

What we need instead is a redefinition of society, "nothing less than a religious reformation." And while Jackson admits he wants to be a leader in that reformation, "One has to be careful that he does not go parading himself around as the savior of the world." If not the savior, Wes Jackson at least wants to be one of the prophets.

We parted ways with a handshake and a promise to stay in touch.

Eight years later, I again venture across the Flint Hills to Salina to see how things have progressed at The Land Institute. Jackson hasn't changed much. He is still gracious in his welcome and happy to talk. He is still a rumpled voice in the wilderness who can charm with his wit and broad eclectic knowledge, and he can still annoy with his self-righteousness. He has laid aside some of his messianic verbiage. But he is not shy about the scope of his studies, which he compares to the intellectual revolution led by Copernicus in the 16th century. That revolution did no less than reverse the relationship Earth had with the sun. Today we accept that our planet revolves around the nearest star, not vice versa.

"There was a lot of resistance to those ideas," Jackson tells me. "But in the end, we gained a different idea about our relationship to the universe. Now we want a change in agriculture that is equivalent to the Copernicus revolution. We want agriculture that does not lay waste to the soil, that does not rely on man-made chemicals, that runs only on sunlight."

Jackson's self-confidence has played well with donors and patrons. The Land Institute compound has expanded, and more interns and paid staff members than ever work its fields. As he introduces me to his new crop of acolytes, they strike me as much like their predecessors: young idealists who do their studies on the prairie in scruffy clothes, longish hair and an earnestness that harkens back to college campuses of the 1960s and 1970s. They are true believers, slightly superior to those not yet converted to the purity of their mission.

They don't claim any major breakthroughs. Instead, they talk about steady progress. Some of the star crops of the past have faded. Now eastern gammagrass and mammoth wild rye are in the spotlight. The most stellar crop is the perennial Illinois bundleflower that can produce sizable quantities of seeds, up to 1,000 pounds per acre. Unfortunately, those seeds are barely edible.

Jackson admits The Land Institute has had more research starts than finishes since I last visited. For instance, in 1991 it established Sunshine Farm, a 150-acre experiment in energy self-sufficiency. Using the power of horses in combination with renewable energy sources, it aims to grow grains, forages and meats with no net loss of energy. It's too early to judge its success. But as always, Jackson is unruffled.

He tells me: "We knew our work was going to be a long pull. This represents a first, after all. Nobody in human history has ever worked with perennials like this. All we know for sure is that in 100 years, agriculture will be a lot different than it has been for the past 10,000 years."

I checked with The Land Institute again in 2022 to see if the same determination against all odds is holding fast. It is. Jackson has released the reins and is now president emeritus. The staff has grown to more than 50, and it now has 53 global partners. The Land Institute's financial sponsors remain committed and unfailingly patient. As its website says: "In the next 40 years, we intend to develop an agricultural system featuring perennials with the ecological stability of the prairie and a grain and seed yield comparable to that from annual crops. Through such a system, we can produce ample human food and reduce or eliminate impacts from the disruptions and dependencies of industrial agriculture."

I admire their resolve. But the whole notion still sounds a bit naive to me. Or maybe it's my vision that is too limited. Maybe Wes Jackson was prophetic when he wrote: "If your life's work can be accomplished in your lifetime, you're not thinking big enough."

A POPULIST VOICE

If populism is defined as telling the world something like, "Elites, commercial giants and the government are taking advantage of us common folks," then populism is part of the genetic material of American agriculture. As far back as the mid-1780s, before the Articles of Confederation gave way to the Constitution of the United States of America, farmers in Massachusetts rebelled against taxes imposed by the state to pay off debt accumulated in the Revolutionary War. It was big-city elites trying to gouge common folk. Led by a yeoman named Daniel Shays, who had fought with the Continental Army, a few hundred farmers took up arms, closed local courthouses to impede tax collection and eventually marched to battle state militia forces. Outgunned, Shays' Rebellion did not end well for the populists.

A few years later, the president of the new United States had to face a similar populist uprising among farmers. The Whiskey Rebellion was centered in western Pennsylvania and also involved taxes meant to pay the debts of the new nation. The offending taxes in this case were on whiskey. Many farmers in the 1790s made whiskey from leftover crops as a profitable side venture. They did not take kindly to the new government in Philadelphia demanding a cut in the action. Over a period of years, resistance to the whiskey tax turned violent. Skirmishes between state militia and insurgents intensified. Impoverished citizens with other economic grievances joined farmers. And by 1794, an all-out shooting war loomed between common folk and the government. Federal forces—the first to be formed under the new Constitution—got involved. President George Washington himself put on his old uniform, left the nation's capital of Philadelphia, and rode west. The show of federal force was intimidating, and the insurgents dispersed without a shot. Some of the leaders were arrested and tried. Two were sentenced to hang, but Washington pardoned them. In 1801, under the administration of President Thomas Jefferson, Congress repealed the whiskey tax.

Ninety years later, farmers again rebelled against what they considered economic injustices imposed on them from the outside. This time, the rebellion was peaceful and political. The Greenback Party, the Farmers Alliance movement and the Populist Party included farmers as organizers and leaders.

Agrarian populist revolts also marked the 1980s. The American Agriculture Movement used political pressure, tractorcades and farm auction demonstrations to protest the worst economic conditions to hit American farmers since the Great Depression. Posse Comitatus, a loose band of insurgents, avowed that violence against the oppressive government and large corporations was the only means to reverse the depression in rural America. And hundreds of farmers showed up at bankruptcy proceedings to disrupt the sale of neighbors' farms by greedy banks.

In my role as a journalist, I had brushes with all those 1980s populist movements. Most were brief encounters, hit-and-run reportage of events marked by anger and agrarian pride. But I did spend valuable time with one self-described rural populist, and I came to respect and admire him.

Dixon Terry's part of Iowa is rough country compared to the lush flatland north of Interstate 80. The village of Greenfield is in the rolling hills that farmers use for both crops and livestock. Crops get the best ground; cattle get the steeper land with thinner soils. Hogs, chickens and turkeys settle for indoor facilities wherever it is convenient for the farmer to build large metal growing facilities. Those barns are almost aways set back from the main roads so as not to disturb the pastoral fantasies of pass-ers-through, who imagine that pigs still wallow in mud, and poultry still peck at grain cast on the ground by farm wives in bright dresses.

Dixon's farm is real, not idealized. He milks about 30 cows and grows hay and corn on a couple hundred acres near his compact farmhouse. He's not a rich farmer. Never will be. His means are modest, and his prospects are in line with that modesty. His dreams, however, are big. Not big in the sense of wealth or of owning hundreds of dairy cows and thousands of acres. His big dreams are for a more equitable share of the economic pie for farmers who work hard, play by the rules and cherish their place on the land.

It's a cloudless summer day in 1988, and my well-used Oldsmobile and I turn down the lane that leads to Dixon Terry's red clapboard house. He's out in the yard with wood chips scattered at his feet and a chainsaw in his leather-gloved hand. Several stumps about 2 feet in diameter project from the ground around the perimeter of his yard with good-sized slices laying nearby and cordwood stacked neatly to one side. He won't cut the windbreak trees on the north and west side of the house. Those are his defense against Iowa's inevitable cold.

"You must be Jim," he says, striding toward me and taking off a glove to shake my hand."

"And you must be Dixon getting ready for winter."

"I am. Building my wood pile. How was your drive?"

For the next few minutes, we're typical Midwesterners talking roads, weather and soil moisture, the universal pleasantries that ease farm country strangers into conversations. Dixon and I are about the same age—late 30s. He is of medium height and is trim as befits a man whose profession revolves around physical labor. He has bright red hair spilling from beneath his farmer cap and flowing down his sideburns to a neatly cropped full beard. His wire-rimmed glasses have round lenses, and his eyes crinkle when he smiles, which is often.

As is my practice with these types of interviews, I ask for a farm tour. Farmers are often most comfortable when showing off the land they love and tend. Dixon is no exception, and as we bounce around in his old pickup, we discover we have several things in common, including being in college during the Vietnam war. He at Iowa State, I at Mizzou. We both viewed the conflict as a war of choice: unwarranted and detestable. We both marched in protests and became radicalized by the experience. The war caused us both to question our government's veracity and our society's values. He became more of an activist than I, and antiwar demonstrations led to political action for him. He organized campaigns and became a leader. He came to see politics as a means to fight injustice. I became an observer.

The pickup carries us past the milk parlor, which is need of repair and updating. It is old technology in an industry just starting to adopt multiple stainless steel milking stalls and the first steps toward automation. Same is true of the other outbuildings; they have shed their coats of paint and look old-fashioned and forlorn. Dixon seems to have anticipated my assessments of his facilities. "I'm not home as much as I'd like to be," he tells me. "It's hard to take care of the farm and do my political work."

His pastures near the parlor are lovely. The rolling hills are dotted with black and white Holsteins and filled with summer grass, pale compared to lush spring growth but still looking like a dairy cow paradise. His more distant hayfields are almost ready to cut and look like they will be productive. The pickup climbs a hill, and Dixon pauses so we can take in the vista. "We've had some good rains," he says with an affirmative nod, and we head back to the farm and the inevitable selection of his kitchen table as the spot we'll settle for the rest of our conversation, aided by traditionally weak but welcome Iowa coffee.

Dixon describes himself as a populist. When he speaks, it's about a philosophy as old as discontent on American farms. Like all populists, he is full of love for the common man and distrust of big business and big money. He draws distinct lines between what he sees as the interests of "family farmers" and those of agribusiness. He's particularly concerned about recent trends in the livestock industry toward vertical integration. Corporate giants own the means of production, including the animals from birth to slaughterhouse to grocery-store coolers. Farmers are merely a link in the production chain. They consent to build hog and poultry barns to company specifications, receive thousands of young animals to feed in those barns and get paid based on the weight of animals as they leave the farm in trucks bound for company-owned processing plants. Under that scheme, farmers are merely hired hands who have lost their independence.

"We need to stop the trend toward vertical integration and cost-control," Dixon tells me. "Look at the meat industry now. The Cargills and Conagras are feeding the cattle and the hogs; they are processing them and marketing them, too. That kind of integration and control frightens the American public."

Activists like Dixon use that fright as a weapon. "We need the public on our side if we are to get anything through Congress," he tells me.

It's revealing that he thinks the political system can provide answers. Previous and subsequent rural populists were so alienated from government that they thought the only solution to farmers' economic and social problems was to throw all the bastards out and give "outsiders" the levers of power.

Dixon has a traditionalist streak. He believes the system is flawed but can be improved.

"The system needs to be changed," he says. "The reason we mistakenly got involved in Vietnam is the same reason we have a mistaken farm policy now: vested interests, huge multinational corporations. From 1981 to 1986, Conagra increased its profits 515%. At the same time, farmers are going broke in record numbers. So it's no secret why we have farm policies that hurt farmers. It's because some powerful forces have a vested interest in maintaining things as they are."

Dixon's passion and anger is understandable. His own father lost the family farm to debt in the early 1980s, when the farm crisis was just getting underway. Farm foreclosures and family dislocations have only gained momentum. "People out here are so damned depressed and demoralized," he tells me indignantly. "They assume this whole thing [traditional family farming] is going down the tubes. The young people are just trying to decide where they are going to move to find work. And the old people are just counting the years until everything is gone. If you think back 10 years, expectations were just the opposite. Rural population actually increased in the '70s. It has decreased in the '80s."

Dixon says it pisses him off when someone tells him what is happening in rural America is inevitable, that history and economic forces have ordained that many small farmers must give way to a few large farms. "We have this blind assumption that progress means fewer farms and bigger farms, or that progress means more chemicals and fewer small towns. That's a lie."

The fight to counteract "lies" and the effects they have on farmers is personal for Dixon. "As this point," he says, "I'd have to categorize myself as one of the questionable survivors. I have a lot of debt, and although I'm paying my bills, my future is uncertain. It's not a future that makes my children want to own a farm."

That admission, that the next generation might not want to farm, is among the saddest statements a farmer can make, and it kept Dixon in an activist role.

When I spoke to him, Dixon was a rising star in Iowa Democratic circles. He and his wife, Linda, were among Esquire magazine's "'The Best of the New Generation: Men and Women Under 40 Who Are Changing America" in 1984. He was co-chair of the League of Rural Voters and vice president of the Family Farm Foundation. He advised Iowa Democratic Senator Tom Harkin on farming issues and helped shape an ill-fated piece of legislation that would have set a floor for commodity prices while keeping farm production at sustainable levels. Dixon even struck up a friendship with politician/preacher the Rev. Jesse Jackson when he stumped Iowa during the 1984 and 1988 presidential caucuses.

Dixon blames much of today's family farm disaster on recent government policies that originated in Washington D.C. Specifically, he blames Republican administrations for cutting government assistance and supply-management programs in the name of fiscal responsibility. At the same time, they encouraged farmers to make up for low commodity prices by planting more acres to maximize production. Richard Nixon's Secretary of Agriculture Earl Butz famously urged farmers to plant "fencerow to fencerow" and to "get big or get out."

A decade later, "The Reagan-Bush people are for full production and letting the whims of the marketplace set prices," Dixon tells me. "We know from history that means boom and bust in the farm economy."

Unfettered production by prolific American farmers historically leads to oversupplies, which lead to commodity price crashes. When prices hit bottom, small farmers with sparce cash reserves are forced to leave the game, and larger farmers buy their land. Eventually, the supply and demand reach an equilibrium, and prices rise again. The whole cycle begins anew. Which is why some farm groups favor government programs that restrain production. The Soil Conservation Act of 1935 established a model whereby the federal government would pay farmers to put some of their land in conservation programs that would preserve resources. That reduced the number of acres planted to crops, which lowered production so it did not overwhelm the markets. Higher commodity prices resulted. The Agricultural Act of 1956 created the Soil Bank program with the same objectives. So did the Emergency Feed Grain Act of 1961. Farm groups and individual farmers valued such government programs because of the stability they brought to their industry. It was a populist idea put into practice.

It wasn't until the 1970s that such conservation/production control programs fell out of favor. The Nixon administration and later the Reagan administration sought unrestrained production to meet what they perceived as infinite international markets for U.S. farm goods. But small farm populists such as Dixon saw the dangers of deregulated markets reliant on overseas markets. They understood a governmental policy of laissez-faire left the little guy unprotected, especially when markets tanked because of the cycles capitalism creates.

"No matter how hard you work at managing your farm, as long as policies are structured in the interest of the Cargills and Conagras of this world, you're not going to survive," Dixon tells me.

Dixon was a leader of a rural populist movement that coalesced around Democratic politicians who promised government programs to ensure a level playing field for farmers of all sizes. Today, the populist landscape has changed. Rural populists now gravitate to Republican politicians who promise fewer regulations and freer markets. The transformation from Democratic to Republican has been astounding. Farm states, which once voted Democratic, now are reliably Republican. Part of the Republican appeal is related to societal values. Gun rights and pro-life promises from Republicans play well in the countryside. That is perhaps understandable.

But it ignores the fact that farmers historically have done better economically under Democratic than Republican administrations.

On a deeper level, a strain of populism always has rejected government officials as either weak or corrupt. "Throw the bastards out!" is a populist refrain. However, forcing veteran politicians from office inevitably leaves a power vacuum. It also creates a craving for a decisive and vocal leader, which is why populists can be susceptible to seduction by a demagogue, as they were in 2016. I wonder what Dixon Terry would have thought of Donald Trump, who won the White House in large part by capturing the devotion and the votes of rural populists. How could the same Iowans who loved modest farmer Dixon Terry in the 1980s fall in love in 2016 with a self-proclaimed billionaire who was born to luxury, attended elite East Coast schools, used multiple bankruptcies to avoid paying middle-class employees and bragged constantly about his wealth?

Perhaps it's prudent for populists to remember that the next demagogue might be lurking behind the woodpile.

Dixon, of course, is unaware of the disturbing future and displays to me an optimistic outlook. "There are plenty of reasons for hope if you understand how the political system works and how farmers can affect it," he tells me. "And you don't have to get a lot of farmers involved. If you get 5% involved, that can be enough to make a difference. The key is being smart and building coalitions with other interest groups."

Our coffee-table conversation is coming to a close, and Dixon's tone transitions from the buoyantly practical to the nearly poetic: "We can have a new day out here in the country, and that's what we must get people to believe. By changing policy, we can change our lives and open up possibilities for our children. We can make our communities vital again."

As we walk to my car, Dixon explains another reason he fights the fight. "I just play a role," he tells me. "I speak for people who wouldn't get heard otherwise. And when someone comes up to me and says, 'Thanks. You said it just right. You're speaking for me,' that's what keeps me going."

We shook hands, and I promised to check back with him to see how his work was progressing. But that was the last time I saw him.

On a June day the year after I visited his farm, Dixon Terry, his father Dixon Sr. and his 13-year-old son, Dusky, raced an incoming storm to bale the last of the first cutting hay before the rains came. They had just finished, and the other two had gone ahead with the truck and trailer while Dixon drove the tractor home. At the top of a hill, a bolt of lightning struck, killing him instantly.

More than 1,000 mourners came to his funeral, filling the United Methodist Church in Greenfield and spilling out into the road. Harkin and Jackson were among the eulogizers. A friend named Dan Hunter played the guitar and sang a song which included the verse: "Dixon was there for us. Red beard, flashing grin, muddy boots on the floor, in a kitchen somewhere around midnight."

More than 30 years after Dixon Terry died in a stormy hayfield, populism is still a potent force in rural America, among farmers in particular. Agrarian populists in the 21st century still view themselves as the underdogs waging battle against powerful corporations, urban elitists and overreaching government. But their political affiliation has changed, and their heroes are people Dixon would not recognize.

CHAPTER 18

OLDEST FARMS IN AMERICA

The deeper I got into farming culture, the more I became a collector of historic farms. Like any good collector, I looked for the unusual—mushroom farms, fish farms, farms that raise goats for goat yoga class. But what is more unusual than the oldest of anything? I went looking for the oldest farms in the country. Specifically, I wanted to visit the oldest farms that were continuously owned and operated by the same family from foundation to present day.

In 1988, that search took me to Appleton Farms, in Ipswich, Massachusetts.

As best as I could tell from weeks of research, it was the oldest dairy farm in America to be passed from generation to generation. Farm manager James Geiger told me on the phone that he'd be pleased to tell me what he knew of the Appleton Farms' history. So I planned a flight to Boston and a drive to Ipswich.

The lane into the farm is classic rural New England: mossy stone walls, green pastures with stray rocks protruding, leafy centuries-old trees. It feels like a slice of colonial history just off a busy 20th century highway.

James meets me when I find my way to the farm office. He's a trim man in his 40s wearing a pressed, blue cotton shirt and grey khakis, and a tobacco pipe hanging from his mouth. I detect an upper-Midwestern melody to his speech as he welcomes me, and he confirms that he is a son of Wisconsin. We talk about my hopes for the visit, and James guides me to the "Old House," a white frame building that began as a one-room structure in 1688 and grew over the generations. It's now an impressive, rambling two-story house with touches of Georgian and early Federalist styles. It has been remodeled and reshaped at least six times over the generations, and now is home to farm owner Joan Mary Egleston Appleton. The lady herself, who is in her mid-70s, strides gracefully down the front walk to say hello. She is tall and straight-backed and moves with poise. Here is elegance.

James refers to her as "Ma'am," and I immediately feel I should do the same. She responds to us with the hint of an English accent. I later learn that she is indeed England-born. She met and married Francis R. Appleton Jr. on a trip to visit American friends in the 1930s. Family lore has it that they were both equestrians, and at their first encounter, his horse threw him. Joan retrieved the animal for him and captured his heart at the same time.

The three of us chat for a while about the farm, and I begin to gather history. Mrs. Appleton is gracious and generous with information but soon leaves us to complete our work, which includes a tour of the farm, photos and some conversation about its business and how the farm manager hopes to take it into the future.

Here is how I later described my visit in a 1989 article.

APPLETON FARMS

In 1638, when the Appleton family first started milking cows at their Ipswich, Massachusetts, farm, Galileo was still pondering the moons of Jupiter, the Thirty Years' War still had 10 years to go and King Charles I of England still had a crown his head.

Things change in 350 years. Galileo's moons have posed for NASA photos, other senseless wars have come and gone, and a new Charles is next in line for England's throne.

One thing hasn't changed: The Appleton family still tends cows on the gentle hills of Ipswich.

Three hundred and fifty years. That makes Appleton Farms the oldest dairy farm in America, which causes the farm's general manager, James Geiger, both pride and anxiety. Pride because he has a keen sense of history. Anxiety because he knows that, along with owner Joan Mary Egleston Appleton, he has an unusual responsibility: to preserve the past while preparing for the future.

Fortunately for James, the Appletons have never sat still and watched the world change around them. Through the centuries, they have kept pace with—and even set the pace for—American dairy producers. That's why James felt he and Mrs. Appleton could make decisions that changed the very nature of Appleton Farms, transforming it from a small-scale dairy that scraped by in the 1960s to a successful genetics operation that uses the most modern technology of the 1980s.

Maybe, too, that's why James had no qualms about writing this motto for the farm's brochure: "Historic Appleton Farms does not merely keep up with the times ... it helps define them."

THE BEGINNING

Samuel Appleton, the Englishman who founded the farm, understood the need to change. In 1635, the 49-year-old Appleton left the security of his home in Suffolk County, England, and sailed across the Atlantic to the new colony of Massachusetts. His friend and neighbor in Suffolk County, John Winthrop, had recently been appointed governor of the colony, and Appleton no doubt thought a man with such influence could help him start a new life.

The record isn't clear if Winthrop used his influence on Appleton's behalf. But the Ipswich "towne booke folio" does indicate that in 1638, Samuel Appleton was granted "a farme containing foure hundred and sixty acres more or less medow and upland' near town. That is the same year that the chief of the Agawam Indian tribe sold the land where Ipswich now stands to English settlers for 20 pounds sterling.

It also isn't clear whether Samuel Appleton brought milk cows with him from England. But Governor Winthrop's diary indicates that Appleton was involved with the arrival of cows 'come on shore.' If Appleton did have cows, it was likely he grazed them on the town commons where livestock was safe from wolves.

As the colony grew tamer, the Appleton family improved their farm. They also branched into other enterprises that eventually made them wealthy citizens in the new land.

Samuel, perhaps with help from his friend the governor, received special five-year tree-cutting privileges that he used not only to clear his land but also to found a prosperous milling business. A later generation of entrepreneurial Appletons became successful watchmakers in Waltham, Massachusetts. Appleton & Tracy Company eventually helped form the renown Waltham Watch Company of New York. Still later, Lieutenant Colonel Francis R. Appleton Jr. (who died in 1974 and whose widow is the current owner of the farm) acquired prestige and wealth as an attorney practicing international law.

Wealth from these outside ventures reduced the need for income from the family farm. But the family persisted in farming and used its wealth to experiment with the latest in dairy techniques, which kept it at the forefront of the industry. In the early 1860s, for instance, Daniel Fuller Appleton started two of the first purebred dairy herds in the country. His Kerry cattle were a short-lived dalliance. But his Jersey cows became the dairy farm's backbone.

While Daniel Appleton was discovering Jerseys, Louis Pasteur was discovering how to prevent bacteria from causing milk to sour. When the pasteurization process became commonplace in the late 1890s, Appleton Farms was ready to ship to distant markets with a herd of cows capable of producing plenty of milk, which they transported to Boston on newly laid railroad tracks. Money from milk sold in Boston flowed back to the farm.

Just after the turn of the 20th century, Daniel's son Francis R. Appleton Sr. became lord of the manor. He ran a diversified livestock operation but took special interest in dairy. He imported Holstein bulls from Holland to create strong new bloodlines for maximum milk production. In 1907, one of his Holstein cows held the world record of 27,400 pounds of milk produced in one year.

His son, Francis R. Appleton Jr., took things in a slightly different direction. He preferred Guernsey cows, and his Guernsey herd became one of the foremost in the country. Frank Jr. also used readily available labor during the Depression to turn wooded hills into pastureland and to build many of the buildings that give character to Appleton Farms.

Today, the oldest dairy farm in America is reminiscent of an English estate. Grand old elm trees create green tunnels along lanes. Stone walls define paddocks where a few cows lazily graze. A large barn covered with shake shingles dominates. While small frame houses built for hired help cluster around an herb garden complete with a group of Adirondack lawn chairs and a view of rolling pastures.

The farm's carefully maintained 500 acres and traditional buildings still speak of wealth and gentility. But by the time farm manager James Geiger arrived 10 years ago, the glory days had passed. James, a Wisconsin native who had moved East a few years earlier, found dairy farming in eastern Massachusetts on the wane.

In a region where urbanization gobbles up farm fields, dairy operations find it difficult to buy feed at manageable prices. And the recent boom in

Massachusetts' economy means labor is hard to find or afford. "With nearly full employment in the area, I can't compete for help," James says.

In his first years at Appleton Farms, James struggled to keep the dairy operation solvent. He modernized equipment in the dairy barns, bought Holstein heifers to improve the herd and succeeded in raising milk production beyond the 20,000-pound annual national average for 40-cow herds. Still, the operation was in trouble. "I did everything I could to make us more efficient. But we just couldn't make it," James says.

As an alternative to selling bulk milk, James investigated making specialty cheeses. The start-up costs and future labor costs proved to be too high. Finally, he and Mrs. Appleton decided to go in an entirely different direction. With the farm's rich history of genetically superior animals, it seemed natural for Appleton Farms to explore purebred sales of genetics.

NEXT STEPS

In 1983 and 1984, James developed a plan to buy top-quality young cows and use them as the basis of a new venture: selling embryo transfers to overseas markets. He set up a limited partnership that left him and Mrs. Appleton in control while providing the capital needed to gamble on really good, really expensive DNA.

They hit it lucky with the first roll of the dice. Their initial purchase, Juniper-Mist Bell Paula, a four-year-old cow with excellent pedigree. She has tested at almost 32,000 pounds of milk with 1,388 pounds of valuable butterfat. Appleton Farms sold one of her first progeny to a Japanese businessman for $30,000. More than 60 of her other female embryos sold for an average of about $12,000 to investors in Japan, France, Australian, Canada, France and Japan.

Besides Bell Paula, James now keeps two or three other donor cows and 80 replacement/recipient heifers. He has help from two foreign-exchange students and his wife, Caroline. And, of course, there is the elegant Mrs.

Appleton, who says, "I don't drive a tractor. But James and I confer on all the major decisions."

Mrs. Appleton is the ninth generation of Appletons to live on the farm. She is childless. When she is gone, the historic link to Samuel Appleton finally will be broken. To ensure that at least the farm—if not the family name— continues, she has arranged with a nonprofit trust to eventually maintain the land as farmland.

Meanwhile, she and James will continue to chart the farm's path. For James, that is a responsibility that carries some weight. "I find it almost impossible," he says, "to make a move on this farm without thinking about the historical implications."

POSTSCRIPT

As James and I finish our business that day in 1988, Mrs. Appleton glides up in an electric golf cart and disembarks. She has come at my request to have her picture taken with James and one of her cows across a stone wall. We move to the location where she and James converse as I frame photos of the last of an ancient household, a capable farm manager and a black and white cow.

I'm pleased with the results and thank the two for their time. Mrs. Appleton chats with us for a few moments then offers her hand as a proper lady does, and bids me a pleasant journey.

In 1998, The Trustees of Reservations assumed responsibility for the farm. The Trustees is a conservation group that operates parks at about 100 historic sites in Massachusetts. Appleton Farms still functions as a dairy and livestock farm, but the Trustees have expanded its acreage to 1,000 and added other functions. It now has a consumer-supported agriculture (CSA) business to sell in-season vegetables to subscribers; it has a store stocked with farm goods for sale to walk-ins; and it welcomes students for educational tours. Brides and grooms cherish the farm as a wedding venue.

Aspiring chefs take cooking classes here. And town kids can attend camp on a real, working farm.

Mrs. Appleton lived on the farm until her death in 2006.

THE TUTTLE FARM

A year after my trip to Appleton Farms, my quest to collect ancient American family farms brought me to Dover, New Hampshire. I suppose I should have gone to New Hampshire first, because the Tuttle Farm predates Appleton Farms by six years. But it took me awhile longer to find documentation of the Tuttle farm. Founded in 1632, it has provided sustenance to 10 generations of Tuttles. The ninth generation is Hugh Tuttle, a tall, thin middle-aged man with a Yankee sensibility and a gift for gab. His vigorous handshake is followed by a forceful suggestion that we start with whatever it was I had come to do. He is a busy man. With that, we begin a tour of the farm that often strays into history, anecdotes and sly humor.

Here is how I described my visit in a 1990 article:

We all have our ghosts. Hugh Tuttle's are just older and more alive than most.

Tuttle owns the oldest family farm in America, and every day that he walks out his door and sees his fields, he is reminded of his ancestors. From John Tuttle, who founded the farm more than 300 years ago, to George Tuttle, who made his strawberry pickers whistle while they worked so they couldn't eat his profits, to William Penn Tuttle II, who brought the farm into the 20th century, they are all still around—or so it seems to Hugh.

"There is an awful lot of déjà vu here," he says of his farm. "Sometimes I go out early in the morning and almost think my ancestors are looking over my shoulder to see what I'm doing."

They would hardly recognize the place. What was a white pine forest in 1632 when John Tuttle landed there is now a hectic metropolitan area 70 miles north of Boston and within shouting distance of Portsmouth, New

Hampshire. The hills all around are obscured by houses, and a road carrying 14,000 vehicles a day cuts through the heart of the 245-acre farm.

City folks and urban traffic have influenced the Tuttle place. What had been a subsistence farm for six generations of Tuttles began to change when Hugh Tuttle's great-grandfather decided to raise fruits for sale to big city markets.

His son later got into the poultry business, and Hugh's father transformed the place into a vegetable farm that sold wholesale to area groceries. Hugh then converted the farm into a retail operation that sells vegetables, bedding plants and flowers to shoppers coming off that busy road.

Today, in the $2 million building Hugh named "Tuttle's Red Barn," the Tuttle family also sells gourmet cheeses from France, olive oils from Italy and coffees from Colombia.

No, the ghost of old John Tuttle wouldn't recognize the place now. He was an apprentice barrel maker, and in 17th century England, that meant he was near the bottom of society's barrel. He lived like a slave, with little in life to call his own, including his future.

Fortunately for John, King Charles I was looking for a few good men and women to settle territories in the New World. The king offered 15-acre tracts of land to almost anyone who requested them. When John put his "X" on a land grant document, King Charles' people gave him parcel number 14 in New Hampshire.

It was a lucky draw, according to Hugh, because the parcel was river bottomland and therefore some of the most fertile soil around.

But John's luck was short-lived. With high hopes and dreams of a new life, he and his wife boarded the ship The Angel Gabriel in Bristol in 1632. After weeks on the open seas, the ship reached the coast of Maine ... and foundered.

The Tuttles escaped with their lives, but John lost the tools he had so carefully saved to buy in England. Imagine his predicament: an ocean away

from home in a wild and unknown land. For the first time in his life, he pos-
sessed property and the chance to make his own way. But the property was
covered in tall trees, and he had no axe to cut them down.

"I have no idea how he survived," Hugh Tuttle says of his ancestor.
But survive, he did. So did the next generation and the next all the way to
the 1860s when Hugh's great grandfather decided survival was not enough.
Joseph Edward Tuttle wanted to prosper. He planted fruit trees, put in a cran-
berry bog and began a vineyard for table grapes and wine. These were radical
changes for a subsistence farmer. But they proved successful and brought the
family much needed income.

Joseph's son inherited his entrepreneurial spirit and kept an eye open
for new income streams. He noticed that roast duckling was the rage in New
York City. Before long, the son was in the duckling business in a big way.

And his son—Hugh's father William Penn Tuttle II—also inherited a
head for business. Right out of high school he began growing vegetables to sell
wholesale to grocery stores. He bought a Maxwell car, cut off the back passen-
ger compartment and had a makeshift pickup truck to deliver fresh vegetables
from his fields to four local stores.

Truck farming might have remained the Tuttle family business if times
hadn't changed and Hugh hadn't been next in line. He didn't want to farm,
he tells me. "I had in mind to be a doctor of some sort, although I can't tell
you why."

He went off to a nearby college—Harvard University—and majored in
botany. But after less than a year he missed farm life. "That spring when the
first crocus bloomed, I thumbed my way home to see how things were going.
That's when my father knew I was destined to be a farmer."

Tuttle is wiry and leather-skinned in his mid-60s. He loves to talk, and
he does so with a saltiness and verve that is New England charm incarnate.
"You ought to be here at Thanksgiving," his daughter Lucy informs me. "He

tells story after story about the family, and we sit around saying: 'Tell it again. Tell it again.'"

It wasn't Hugh's storytelling ability that was required when he took over the farm. It was a business sense and a willingness to take a gamble.

His father's business model of selling produce to local stores was falling apart because a new kind of store was developing: the supermarket chain. "Ah," Hugh says with disgust. "If that's progress, we don't need it."

According to him, supermarket chains made it impossible for local farmers to sell their produce. "All they wanted from their vegetables was uniform mediocrity at the lowest possible price. That's not the way we do business. So we decided to bite the bullet and go out on our own."

With that, he set up a retail shop in a 150-year-old barn on the farm. Direct sales were an immediate success. Hugh bought land to expand his 65 acres to the current 245. Even with the additional acres he couldn't keep up with the demand for fresh, homegrown produce. "We had a tiger by the tail," he says. "The retail business was lot better than we ever imagined."

Soon Hugh, and by now his daughters Lucy and Rebecca and son William Penn Tuttle III were buying produce in Boston to meet the demand. They built a glossy new addition for the old barn and expanded the product line.

"We still grow most of the delicate crops," Hugh says, "plus those vegetables we can't find of good quality." That ensures you won't find any "plastic tomatoes" from distant hothouses at Tuttle's Red Barn store.

Hugh tries to stay clear of the store. Even though he loves to talk, Hugh's inclinations run to growing crops rather than selling them, and the store strikes him as "a flippin' zoo." Daughter Rebecca helps in the fields, and Lucy's bailiwick is the specialty foods. Son Bill is the produce buyer and "a real businessman," Hugh says.

Hugh's children do feel some weight from being part of the Tuttle Farm legacy. "I am really proud to be part of the oldest farm in America," Lucy tells me. *"I also know it's not something I had anything to do with. It was just a fortunate accident of history."*

Hugh, who has lived all his life with that family history on his mind, now says, "I have to start learning to retire."

In the summer of 1987, he took his first growing-season vacation and plans to be gone more often from the everyday activities on the farm. But he doesn't expect to stray far. "I have my house set up so I can lie in my bedroom and peek between my toes to look right out on our fields. I would rather have that view than a view of anything."

It's hard to imagine Hugh Tuttle moving from his roots. His ancestors never did in more than 300 centuries. "You know," he says in a reflective moment, "I have one strange desire. I would like each of my ancestors to be reincarnated for a day. I would like to walk the farm with them and try to explain to them what I am doing now. If I had one ancestor to pick, it would be John Tuttle. I would like to hear him explain what was going through his head when he arrived here in 1632."

POSTSCRIPT

In the winter of 2021, I did research to see if Tuttle's Red Barn farm was still in the family. It wasn't. After more than 370 years and 10 generations, no Tuttle wanted to farm anymore.

In 2010, Bill Tuttle told CBS News: "We are tired emotionally, mentally exhausted and we are ready to walk into the sunset." He and his sister, Lucy, sold a conservation easement on the land to Strafford Rivers Conservancy. That means the land can only be used for farming in perpetuity. "It's not going to be houses, condos or shopping malls," Bill said.

The farm itself sold to another farmer in 2013, and some other farm somewhere else now holds the title of Oldest Farm in America.

CHAPTER 19

THE BEST GRASS
IN THE WORLD

It is close to sunset in the Flint Hills of Kansas, and we are bumping in a pickup down the winding gravel roads and dirt paths that wander across Happy and Kathryn Jackson's ranch. Kathryn, a rosy-cheeked lady nearing 80 years old, can't resist the opportunity to brag a bit about what we see all around us.

"Take a look," she says, indicating the rich green pastures on both sides of the road. "The Flint Hills have the best grass in the world." And from all appearances, she is right.

Hill after green hill roll into the distance, and each is dotted with cattle that have their heads down and are chewing contentedly in the golden light. They look like a postcard from bovine heaven.

"I heard a gentleman one time explain why our grass is so good," Kathryn tells me. "The limestone that underlies our hills provides the nutrients to help the grass grow strong, and when the cattle eat that grass, it puts weight on them quickly and strengthens their bones."

Happy nods in agreement and keeps driving. He is a tall, thin man, bent a little by age and arthritis, but as strong and vigorous as a stand of bluestem grass. He doesn't talk as much as his wife, but he is just as proud of the Flint Hills as she is. He was born here in 1910, and the grass and the cattle that graze it have sustained him his entire life. He currently tends 4,000 acres of pasture and hay ground. Other ranchers—some as far away as Georgia—pay him to graze cattle on their lush pastures until they are ready for "finishing" in a feedlot. In cattlemen's terms, Happy is a "backgrounder," as are many of the Flint Hills ranchers.

Wife, Kathryn, has been by Happy's side for 58 years. She has a curly cloud of grey hair and lively eyes that sparkle through wire-rimmed glasses. She possesses a well-mannered way of speaking that is brimful of enthusiasm, a practice undoubtedly developed while teaching in a one-room schoolhouse all those years ago. When she wasn't teaching school, she was helping Happy on the ranch and raising their three children, now grown and gone.

Although she is not a native of the Flint Hills, you couldn't move Kathryn from here now with a team of mules. She and Happy (his given name is Harry) have lived in the same white frame house in Greenwood County since 1935.

They want to show me as much of the hills as possible before the sun goes down, so we drive on ribbons of gravel roads to Sugarloaf Hill, a high point in the county.

A VALENTINE'S STORY

I'd found myself on the Jackson ranch by chance. During that summer of 1990, I'd spent pleasant days poking around the Flint Hills hunting for pieces of a story I planned for that special region of Kansas. I searched for historical, social and geographic bits of the Flint Hills to adorn the farming and ranching montage I hoped to create.

A source had told me about an older married couple in Greenwood County. The wife was a former schoolteacher and could wax eloquent about area history, my source told me. And the husband was a "retired" rancher. The quotes are because ranchers never really retire, especially in the Flint Hills. Like old soldiers, they just fade away.

So I contacted Kathryn and Happy Jackson to see if I could visit their ranch.

Early on this early-summer afternoon, Kathryn and Happy graciously give me time and coffee in their parlor. Her round face and bubbly manner remind me of a cartoon fairy godmother. If only she'd had wings, the picture would have been complete. He is craggy and friendly with a face crinkled from decades of smiles. They—especially Kathryn, because Happy is the strong silent type—are overflowing with the types of stories I had hoped to find. They share local lore sprinkled with their own experiences and their love for the Hills. They talk of neighbors and relatives, history and rumors, tales of the kind only longtime residents can tell. It isn't until I am about to leave that Kathryn suggests we drive to Sugarloaf Hill to get an overview of the terrain.

By now, the ordinary day has become glorious. The sun is sliding into the emerald hills, and the western sky has an orangish glow. Happy drives the Jacksons' old pickup, Kathryn sits in the middle and I hang my elbow out the window and feel content with the delightful way I make my living. We park at last and walk our way up a dirt path to the flat summit of a knoll.

The Jacksons are right. This is a special spot. From up here, the incredible green hills seem to lie in folds below us like a rich woman's emerald-colored cloak casually tossed onto the earth. A polite breeze blows Kathryn's hair around her beaming face, and Happy gazes quietly from beneath his white cowboy hat.

"I always get nostalgic when we come up here," Kathryn says. "This is our little bit of heaven."

Then she tells me the story of a Flint Hills romance that bloomed in a 1930's blizzard.

Kathryn first laid eyes on Happy Jackson in 1930 when she was a girl of 18, a schoolmarm come from town to teach in a one-room schoolhouse that sat just on the edge of a pasture down the lane from the Jackson ranch.

It was the custom in those days in the Flint Hills that itinerant schoolteachers stayed with a local family as part of a room and board arrangement that was necessary because young women teachers didn't receive much pay, and there were no such things as rental apartments in the wide-open country. The Jacksons were the host family for Kathryn that school year.

"I'll never forget the day I went to look at the Jackson house where I was supposed to live," Kathryn says. "When I came to the front door, there were Happy and his two brothers lined up to get a look at me. If they had known how long I'd be around, they wouldn't have been in such a hurry to see me."

Skinny young Happy was about the same age as Kathryn. He had never traveled much beyond his family Greenwood County ranch. So it was quite an event to have a new girl all the way from Fall River move into the neighborhood, especially one with rich auburn hair and a broad-brimmed hat that dipped jauntily on either side and trailed ribbons down the back.

"I was a little shy in those days," Happy recalls with a sheepish grin. "But I was interested in her."

If this were a gothic novel, there would be a torrid romance to describe next. But this was real life in late-1920s Kansas. And while Happy and Kathryn did court according to prevailing conventions, they didn't fall head over heels in love. They merely went to country dances (with his whole family), attended ice cream socials with neighbors and only occasionally got off by themselves.

"We weren't even steady at first; he went out with other girls," Kathryn remembers. "He never mentioned his other dates. But his younger brothers made sure I knew about them."

Kathryn lived with the Jacksons for a year then moved to another school and another host family seven miles away.

Absence might have made Happy's heart grow fonder, or maybe it just made him a little bolder. After Kathryn wasn't living under the same roof anymore, he started courting her in earnest.

"I was living with the Ericksons then," Kathryn says. "And we had certain days when Happy would come over, and we'd sit and play cards and talk for hours. We enjoyed each other's company. Oh we didn't need to go anywhere to have fun." Here, she laughs, "Of course, we were 10 or 12 miles from town and didn't have money to do anything even if we did make the trip.

"One of the hired men used to sit up nights with us and play cards. He was nice, but sometimes we wanted to be alone," she continues. "And one night, we tricked him. He would always go to bed before 10 o'clock because he had to get up real early to chore. So on that night, we set the clock ahead one hour without him knowing about it. He went to bed because he thought it was late, and we had an extra hour to ourselves." Kathryn giggles like a mischievous schoolgirl as she remembers the story.

On Valentine's Day two years after Kathryn and Happy began courting, the roads were muddy up to a truck axle, and a big snowstorm was brewing in the hills. As it happened, this day was one of Happy's days to visit Kathryn—and a special day at that. He saddled his horse and set out for the Erickson ranch as the wind picked up and snow roared in from the west almost horizontal to the ground.

"He was later than usual getting there, and since his family didn't have a telephone yet, I didn't know for sure that he was coming," Kathryn says. "I thought that any sensible person would have stayed home on a day like that. But when you are that age, you are not always sensible."

Happy finally arrived, wet and cold. As he warmed himself by the woodstove, the two of them sat and talked. Outside the blizzard that had been building hit with a vengeance. The wind howled and snow blew. It went on for hours.

After a while, Happy announced he would have to start back home. He bade a reluctant goodbye to Kathryn and moved toward the door.

"Where do you think you're going?" Mr. Erickson asked.

"Why, I have to go home," Happy answered. "My mother will worry."

"You're not going anywhere in this storm, young man," Mr. Erickson told him.

"But I have my chaps on my saddle and my slicker, too. I'll be alright."

"Son, you're staying here tonight. Go out and put up your horse."

Years later, Happy remembers, "I slept with the hired men that night. The next day, they kidded me about how I tossed and turned, and kept them awake. Said I was talking in my sleep about Kathryn. I knew they were just teasing me, though."

Kathryn was not laughing the next morning when Happy left. She had seen a side of him that touched her heart.

"I was flattered that Happy had come to see me, even though he knew there was a blizzard coming. It made me feel special," she says now.

A few months after that Valentine's Day, Kathryn and Happy eloped.

"It just didn't feel right anymore not to be married," she remembers.

They have stayed married for more than 60 years. They have ranched, raised three children and survived other blizzards together.

And after all those years, "I still love that Valentine's Day story," Kathryn says.

As I watch, Happy drapes his arm around Kathryn's shoulder, and she slips an arm around his waist. They stand looking at the horizon where the sun has now set but the sky grows more colorful by the second. I focus my camera and get a photo of the most romantic couple I ever met.

BACKBONE OF KANSAS

The Flint Hills run like a spine through east-central Kansas from Oklahoma (where they are called the Osage Hills) north to just short of the Nebraska line. They are 40 to 60 miles wide, a rolling terrain that has no firm boundaries.

"You are never really sure when you enter or leave the Flint Hills. But once you are in them, you know it because all around you, you see these grass-covered hills." So says Jim Hoy, who grew up in the Flint Hills and writes about them when he is not busy with other duties as professor in the Emporia State University English department.

"The Flint Hills don't have the spectacular knock-you-over-the-head kind of beauty of, say, the Rockies," Hoy tells me. "People drive through them all the time without being much impressed. But if you take the time to stop and look, the Flint Hills have a quieting, peaceful kind of beauty that I love."

Age might have something to do with that soft beauty. The Flint Hills' formation goes back 250 million years to when a shallow sea covered much of eastern Kansas. Limestone materialized eons ago when creatures in the sea died and their bones drifted to the bottom. When the sea dried, it left behind a gently rolling seabed that forms the hills we see today. Shale and a smattering of flint give the Flint Hills their character, and if you walk out into the hills, you realize that the grass is growing through a fine layer of white and gray pebbles mixed with larger stones.

Millions of years after the sea disappeared, the Flint Hills were part of the vast prairies that once covered the continent's midsection. Most of that prairie has since been plowed, and the Flint Hills are the largest unbroken expanse of tallgrass prairie surviving on the continent.

For that reason, some contend the regions should be called "The Grass Hills." Credit Zebulon Pike for its current name. He christened the region in 1806, when he wrote about it in his travel diary: "Passed very ruff flint hills. My feet blistered and very sore."

It wasn't until 50 years after Pike that white men and women began moving into the Flint Hills. Native Americans, of course, had lived there for centuries, using it for summertime hunting grounds. They understood the nature of the hills, and they would light fires in the springtime to burn the winter-dormant prairies, thus destroying woody plants and encouraging the growth of bluestem and other tall grasses favored by buffalo and antelope. That's why trees and scrub brushes are so scarce in the Flint Hills.

Ranchers learned the value of pasture-burning and continue it to this day. In the early spring, the horizons of the Flint Hills are veiled in smoke and flames. Signs along the interstates warn drivers not to venture into thick smoke. A few weeks after the fires, bluestem grasses poke through the charred earth. When they mature, they become the best grass in the world, just as Kathryn Jackson boasts.

Half a million cattle each year fatten on the bluestem and brome grasses covering the hills. Most of the animals come from other parts of the country, in particular Oklahoma and Texas. But ranchers from the Deep South also send young steers to the Flint Hills to "background" (mature and gain weight) for three to five months before they depart for western Kansas feedlots to fatten further on corn-based feed.

Backgrounding has been a part of Flint Hills history since the 1850s, the era of the famous Texas cattle drives. Cattlemen paused longhorn herds in the Flint Hills to rest and graze on rich grass before pushing to railheads and slaughterhouses in Abilene, Kansas City and Topeka.

THE ENDURING PAST

Indeed, the Flint Hills are full of history, some of it made permanent in limestone structures. Driving the back roads, I see old limestone schoolhouses sitting abandoned in lonely pastures and ancient limestone fences wandering the hills as if looking for the past.

Happy Jackson's father grew up not far from where the Jacksons now live. To hear Happy tell it, his father was a rounder and a cowboy. "He wasn't an outlaw," Happy says. "But he carried a pistol everywhere he went: a .38 special that I still have. He was a dead shot with it, too. He killed 293 coyotes in the time we lived on that one ranch."

Family folklore has it that Happy's father and Uncle Charlie made their own coats and chaps from cowhide with the hair left in place. Their furry outfits gave them a wild look. One day in the late 1880s, the two of them rode their horses to a newcomer's ranch to pay their respects. The husband wasn't home, and when the wife saw two cowhide-clad strangers with guns on their hips approaching the place, she mistook them for desperadoes and crawled into the oven to hide. After the cowboys left, she realized the oven door was stuck, and she had to wait five miserable hours until her husband came home and freed her.

"Dad and Uncle Charlie had a good laugh when they heard that story," Happy says. "But the husband was a little upset with them for laughing."

The woman had good reason to be fearful. "The Flint Hills were pretty wild in those days," Jim Hoy told me. "There are at least a half-dozen places here called Dead Man's Gulch or Dead Man's Hollow. And they earned their names."

The Hills, after all, bordered the Wild West. The rough-and-tumble cow towns of Abilene and Dodge City lay to the west. To the east was Missouri, where outlaws like Jesse James and the Younger brothers marauded until the 1880s. But the widespread unruliness didn't discourage Happy's father and his family. They were tough people who put down roots in the Hills and stayed.

As we finally drive back to Happy and Kathryn's ranch house, the sky has gone black and is bejeweled with stars. Happy stops the truck and turns off the motor so we can savor the silence of the eternal night.

"It's 20 miles to the nearest house," Kathryn tells me in a quiet voice, "and between here and there, there is nothing but grass and cattle. Some folks—city folks mainly—find that frightening. I guess we kind of like it."

THE NEXT GENERATION

The Flint Hills town of Council Grove was one of the staging areas along the Santa Fe Trail as late as 1880. Even today outside of Council Grove, you can still see ruts that wagon wheels made as they rumbled west. Road markers, monuments and the occasional gravestone show where immigrants from all over the country passed through the Hills.

By the time they got to Kansas, some of the pioneers who planned to traverse Kansas on the Santa Fe Trail realized they'd had enough of life in a wagon, and they decided to stop and farm the Flint Hills. That was a good decision for some. Those who stopped to farm in the river bottoms and flat areas where limestone and flint are buried under a deep layer of topsoil prospered. Their descendants today plant corn, wheat and soybeans. But others who didn't find the deep topsoil and settled instead in the rises regretted their decision to try to farm in the Flint Hills. Some of their abandoned limestone houses give testament to their failure.

"It was a disaster for many who tried to farm the Hills," Annie Wilson tells me when I visit her ranch near Elmdale. "That land was too rocky and never meant to be farmed. It made for a horrible life. This land was made for grazing, not farming."

Annie is in her 30s and has straight yellow hair that hangs to her back and a smile that says, "I don't know you, but you're probably nice." She comes from a family that has lived in the Flint Hills for more than 100 years. Her father left the hills to become a doctor, and she grew up in Wichita. She studied at Tufts University in Massachusetts and earned a law degree from the University of Kansas.

Annie's husband, John, doesn't look like a cowboy. He's big in the shoulders and wide in the waist. He wears a farmer cap and rides a horse with a stiff back and a rough rhythm that doesn't quite match the horse's rhythm. He bounces rather than glides, but he gets along just fine. John describes himself to me as "kind of a flatlander" from eastern Kansas. When he met and married Annie, he worked the oil fields that dot Kansas, and she taught school in town. But once they were together, something about the Flint Hills—perhaps Annie's love of them—called to them both. He left the oil patch; she left the classroom. Together they became Flint Hills ranchers on land her family owned.

"We didn't come here expecting to strike it rich," John tells me. "We came here because we thought this would be a good place to raise our children. So far, it looks like a good decision."

They had their doubts in the midst of the farm crisis of the 1980s that devastated much of agriculture. But the Wilsons weathered that storm and now have 6,800 acres of pasture in Greenwood County, where they custom-graze 1,650 cattle.

Like the Jacksons, the Wilsons are proud of their land and want to show it off to a stranger. Also like the Jacksons, they offer me a sunset pasture tour in their pickup. This time, I sit in the truck bed while John, Annie and their two younger daughters, Emily and Julia, ride in the cab. In the truck bed with me is 6-year-old Katie as we carefully bump our way through a pasture to a favorite overlook.

I take a photo of Katie with her blonde hair blowing and her pale skin turned gold in the light. She is looking into what might be the future with a contented smile and the sun reflected in her eye. Every once in a while, a photo just happens. It's a gift that warms my heart even years later. My photo of Katie—an image of a ranch girl's simple joy of riding through the Hills—is one of those gifts.

We reach the overlook, and I stand with the Wilsons for a long while in the pasture enjoying the quiet and the way the wind ripples the tops of the grass. In the distance is an old wooden windmill that still pumps water to a trough for the cattle. American golden plovers and Bell's vireos chirp in the distance. Had we been really lucky, we might have heard male prairie chickens "booming" for mates. We do see a red-tailed hawk perched on a fencepost, his head on a swivel and alert for deer mice and prairie voles.

The peace is palpable. I understand why folks such as the Wilsons choose to live here and why they want the Flint Hills to remain unspoiled.

Finally, without a word, we decide we're satisfied and walk back to the pickup for the ride back to the ranch house.

"We aren't buying a Mercedes," John says as we shake hands and prepare to part company. "But we make a good living, and we're planning for the future. We have spent six years improving the pastures and ponds. The grass is our capital, and we respect it. We make sure we don't overgraze it or abuse it. We figure the more grass we grow, the better off we are. So far, the Flint Hills have treated us right."

I have crossed paths with Annie twice more in the years since my visit to the Wilson ranch. The first time, I called Annie because I heard she was managing a marketing project for a cooperative of local ranchers. The ranchers were bent on breaking free from the standard practice of sending cattle to western feedlots for finishing on corn feed. That practice left the ranchers at the mercy of a vast and impersonal marketing system that stretches across the country and even across oceans. It gave ranchers no leverage.

Four corporate giants control 85% of the beef industry in the U.S. They own the feedlots, the processing plants, the distribution system and the wholesale markets. The prices they give ranchers for their animals can seem arbitrary. Sometimes they are enough to keep the producers in business, sometimes not. The corporations really don't care, as long as enough ranchers survive to keep the cattle coming.

The ranchers' cooperative Annie represented wanted to circumvent the system by keeping cattle at home and raising them solely on grass. That way, they could brand their product as healthy, sustainable "grass-fed beef" and sell it for a premium to local consumers and retailers. Annie was enthusiastic about the idea when I called to discuss it. But I learned later that the group did not endure long. Personalities and corporate market forces killed it before it got established. It was probably a rough time for crusading Annie Wilson.

The next time Annie and I talked, she was again tilting at windmills. This time almost literally. She was a leader of a protest movement that opposed wind farms in the Flint Hills. Her part in the movement was based—not surprisingly—on her sense of place. Annie told me that she did not oppose wind energy. But she thought the Flint Hills was the wrong place for giant wind turbines. Lines of them interrupting the horizon would destroy the natural beauty and solitude that were the Flint Hills, she argued. The region was sacred to her, and "windmills just don't belong." That fight continued for years and had some success. Under pressure from Annie's group and other regional interests, three different Kansas governors ordered a moratorium on wind farms in the Flint Hills. But new projects continually have popped up, and folks such as Annie Wilson, who would much rather remain secluded in their Flint Hills homes, again and again have gone to the capital in Topeka to do battle against wind turbines.

"Well, it all really comes down to the land, doesn't it?" she told me. "That's our Mother Earth right there, and I feel blessed to be in this area. I won't have it disturbed."

I lost touch with Annie. Recently, however, I read to my surprise that she had become a well-regarded singer/songwriter who specialized in songs about the Flint Hills. She and her band headlined at local cultural events and county fairs. The governor even named her "The Flint Hills Balladeer."

I see photos of her on the internet. She still wears her hair long. But it has gone yellow to a dignified grey. She's dressed in a big, floppy straw hat and a beaded vest, and looks like a folk singer instead of a rancher. She's kept her wire-rimmed glasses and her welcoming smile. A song she wrote contains these words:

There is peace on the prairie

We can feel it deep inside

Peace on the prairie

We can see it in the sky

The waters flow, the grasses grow

Everything feels right

There is peace on the prairie tonight

KANSAS COWBOYS

More than two decades after I first met the Jacksons and the Wilsons, I ventured back to the Flint Hills for another story about a ranch family, this one in Chase County. I'd found the Mushrushes through a Kansas State University Extension agent, who recommended them as fine people and remarkable graziers.

In an introductory phone call to Joe Mushrush, I learned that shortly after the disaster that was the Civil War, his great-, great-grandparents struggled into the Flint Hills looking for a better place to live. On his mother's side, they were Virginians fleeing the war's devastation. They walked all the way. On his father's side, they were Indianans looking for opportunity. "The Hoosiers were better off than the Virginians," Joe says. "At least they had a wagon." But not much more.

Though many of the eastern immigrants bypassed the Flint Hills and continued farther west, the Mushrushes took a chance on this land of luminescent green grass. They adopted some of the Native Americans' practices for burning and restoring the grassland. And they prospered.

When I arrived one day in May 2013 and unpacked my cameras, the family was busy vaccinating and inseminating about 60 heifers. Sons Cole and Daniel and daughter Madelyn (all in their 20s) are helping Joe and wife, Connie. It's dirty, noisy work marked by bellowing animals, yelling Mushrushes and the banging of metal on metal as chute gates open and slam closed.

The family takes turns at different workstations, with a rider on horseback herding animals into a holding pen. Once there, a pair of Mushrushes on foot moves the milling animals toward the working chute, which is in a small pole barn with metal walls and roof. The ranchers shout and use flexible sticks to steer the heifers in the right direction, moving quickly to head off stragglers.

When the nervous heifers get to the narrowing entrance to the barn, they form a single line and are individually prodded toward the work chute. When a heifer reaches the end of the line, she sees an opening at the other end of the 8-foot-long chute and lunges toward it. As her head comes out the other end, Joe pulls hard on a lever and quickly closes the gate around the heifer's neck. It's a maneuver that takes timing, skill and strength. There is a loud clang as the headgate closes, and the heifer's thrusting shoulders slam into the gate.

The work chute team springs into action. Connie on one side of the chute injects vaccine into the heifer's haunch while Daniel on the other side picks up a glass "straw" of semen that has been stored in a container cooled by liquid nitrogen. He inserts the thawed contents into the heifer and releases the semen. Meanwhile, Joe at the head of the chute gives the cow an earring—a numbered tag that indicates the treatments she has received.

It's all over in a minute or two, the headgate opens, and the heifer scampers into a large pen.

Next!

Joe and Connie both have animal science degrees from Kansas State University. Joe is a friendly guy with a bushy cowboy mustache and an easygoing personality. Connie is tall and thin, and the mother of six children. She has a serious look to her, and I'll bet she can outwork most men.

The couple shares responsibilities, and they do much of the ranch work side by side. Joe does most of the cowboying and haying. Connie is the bookkeeper and the details person. She keeps meticulous track of the animals and can tell you the history of each one of them. Come vaccination and insemination day, you better not mess up the ear tag numbers. "She's pretty intense," son Daniel tells me with a wince and a grin.

The Mushrushes own much of the 8,000 acres they use for pasture. Unlike many of their neighbors, they run a purebred operation, which means they raise animals to sell as seed stock to other ranchers who want to improve the genetics of their herds. In fact, Mushrush Ranches is internationally known for its registered Red Angus, and progeny from its cows and bulls graze pastures far from Kansas. To supplement their income, the family operates a small feedlot to finish other people's cattle headed for the slaughterhouse. They also grow crops in the bottomlands and hay on some rougher ground.

The Mushrushes are a busy family. But Joe takes time after working cattle to give me a quick tour in his pickup and tells me more of the family history going back 150 years. He talks about the family's generationslong love of the Flint Hills. "Some people will never understand the attraction; and some of us never want to leave."

After an hour, he has other pressing work to do and politely excuses himself. I've distracted him enough for one day. But he invites me back in the autumn to watch and photograph a cattle drive as the family rotates heifers from one pasture to another.

It's December by the time the cattle drive happens. The glorious green grass is now rusty brown, beautiful in a more subtle way. The weather is cool but not cold. The sky is pale blue with thin clouds, and the filtered light is brilliant enough to release all of nature's colors without casting harsh shadows—a perfect day to photograph cowboys at work.

When I arrive at the ranch early in the morning, the family is saddling horses in the yard. I can hear the squeak of leather against leather, the "cachunk, cachunk, cachunk" of hooves hitting gravel and the soft murmur of voices as Joe, Connie and Daniel prepare to mount up. Some cowboys use four-wheelers instead of horses. But horses are superior cattle movers in lots of ways. They are quiet; they can turn on a dime. A good horse has the instincts to challenge a stray calf even before the rider tugs on the reins. The view from a horse is high enough to see what's happening over the next rise in the terrain and to spot that lost calf behind a bush. Besides, the Mushrushes are traditionalists about their horses. What was good for previous generations is good for them.

I won't be riding a horse today for a couple of reasons. One, I'm no good at it. Two, I want to be able to move quickly around the pastures. Understanding this, Joe has brought out a four-wheeler for me. It has a rear basket that will hold my camera bag, and it has the maneuverability to take me where I want to go to get good angles for my photos.

Joe explains briefly where we will be working and what the cowboys will be doing. Without much more conversation, we head out of the yard, down a lane, through a gate and into a hilly pasture. It takes a few minutes to find the cattle in the slopes and valleys of several hundred acres of grassland. A group of cattle—these are the same heifers the Mushrushes worked a couple of months earlier and are now pregnant—is clustered to the east around a watering tank. Another group is to the west near a grove of trees. Joe and Connie veer off to the west, while Daniel turns his horse to the east and sets off at a canter. I split the difference and head north, directly up the slope so I can gain height to see both east and west.

If you've ever ridden a four-wheeler through a pasture, you know the jolting that it can dish out. So you stand on the foot pegs to get your butt off the seat and to use your bent legs as shock absorbers. In the rough ground of a pasture, this is the only way to survive if you are going to maintain any amount of speed. You must be especially alert in the Flint Hills, because rocks of all shapes and sizes hide in the grass. If you hit one while moving at even 10 mph, you'll wind up flying over the handlebars. Which is why you have that helmet on your head instead of a cowboy hat.

I reach the round summit, and to the west, I see Joe and Connie circling behind the cattle near the water tank. The idea is to move them farther west along a draw with trees on either side of a dry creek. Somewhere down there is a line of fence and a gate.

There is not much fencing in the Flint Hills, just enough to delineate one pasture from the next. Since cows are lazy beasts interested almost exclusively in eating, they will begin munching as soon as they get to an ungrazed area. If they wander over to a barbed wire fence, a single strand or two nailed to posts made of stout tree limbs usually is enough to deter them.

To the east, I see Daniel as he descends into another draw to retrieve cattle. I'm too far from either set of riders to get good photos. But Joe had told me they would swing cattle by this hill so I will have a good view. With that hope, I sit on the four-wheeler to wait and soak in the starkly beautiful scenery. As far as the horizon there are no roads, no houses, no outbuildings, no power lines, no water towers. This is the Flint Hills as Joe and Connie's ancestors saw it. Hills rolling like the bottom of a long-gone inland sea, earth tones muted by oncoming winter, lines of leafless grey trees that were planted by seeds that floated decades ago down shallow streams. There is something eternal about the scene, something that soothes the soul. I understand what Joe meant when he told me, "Some of us never want to leave."

Joe and Connie have begun guiding their group toward the pasture to the west. On the other side of the hill, Daniel, too, has gathered his group and is pointing them my way. I move to his side of the hill and start banging away with a long lens as Daniel rides closer. The Red Angus are surrounded by the pale browns and golds of the grass as they make their way up the hill. A fine dust rises, and Daniel's horse moves back and forth behind the cattle to keep them in line. As they draw closer, I can hear them bellow and moo, and I begin to feel the ground shake below my feet.

Now is when I must be careful. Not that the cattle will run me over but that they could see me and spook in a different direction. Daniel knows his cowboy craft, but he is depending on me not to do something stupid and disrupt the flow he has created with his herd. So I back away from the crest of the hill, start up the four-wheeler and move north, out of Daniel's path.

I don't want to cause a stampede.

What I hadn't counted on was that Joe and Connie had changed directions. Wanting me to get the best pictures possible, they had cut loose a few of their heifers and were approaching me from the opposite direction. I hadn't heard them because of the noise from Daniel's herd. Suddenly, I find myself smack dab in their path. The first of their group thunders up the hill just ahead of me. At the same time, Daniel's heifers reach the summit at a trot and surge behind me. I'm surrounded by moving cattle, and the sensation is electric. Sitting on a four-wheeler, I'm probably in no physical danger. But I now feel like a stupid city boy who got himself stuck between two streams of cattle. All I can do is sit still and wait. To my left, I see Connie on her horse a few yards away. Above the din, she doesn't even try to speak to me. But she understands my predicament, catches my eye and starts to laugh. It's OK, her laughter seems to say; just hang tight and don't move. And she laughs some more.

When the last of both streams of cattle have passed me and reach the bottom of the hill, the cowboys merge them into one line and head west to the new pasture. There the heifers will graze in earnest for a few weeks. When the cold of winter comes, they will move off the hills into the draws where they will be sheltered by trees from the wind. The ranchers will provide hay bales for feed, if necessary. Come March, the heifers I saw bred in May will birth calves. The cowboys will keep watch in case any mamas need help. About the same time, the Flint Hills will begin to green up again. Soon the hills will be dotted with mama cows and new calves—just as they have been for generations.

CHAPTER 20

HORSES AND THEIR PEOPLE

Dressed in a dented and sweat-stained cowboy hat, well-used neckerchief and chaps, Ray Hunt stands in the middle of an indoor corral waiting for his first student of the day. She comes in tentatively, a little 2-year-old gray mare with scared eyes. She sees Hunt and immediately begins making wide circles around him, hugging the outsides of the corral. She points her head out of the ring but casts sidelong glances at Hunt; she whinnies nervously at horses in nearby stalls.

"A horse is like a child walking around a classroom, looking out the windows. She doesn't want to be here," Hunt says. "My job is to get her attention, so I can begin to teach her what I want her to learn. I don't make a horse do anything. I fix it so that she *can* do what I want her to do."

For the last 30 years (this is the mid-1980s), Hunt has been fixing it so that horses can learn. Both here and in Australia, he is renowned as a professional trainer with a unique method of training horses. Actually, it's more a philosophy than a method. Call it "Zen and the Art of Horse Training."

Hunt believes that before he can train a horse, he must think like a horse. In every situation, he tries to imagine what the horse feels and thinks. Then he acts accordingly to limit the horse's options. Eventually, the horse will choose to do what Hunt wants him to do. The horse will learn that Hunt's way is the only way. He will, in Hunt's words, "get his mind right."

Hunt is trying to get into the little mare's mind as she trots around the ring. He watches her every expression looking for clues to what is going on in her head. "You can tell how she feels by the way she holds her ears or how her tail hangs. Just the way she moves her legs tells me a lot," he says.

The mare stops and sticks her head into one of the stalls seeking a respite from the stress of the ring. Hunt tosses a halter tied to a rope at her hindquarters. Startled, the mare takes off again looking for a way out of the corral.

"Make the wrong thing difficult and the right thing easy," Hunt tells me.

The right thing in today's lesson would be for the mare to turn and face Hunt. But she doesn't understand that yet. Round and round she goes looking for a way to escape. Every time she stops, Hunt throws the halter at her to let her know this isn't what he expects of her. The halter smacks lightly into her flanks, and she begins making circles again.

After 45 minutes of this, Hunt senses a change in the mare's attitude. She is sneaking more glances at him. Her hindquarters are not pointed at him as much. She is more open to him; her body is gradually turning more toward him.

"She is almost there," Hunts says. "She is almost ready to let go."

Suddenly, the mare stops making circles. She turns and faces Hunt.

"There," the man says with satisfaction. "There is her mind."

The mare has finally realized that the difficult thing is to keep running from the man. The easy thing is to face him, to let him guide her.

Ten months a year, Hunt and his wife, Carolyn, travel the country in a two-vehicle caravan. He drives the bus that serves as their motor home;

she drives the pickup that pulls a horse trailer. They stay mostly in the West. But they occasionally make forays into the Midwest and Southeast. Every other year, they go to Australia for a few weeks of clinics.

"I have been married to Ray for 11 years, "Carolyn tells me. "In that time, the longest I've been in any one place is six weeks." That six weeks was spent at their ranch in Mountain Home, Idaho.

Every February, their new business year begins, and the Hunts leave Idaho for warmer climes. Once a week thereafter, they make scheduled stops so that Hunt can put on four-day horse-training clinics. Most of his students are ranchers who want to improve their working quarter horses. They pay $300 to $350 to have Hunt train one of their animals.

At the same time he trains the horses, he trains the owners.

"There is a bunch of little things that won't mean a hill of beans to you now," he tells owners at a session I attend. "But when you get down the road, you'll start bringing out some of the great things in your horses."

During the horsemanship sections of his clinics, Hunt reteaches cowboys how to ride. They learn that, with almost no movement on their part, they can direct a horse to run, stop or turn. They can get a horse to lower her head when cutting cattle and cross her hind legs for quicker turns. This is news to these cowboys. They've been riding horses since they needed their dad's cupped hands to boost them into a saddle. But they had no idea that horses could read their minds—until Hunt told them so.

Back in the corral, he explains to me: "This little mare is kind, real kind. There's not a mean bone in her body." She trots around the ring again, fidgeting, wondering what this man wants her to do now.

"A horse can do whatever you ask him to do," Hunt says. "But he doesn't always know how. He asks, 'How should I do this?' And you have to answer him. But in a way that he understands.

"You see this horse? She's thinking about so many other places she'd rather be. 'Leave me alone,' she says. Just like a kid. That's when she might bite or kick. You have to get her attention and hold it. You have to be the most important thing on her mind."

An hour has passed, and Hunt slowly has gained the mare's full attention. When she tries to move in a way he doesn't want, he outwits her by moving into her path or throwing the halter at her. Again and again, she tries to get by him. Again and again, he thwarts her. Patience is his greatest tool.

Soon, Hunt has the little mare stopping, turning right, left, backing up. He uses only his hands and a shifting of his body position get her to obey.

"Most people think they should force a horse to do something whether he likes it or not," Hunt says. "I just want my horses to work at it. He'll figure it out. If you have a horse's mind, his body will follow. This mare is beginning to get the feel. The 'feel' I'm talking about isn't in our dictionary. It's something deep inside a horse. She is learning."

Sixty-one-year-old Hunt doesn't look much like a philosopher. He has the leathery look of a man who has spent all his time outdoors, winter and summer. His manner is hard-edged and abrupt, except when he is talking to a horse.

Hunt grew up around horses and cowboyed until he was 30. "A cowboy wears big boots and a big hat, and he makes a lot of noise when he walks," Hunt says. "He is a tough son of a gun, and he wants to make his horse a tough son of a gun, too. He tries to break his horse rather than train him.

"I used to break horses. If they didn't do what I wanted, I'd just get a bigger club to hit them with. I'm not proud of that. But it's how I thought it had to be. I now know that a young horse can feel a little fly on her. She can feel a gnat. That's how sensitive she is. When we try to break her, we destroy that. We thump and pound and pull and push. And we think we're a hell of a man. But we are destroying something. If a person treated you that way, you'd quit.

"A fella said to me once, 'I tied my horse to a tractor and drug him around the yard, and he still won't lead.' Why the hell should he? That man taught his horse to be drug, not to lead. The horse never, ever forgets. Never. He remembers the good things and the bad. Some horses hold grudges; some horses don't."

By now, the little mare acts as if she has known Hunt all her young life. "A horse deserves an opportunity to learn," Hunt says. "But he has to be right in his own mind when he learns. I'm not saying you can't scare a horse or beat him to teach him. But he's not going to be right in his mind about it.

"A horse is more than a tool to me. A tool is just something you use. It doesn't feel or think or make decisions. A horse can do all that. And that makes a horse special."

Her workout done, her education begun, the gray mare is excused for the day. In the next three days, her job will be to learn to accept a rider and to follow his directions.

To his clients, Hunt says, "Your job is to respect and respond. You're trying to stay out of trouble. It's easy to get into trouble with your horse just like it's easy to get into trouble with your wife. Trouble is easy. The whole world is trouble, and nobody knows how the hell to make peace."

Hunt pauses for a moment, coiling his rope. Then he looks me in the eye and says, "When I first set out to learn about horses, I thought it was a destination. I found out it was a journey."

Was Hunt paraphrasing Emerson? Or was it that Emerson had learned his philosophy from horses? Whatever the case, I left Hunt's school having learned a lot about horses and men.

HORSES AND ME

I did not grow up with horses. We suburban kids might have played cowboys and Indians, and fantasized about horses. But the only horse I actually knew was the old mare pastured up the road from my grandparents' house on Old Halls Ferry Road, in Black Jack, Missouri. She was grey and docile as I remember, and probably lonely since horses are such social creatures, and she had no one to share her pasture.

When visiting my grandparents as a youngster in the summer, I'd walk up the road and call to the horse from the other side of the box wire fence that had a single strand of barbed wire at the top, just in case the horse got careless and forgot it was not supposed to lean on the fence. She'd amble over to me and nibble at the long grass I reached out to her with one hand. Her teeth were a combination of white and yellow, with a trace of green toward the top. "Horse teeth," I thought with a smirk in my adolescent brain.

It was her lips that really interested me. They were so nimble as she pulled them back to allow her teeth full access to the grass. Those lips were surrounded by a speckled gray muzzle that had coarse white hairs under her nostrils. If I moved slowly and gently, she'd let me pet that muzzle as she chewed. I remember her large black eyes as curious and a little sad. Lonely, as I thought.

The spot between her eyes was flat and hard, and my young hand— again, if I was slow and gentle—rubbed the horse hair there for as long as she would let me. But lonely though she might have been, she soon got bored with me and my proffered grass, and she moseyed back into the pasture where grass was free, and she didn't have to put up with a little boy's hands.

"Leave that horse alone," Grandpa would say when I trotted back to his shady backyard.

"But she likes me," I'd respond, not really sure whether that was a statement of fact or a childish hope.

Other than that gray mare, I didn't interact much with horses. On a rare occasion the family would go to a trail ride ranch, probably near a state park. It wasn't much of a ranch, and the lethargic horses reminded me of human retirees who had taken up part-time work to fill in expenses or maybe because they were bored with doing nothing. I had no idea what these horses had been before they became trail horses. But it had to have been more interesting and rewarding work than this. Still, the horses seemed, if not content, at least at peace with their task.

As a rule, a scruffy wrangler gave us kids a few basics about how to handle the horses. Tug the reins to the right if you wanted the horse to turn right; tug to the left if you wanted to go left; pull back if you wanted him to stop; flick your heels against his side to urge him onward, but do it gently; don't kick 'em. Inevitably, there was one horse in the herd that the wrangler would say is "a little ornery," so the kids probably didn't want him, and maybe Dad should climb up on him.

The squeak of the saddle and the earthy smell of the horse were always lovely. And once the wrangler helped me up top, the view from the horse's back was exciting and gave me a feeling of youthful power, albeit mixed with apprehension to be sitting atop a massive creature that I had only a vague idea how to control.

Then it was off on the trail, most often into a wooded area where the path was well worn, and the horses knew them by heart. Horsemanship instructions, of course, were hardly needed. The wrangler led, and the line of horses followed as they certainly would have done had their saddles been empty instead of being filled with city kids and Dad bringing up the rear on the ornery one.

I loved the rhythm of the trail horse's walk, the up and down and gentle sway of it. I loved to reach forward and pat the horse's neck and see it quiver the same way it quivered when a horsefly landed on it. The coarse mane, the round hindquarters, the clip-clop of hooves on dirt were mesmerizing and enjoyable.

I knew I wasn't riding a horse the way my cowboy heroes on TV rode horses. This was a trail horse, not a roping quarter horse. But there was something satisfying, even for a suburban kid like me, in swinging with the same motion as the primordial creature between my knees.

I had a few trail rides as an adult. Some more adventuresome. Some just as tranquil. Once, though, while on assignment to photograph cowboys moving cattle from winter pastures in the valley to spring pastures higher up the Colorado Rockies, the rancher asked me if I could ride a horse.

"Sure," I said with as much bravado as I could manage.

He saw through the facade and said, "I have just the mare for you. She's gentle but a good climber."

He fetched her from the corral as I waited nervously, and she turned out to be as gentle as he said. She was also patient and understanding of the tenderfoot who mounted her. She followed the cowboys as they led about 200 cows and calves out of the flatland and up a rocky ranch road into the mountains.

This was early, early morning. The sun was bright on the slopes but had not yet reached the pasture, so we climbed into the light. The day was clear and crisp, and I could see the breath of the horses and riders ahead of me shine in the new light. Up and up we went, the cattle ahead of some of the riders and following others. The ranch road wound through boulders and scrubby blue-green growth ever higher into the blue sky. The scene was gorgeous, and I wished I were more accomplished on my horse so that I could head off on my own to find new angles to photograph. But mostly, I shot the rear ends of horses and cows that morning. I hadn't thought through what this trail drive would look like. My lack of preparedness frustrated me. But heck, this was my first honest trail drive.

Once, though, as the road doubled back, I saw the cowboys in silhouette along the jagged horizon. I pounded away with my Nikons as best I could and came away with a decent western scene.

After a couple of hours, we reached the peak of our climb and started downhill into spring pastures. Now I was above the trail drive and could shoot it looking down into Rocky Mountain vistas. I still had a view of the back of cowboys and the butts of cattle. But dust was rising into the sun with the mountains as a backdrop that framed an Old West image of men and cattle. My day was made.

When we made the valley, and the cattle were turned out into the pasture, the rancher came over with a kindly grin and asked how I'd enjoyed it. Did I get what I needed?

I'm sure my grin was bigger than his and happier. I allowed as how I had had a great day and thanked him profusely for letting me be a part of it. I was thankful, too, that there were horse trailers in the valley, and I would ride back to the ranch in a pickup instead of a saddle.

The next day, I had stiff and achy legs, a sore back and black and blue bruises on my back and sides where my twin cameras beat against them with each step my horse took. Next time, I told myself, I'd be better equipped with camera straps made for horseback or at least a backpack to carry my gear.

As it turns out, I did other cattle drive photo shoots. But by then, four-wheelers had taken hold. While cowboys still rode horses, I could follow along and even get ahead of them from the comfort of a four-wheeler's padded seat. I didn't need a horse anymore.

THE FUTURITY

We can only imagine how it started: Somewhere, a century or more ago, a couple of dusty young cowboys sat around a campfire drinking whiskey and bragging about their horses. Eventually, the boasting turned to betting, and one said to the other: "I'll wager my cutting horse is better than yours."

Sober the next day, they settled that bet in true cowboy fashion with a head-to-head competition. Each rider and his horse took a turn at a group of calves, cutting one away from the herd and relying on the horse's fast footwork to keep the spooked steer from dashing back to the herd. In the end, the winner probably got a reluctant handshake and temporary bragging rights.

A lot has changed in the cutting horse universe. Take that same head-to-head competition and add 10,000 spectators decked out in spotless cowboy hats, boots, furs, turquoise jewelry and alligator boots. Throw in plenty of spotlights, television cameras and loud music. Make the party last two weeks, and make the top prize $100,000 instead of a handshake. Figure that any number of the winning horses will command big bucks for stud fees and first foals. Finally, take the whole thing out of some broken-down corral and plop it into the manicured arena of Will Rogers Coliseum, in Fort Worth, Texas. Now, what you have is the National Cutting Horse Association's (NCHA) annual blowout named the Futurity. Since the mid-1970s, it has been an annual make-a-fortune event that is the stuff of dreams for all serious cutting horse owners.

They work toward the Futurity all year, through dozens of nickel-and-dime events, mainly across America's West, through major championships and finally to two weeks in late fall in Fort Worth.

"This is it," Monte Strusiner told me when I attended the 1989 Futurity event. "This is the World Series, the Super Bowl and the Kentucky Derby all rolled into one."

Monte was a Northbrook, Illinois, mortgage banker whose love of cutting horses and the sport they inspire had cost him a bundle. But it paid dividends when one of his horses made the finals the previous year. That put him and his stables on the NCHA map and made his horses' DNA worth collecting.

Back then, the NCHA had more than 15,000 members. That number has held steady over the recent decades, and most of them, such as Monte, are not cowboys—except in their fantasies. They are folks with a love of horses and a lot of money. By one estimate, more than 25% of NCHA's members are multimillionaires with profligate tendencies.

Paul Madison, a retired engineer, blends a cowboy's simple joys with extravagant ambitions. He drove his superduty pickup and empty horse trailer 2,850 miles from Yakima, Washington, to buy a horse at one of the many auctions during the Futurity's two-week celebration of horse flesh. By the last day, he tells me, he has not bought a horse. He lost two bids beyond the $20,000 mark to Brazilian and Italian bidders. The Futurity has gone international, and that made the bidding competition more expensive.

"You wouldn't believe the money in this room," Paul tells me with a rueful grin. "A couple of years ago, some Japanese investors came and bought a whole planeload of horses."

No matter how much money you spend on cutting horses, the only way to make money is to own a winner. To that end, Paul Madison seeks only the best bloodlines. Then he treats his horses right. "I built a $100,000 [in 1980s dollars] horse arena so I could train my horses year-round," he tells me. "But that doesn't hold a candle to what one guy did. He built a scaled-down replica of this [Will Rogers] coliseum so his horses could feel at home when they got here."

Despite his sizable investment, Paul tells me, he's not in it for the money. He rode bucking broncs in his youth; the thrill of riding—and watching others ride—is what has him hooked.

The genesis of the cutting horse competition as an organized event might be an 1898 Cowboy Reunion held in Haskell, Texas. According to the NCHA website: "Arriving by horseback, wagon or hack (since the nearest railroad was 50 miles away), over 15,000 people attended— lured by ads in The Dallas Morning News and The Kansas City Star. The contest offered a prize of $150, a substantial sum in those days, and 11 riders entered. Sam Graves brought Old Hub, a 22-year-old horse whose fans swore could work blindfolded and without a bridle, out of retirement just for this one event. Graves fed Old Hub oat mash and prairie hay, tied him to the back of a hack and led him all the way to Haskell. Little did Graves know that the two-day journey would be a trip into the history books. After the pair won, Graves set aside half of the winnings to ensure Old Hub had the best of care for the rest of his days.

"In 1919, the Southwestern Exposition and Fat Stock Show in Fort Worth, Texas, became the first recorded arena cutting—when they added a cutting horse exhibition to the annual rodeo. After just one year, cutting became a competitive event," according to the website

The NCHA was founded in 1946 in part to bring under one umbrella the dozens of cutting horse events that had sprung up. By 1963, the organization sponsored more than 700 competitions, including the Futurity, which is limited to 3-year-old horses. Prize money has grown from around $400,000 spread over all the events in 1963 to more than $39 million in 2021. Of that money, $9 million is earmarked for winners in several Futurity categories.

Of course, with the Futurity crowd, prize money probably is not the key. It's prestige. As the NCHA says of its members, "demographics compare strongly with other equine sports associated with the luxury lifestyle, such as polo and thoroughbred racing."

It's not how much money your horse wins. It's how good you look when you stand next to your horse in the winners' circle.

Like a night at the opera, the Futurity has become an occasion for the well-off to gather and flaunt their good fortune. I look around and see older women in floor-length furs, men in cowboy hats as fashionable as any top hat, and young women dressed in leather so tight, it fits better than it ever fit a cow.

This is Texas chic at its peak. Go to the adjoining exhibition hall, and you can buy a pair of pink ostrich-leather boots for $1,900, a reversible beaver jacket for $2,500, a pear-gray Stetson for $500 and a pair of spurs inlaid with gold and silver for $4,000. For $14, Luis Foreman or one of the other bootblacks with fancy stands will shine your old boots. "If you're wearing ostrich, we use lanolin," Luis tells me. "Regular shoe polish would ruin the color." He doesn't bother to give me a price for polishing the dinged-up work boots he sees on my feet.

The Futurity is the rare place where you can catch a whiff of Chanel wafting side by side with the scent of manure and horse piss.

The horses are elite athletes, sleek and well-muscled, intensely sensual with haunches that urge you to run your hands over them and feel them quiver. Outside the ring, they float like bored but beautiful runway models as they pass you by. Inside the ring, they dart and dash with athletic grace and strength. It's easy to understand the obsessive need the wealthy feel to possess such gorgeous creatures.

Mixed in with the wealthy set are real cowboys. They are there to ride the horses and pamper them. These young men bathe the horses in squeaky-clean tiled shower stalls. They roam the arena's practice areas. They tell jokes, point to pretty girls and spit tobacco into Styrofoam cups. These cowboys reflect the sport's past and add the grit that a horse event should have. Without them, the Futurity would be all show and no go, as Texans like to say. Besides, somebody has to do the dirty work.

Most owners pay professional riders—both men and women—to handle their prize equines in the marquee competitions, certainly in the finals. You can tell which ones the professionals are by the expensive chaps and the freshly pressed white shirts they wear. A few rare owners ride their own horses in the preliminary events. These owner/riders wear fresh blue jeans and western shirts with stud buttons newly purchased for the event. Their cowboy hats are newish, too. But they've been used before, which you can see by the faint sweat ring near the crown.

Enrico De Marchi, who covers equestrian events for the Italian magazine Cavallo and looks dapper in a form-fitting suit, whispers to me that the rich don't mingle with the masses where he lives. "In Italy, cutting horse competitions are only for the wealthy. In the U.S., you have middle-class and working-class people competing, too. I like it much better that way. It is more real."

Perhaps. But "real" is in the eye of the beholder, and this appears to me to be one large theatrical event.

When the house lights dim, and the spotlights come on for the finals, a quiet descends on the arena. The gala atmosphere dissolves into hushed attention. This is the grand finale of two weeks of competition. More than 600 3-year-old horses and their riders began the tournament; only 24 make it to the finals.

A horse and rider pair struts into the lighted circle and approaches a herd of 50 yearling calves. The rider is in control at this point, and he gently steers his mount in a kind of casual, "Don't mind me" manner meant to lull the wary calves into inaction. He selects a calf and gradually eases his way between it and the herd. Once a calf is separated, the rider drops the reins, and the horse takes charge.

For a second or two, the mesmerized calf doesn't realize it's now alone. The panic sets in, and it makes a dash for the security of the herd. The horse, as nimble as an NBA point guard, jumps into the calf's path. The calf bolts the other way. Again, the horse blocks the way. Back and forth the calf darts. The horse is there, ears laid back, eyes alert.

Whoops, whistles and coyote yelps erupt from the crowd. When the calf at last stands motionless and defeated, stunned and confused, the horse disdainfully turns and prepares to cut another calf from the herd during his 2½-minute run. He's a matador showing his condescension for the bull he has just outwitted.

When each horse has finished its run, attention turns to five well-qualified and experienced judges. They sit in elevated booths at the arena's edge segregated from each other by plywood walls so no collusion can occur. A chaperone makes sure no one talks to the judges, and they don't talk to each other. "We don't want no funny business," chaperon Hal Husbands tells me later.

After each run, the judges reveal their scores. As in diving or figure skating, the highest scores and lowest scores are discarded. The middle three scores are added together to obtain the total. The NCHA describes the scoring process: "The competition is judged based on many factors: difficulty and how well the horse anticipates and reacts. This is the only equine competition where the horse is required to think."

If winning the Futurity is a cutting horse owner's dream, then this year's Futurity finals have more dreamlike moments than most. Incredibly, at the end of the final day's ride, two riders and their horses stand deadlocked at the top. The announcer tells the murmuring crowd that professional rider Bill Freeman, who already has won the event three times for three different horse owners, is tied with non-pro rider Spencer Harden. A non-pro in NCHA's world is a man who works for himself and probably owns, bred and trained the horse he is riding. This is not some rich dilettante horse owner who pays someone else to do the hard work while he takes the credit. This man has direct lineage to the cowboys who invented the sport in dusty pastures a century ago.

At the announcement of the tie, the crowd explodes in applause. Talk about underdogs. It has been 24 years since a non-pro has won the crown. History is on the way in the form of a winner-take-all work off. This is the equivalent of extra innings in game seven of the World Series.

As the two riders wait on the edge of the ring for their last chance at glory, I worm my way to Harden's side. He is a 60-year-old grandfather dressed in a blue blazer, workaday chaps and a spiffy white Stetson. His horse, July Jazz, had just performed magnificently. A bay with four white stockings and a splash of white on his face, the gelding was a dancer. He had led his chosen calves step for step, blocking their path to rejoin the herd.

I ask Harden if he is confident in his partner. "Sure," he answers with a tense smile. "But I've been in three tiebreakers and lost them all."

Turns out he needed not have worried. Over the humming that fills the area, the announcer makes an astonishing announcement. "Ladies and gentlemen," he says. "There has been an error."

He paused, and the crowd stopped breathing. Finally, the announcer explained. Somehow, someone miscounted the points in the final round. After review, Freeman still has 221 points. But Harden's score is amended. He now has 221 ½ points, and by that half point, he and July Jazz are declared the 1989 NCHA Open Futurity Champions.

The crowd explodes again. Hats fly into the air, women leap from their seats to holler and men thump each other on the back. Harden's son, Mark, appears by his side, hugs his father and lets out a whoop louder than the rest. And Harden stands there shaking his head and grinning like a man who just filled an inside straight and raked in all the chips.

When a man sticks a microphone in his face and asks Harden how victory feels, he says in a humble voice, "It's unbelievable to win this cutting tonight. I guess that sums it up. It's unbelievable. I feel like I am in a daze, a dream. The Lord just had the right horse, the right help and the right calves at the right time. It all worked."

When the cheers have quieted, and the knot of people around Harden has loosened, Freeman, the other finalist, rides over to Harden, dismounts and offers his hand. It is just like the handshakes of 100 years or so ago.

CHAPTER 21

WHEELCHAIR COWBOY

Over the years, I've discovered that ranchers are as tough and durable as saddle leather. This applies to both men and women. They are people of few words and few fears. Doesn't matter the weather, they plow through the coldest winter storms and plunge into the fiercest summer thunderstorms. Doesn't matter the economic climate, by God, they were born on ranches and will die on them whether there is money to be made or not. Doesn't matter if they get sick or get hurt, they have a job to do, a lifestyle to live.

Nothing brought this home to me more than a trip I took in the mid-1980s to visit David and June Voldseth, a ranch couple who had hit a huge bump in the road and kept on going.

It happened one January in Montana. The thermometer was stuck at zero, and the wind rolled like an avalanche off the Crazy Mountains. Rancher David Voldseth slumped in what was left of his tractor seat. His body was broken, and he lay face-first against the steering wheel. On the frozen ground beside the tractor was a 1,000-pound hay bale that had just fallen off his bale spear, rolled backward and crushed him where he sat.

He was conscious, but everything was strange, like a world seen through a smudged window. His first thought was to lower the loader, still up where it had dropped the bale. His next thought was of his legs. "I knew they weren't working right, but I still didn't realize what had happened," he says. It would be several hours before David would get the news that his spinal cord had been severed, and he would never walk again.

That was 20 months ago. It's summer now, and David is getting ready to move cattle. He rolls his wheelchair from his house down the ramp, into the garage and across the drive where a four-wheeler awaits. He stops alongside and pulls himself upright. Then, leaning on the vehicle, he grabs his limp right leg with his left hand and throws it over the four-wheeler's seat. He then grabs the handlebars and pulls the rest of his body up, dragging his left leg behind. In a moment, he guides the vehicle toward the hills where the others—on horseback—have already begun rounding up cows and calves. Before long, David is there, shouting directions to the others and using the four-wheeler to help head the animals toward green summer pasture.

Some would have given up on ranching after an accident like David's. You just can't run 1,300 cows on a 30,000-acre ranch from a wheelchair, they would say. It's too much physical work; it's too tough a job. Since the accident, David has chased away such thoughts with his personal credo. He was born a rancher, he says, and he will die a rancher. Period.

Visiting his ranch on a perfect summer day, I understand his attachment. The setting is magnificent. The Crazy Mountains on one side and the Castle Mountains on the other give it depth; the green hills and pale sage give it color; and the Montana skies let it breathe. Soft whiffs of high desert plants enchant the nose. Antelope, elk and eagles claim it as home, and only a man without a soul could visit here and not be charmed.

There is family history here, too. This is where David's great-grandfather M.T. Grande built a stick hut and settled, one of the first white pioneers in Musselshell Valley. It's where David's grandfather and father struggled to make a living in a land that, for all its beauty, is brutally cold in the winter and bone dry in the summer. This is where David grew up. It's part of his soul.

But David is not tough old M.T. or grandfather Nels Voldseth, or even father, George. They could ride horse, string fence and wrestle cattle. David lives in a wheelchair, and all the determination and stubbornness he inherited won't change that. He has to ranch more by his wits than by his muscles, and he has to have help.

Fortunately, he married well. His pretty and strong wife, June, grew up on a ranch and can cowboy with the best of them. And she has a will to laugh at adversity. "You know, I'm only 5 foot 1, but now I'm the tallest one in this family," she says, a broad smile uplifting her round tanned face.

June remembers the day that changed everything. "It was 9:17 a.m., January 12, when I got the radio message to call the ambulance; at least that's what my phone bill tells me." She rushed to the remote field where David had been loading hay and where he now sat pale and still, unable to move his legs.

"I had just completed an emergency medical technician's course, so that gave me something to think about," June tells me. "The important thing was we didn't want to move him until the ambulance got there."

That took 45 minutes. In the meantime, David got so cold: "I didn't think I would ever be warm again." He was in shock; his blood pressure dropped, and "he was almost white," June remembers.

The ambulance took him—strapped to a board—to a hospital in Harlowton, 40 miles away. Later, a helicopter took him to a hospital in Billings. Days after that, a doctor read test results and told David with clinical directness: "You will never walk again."

For the next month, David stayed in the hospital to mend. For a month after that, he was in a rehabilitation center learning the basics of survival without the use of his legs.

It was a rough time for him and those who love him. His father-in-law refused to accept the news; his brother Keith fainted when he heard it; one of his best friends took days to work up the courage to visit David in the hospital. And David had to learn to accept it himself: "You have a choice in a situation like that: You can lie in the hospital and have someone take care of you for the rest of your life, or you can decide to take care of yourself. It was a pretty easy choice, really."

"It's the little things that are the most frustrating," June says, "things you don't think about." For instance, David had to learn how to sit without using his legs for balance. If he isn't aware of his posture, he could simply tip over.

Since he has no feeling in his lower body, David has to be careful to protect his legs. If they got cut or pinched and became infected, he wouldn't know it. An infection could advance without his knowledge. He could die as the result of a small wound.

While David respects such dangers, he won't be homebound. He had his pickup and other vehicles modified with hand controls. He had a lift built onto the side of his backhoe to allow him to climb into the cab. He modified gates and added cattle guards so he can drive around the ranch without getting out of his pickup.

With his hand-controlled four-wheeler, he can help move cattle and work a catch chute. His main job is ranch manager, and he counts himself lucky to have good help like ranch manager Denny Krunke. And of course, there is June, who works more with the cattle now than before the accident. The kids help, too: Sonia, 13; Vance, 10; and Laura, 7.

"It was hard on the kids at first," David tells me, "especially Vance. There are a lot of things we used to do together that we can't anymore, or at least that he thinks we can't."

In an indirect way, the kids have benefited from the accident, June says: "I hate to say anything good about the accident. But it has given David more time to spend with the kids. I can see a very deep love there that has helped both David and them."

David tells me he now takes the time for other pleasures that used to slip by unnoticed. "Something like this changes your whole perspective. Before, you never think you have time to get away from work. Now, you know you should take time. I find myself enjoying not only my family but my surroundings more. I've always liked flowers, but now in the spring, I'll lean out of the pickup in one of our mountain pastures and pick a bunch of wildflowers to bring home."

David understands he could easily have been killed by the bale that fell on him. He figures that what he has now is more than Fate might have given him. He is grateful for that. But he is not the type to meekly accept handouts. He feels he still has the final say in how he lives his life.

So David will continue to run his ranch, though there are easier ways to make a living. And he'll continue to try to invent new techniques to do as much physical work as possible. He'll also continue to hope that some-day he will be able to walk again thanks to computerized systems that send electric impulses to leg muscles now disconnected from his brain.

Who knows, he asks? Someday he may even ride a horse again. It probably won't be a cutting horse, one of those equine tap dancers that works cattle. But at least he could ride the pastures and view the mountains from atop a horse.

"I really miss that. I loved riding. It's in a rancher's blood," he says.

You can't give up what's part of your blood.

A few years after my visit, David and June diversified their operation, creating Bonanza Creek Guest Ranch for wannabe cowboys. They still run cattle on their commercial ranch, and son Vance and his wife, Kim, operate a neighboring ranch. Daughters, Sonia and Laura, met and fell in love with New Zealanders. Sonia is a life coach in Queenstown, where she lives with her husband, Grant, and two daughters. Laura, her husband, Chris, two sons and a daughter own a beautiful farm on the South Island in New Zealand where they raise 5,000 sheep.

CHAPTER 22

FARM AUCTION

I've always had mixed feelings about farm machinery auctions. They generally occur only because of death, old age or bankruptcy, and have a faint carrion whiff about them. Not much to like there.

On the other hand, buying inexpensive used equipment at auction prices might be the first step a young farmer takes on the path to a successful career. And auctions are a form of minimalist commerce. I take a certain pleasure in watching bidders and sellers interact with only a chattering auctioneer as a go-between. Theatrics and strategy are on display. Competing bidders trade furtive glances to assess the other guy's intent. Spectators whisper behind their hands. Ring men shoot up their hands and yell "Ayep" when a bidder nods consent. In the best of circumstances, auctions can be community events that bring neighbors together.

In February of 2016, I ran across a farm machinery auction just north of Kansas City and just south of my home in Plattsburg. The farm is one I'd passed untold times over the previous 30 years, although I'd never met the family that owns it. The place always captured my eye because of its steadfast white wooden barn, quiet cattail pond and curving drive that ends in a neatly treed farmstead atop a hill. For the past few years, the barn had shed some paint. But the place always looked well-tended and prosperous.

So it was with dismay that I noticed the farm machinery auction sign.

The swooping drive was lined with pickups, trailers attached, all backed into place the way farmers confidently do. The trucks' occupants wore heavy canvas coats and insulated sweatshirts with hoods up as they walked under a grey sky and into the biting February wind. Up ahead, the sign-in trailer was busy as men slid numbered bidder cards into back pockets. Near the two-story white house, a concession trailer leaked a little steam from hot dogs and burgers on the grill. But, since it was well before noon, people walked away from the trailer holding only coffee cupped in gloved hands. A few had purchased sweet rolls to cover the bitter taste of the concession trailer coffee.

Strung along the field's edge beside the drive, merchandise was on display, including three semitrucks and trailers, a Rogator and a couple of planters—a John Deere and a Kinze, both relatively new. Farther up the line were a Deere 9770 STS combine (several years old but still in its prime) and two almost new Deere 8R Series tractors. I knew these big-ticket machines would be the stars of the show.

Since this was my neighborhood, I recognized some folks in attendance. One of the ringmen lived in my town, and he told me the seller (Ted) had farmed here for 35 years. But he had overbought equipment just before the recent commodity price slump and now couldn't keep up payments, much less buy seed and fertilizer. Ted was tired and could not fight the battle any longer. He hoped an auction would bail him out of debt so he could move on with his life. That quiet desperation helped explain the urgency. Why else schedule an outdoor auction for February?

The ring man told me Ted would keep possession of most of his land but needed a million-dollar sale to be whole again. No matter how well the sale went, Ted would have to watch someone else farm his land, and that was a bitter prospect for any farmer.

I asked a familiar cattleman from Plattsburg, whose round red face was redder than usual in the cold, if he was there to spectate or to buy. He laughed and told me that if he bought anything, I probably should shoot him before his wife did—unless he got a real bargain.

Another local farmer, who I knew to be a real opportunist with deep pockets, told me he already had secured a lease on Ted's 1,000 acres for the coming season. He was gleeful, because a good piece of land like this was hard to find in our competitive farming neighborhood.

An older farmer who was the grandfather of my daughter's high school friend seemed angry about something. In colorful language, he allowed as how some people were too stupid to farm anymore. He also complained it's a wonder with these low commodity prices and these high land costs anyone could stay afloat. He wanted to blame someone or something for this farmer's failure, and anger was the way he expressed his frustration. I wondered if maybe his own farm was in trouble.

I'd been an ag journalist for a while and remembered the 1980s. Farm auctions in those dark times were scenes of high drama. Disgruntled neighbors, friends and members of farm advocacy groups showed up in a display of solidary with the insolvent farmer. When farm bankruptcies were at epidemic levels, bank representatives took their lives in their hands at farm auctions as farmers tried to stop foreclosures, sometimes with violence. Penny auctions became a form of protest both in the 1930s and the 1980s. A belligerent protester would bid a penny or a dime, and dare anyone to bid higher. The goal was to purchase a farm for a pittance and return it to the man who could not meet his mortgage.

Thank God current times weren't that bad. But the angry old farmer got me thinking about them nonetheless. It made no difference to Ted that this was not 1932 or 1982. These times were as bad for him as any. It was painful to watch him lose the machinery that once had fueled his farm, his livelihood and his family. At least in this case, he retained the land, and he had lease income to soften the blow.

The smaller auction items today were spread out on the lawn and the edge of a field like an outdoor department store. Here were utility trailers and the low-horsepower tractor to pull them. There were lawn tools—a riding mower, rakes, shovels. In another cluster were tillage equipment for the fields—a chisel plow, a three-gang disc and a deep furrow plow. In the old barn were hand tools and workshop paraphernalia, the personal stuff a farmer used in the quiet winter hours when fieldwork was impossible.

Grouping sale items into categories served a purpose for shrewd auctioneers, who are craftsmen and know how to pace a sale. Each practitioner of the auctioneering craft has a strategy to keep as many folks as possible bidding as much as possible. Auctioneers understand that auctioning mid-sized items at the beginning of a sale will draw bids from lots of folks. At this auction, ATVs, livestock panels, an old truck and miscellaneous equipment quickly found new owners. The auctioneer interspersed small items, because less-expensive items keep many bidders engaged. They also keep the cashiers busy. A guy who had no intention of buying anything finds himself raising his bidder card because a weed wacker—that may or may not work—caught his eye and looks like a bargain. All the while, the auctioneer moves from category to category while reminding the crowd, "There's a barnful of tools" to be sold later, which is an enticement to stick around for any man in the crowd who covets hand tools and power tools. The auctioneer also doesn't let the crowd forget that the main event—the large equipment—is coming soon enough.

If this had been a summer day, the scene would have had a party atmosphere. Young mothers would have brought their kids, who would play grab ass and chase each other round and round as their moms stood side by side with arms crossed over their chests as they caught up on community news. Grandmas would have stood in gaggles of three or four, and noodled over the latest gossip and ancient neighborhood lore; grandpas would have sifted through the small auction items stacked on trailers.

But this was a cold February day. Kids were in school, and mothers and grandmothers were going about their tasks at home. This was a mostly male crowd—and a mostly serious one, as well. They were here to do business, or at least watch others do business.

A select few bidders at every farm auction come prepared to buy high-dollar pieces. They have read carefully the sale bill that describes in bold letters the large machinery, and they have come with a specific item in mind. A potential six-figure price for a piece of equipment doesn't scare them, because the auction sale price could be thousands less than the price for a similar used machine on a dealer's lot. These deep-pocket buyers are here to acquire a combine or tractor that will fill a critical hole in their machinery inventory or replace a machine that is on its last legs. When their turn comes, they will bid with determination, and the small fry will watch the show.

Today's auctioneer is Eddie Pickett. A tidy, likeable man, he is a fixture in northwest Missouri and southwest Iowa farm auctions. People say he always runs a clean sale. I've been to many Pickett auctions and admire his professionalism. A lot of auctioneers seem to think they are selling themselves as well as the sale items. They are showmen who preen and strut, and put themselves on center stage. Eddie shines the spotlight on his clients' goods instead. He does this with a noticeable honesty, whereas some auctioneers find exaggeration irresistible.

After an hour or so, most of the small and medium goods are gone. Eddie now tells the crowd of maybe 200 that it is time to go up the drive and sell the bigger equipment. They follow him the 300 yards or so to the top of the drive, heads down into the wind and gloved hands firmly in pockets.

Eddie operates out of a small, heated popup mounted on the back of a pickup with speakers attached to the roof. He stands inside and leans out the window, mic in hand, and asks Ted the seller to step forward. Ted is late middle-aged, tall and friendly looking. Eddie wants the crowd to recognize Ted; maybe they'd bid a little higher if they find him amenable or sympathetic. Eddie tells the crowd that Ted has been very helpful in setting up the sale, and that he always takes extra good care of his equipment. People would get what they pay for today.

That bit of salesmanship accomplished, Eddie clears his throat and begins again that staccato song all auctioneers sing. Object of his first verse is a slightly rusty Rogator, a large piece of equipment with balloon tires that farmers use to apply fertilizer to their fields. This one has some age on it.

But to demonstrate that it is still mechanically sound, Eddie tells a helper to take it for a spin across a field of corn stubble. To me, the machine seems in bad shape as it putters through the field, and there are some derisive titters among the crowd. Ted notices this and, when the Rogator comes to a stop near the crowd, he waits impatiently for the driver to disembark down the vehicle's ladder. Then he climbs into the cab and tears off, dust flying and diesel smoke belching. He wants to prove there is plenty of life in the old applicator yet.

Still, buyers are skeptical, and the Rogator brings only a few thousand dollars. Not an auspicious start to the gravy part of the auction.

Undeterred, Eddie and his auctioneer mobile roll on and stop at the first of the semitrailer combos. Farmers use big rigs like these to haul grain from the field to the elevator. Farm semitrucks most often are secondhand. The original owners are long-haul truckers who put on many highway miles before they sell the semis to farmers. Then the trucks "retire" to farm country gravel roads, get married to a grain trailer and haul corn from field to elevator. This truck is relatively new, and Eddie gets a decent price for it. The trailer attached to it, however, is older, and even though it has eight tires that look nearly new, bidders don't show much enthusiasm. Despite Eddie's cajoling and pleading, the bidding goes slowly. So Eddie pauses strategically to give the bidders a chance to think about it. He carries on a sotto voce dialogue with his ringmen—just loud enough for all to hear—about the value of a good grain trailer and how this one still has years of service left in it. The strategy doesn't work this time. The winning bid on the trailer is only $2,500. "The tires are worth more than that," mutters the guy next to me.

So it goes. Most of the equipment brings less than Ted hoped it would. He hangs in there and chats with the crowd. But he doesn't look happy. Time and again, Eddie urges the crowd to consider the quality of the items and the superb care Ted has taken of them.

The lowball trend continues as the auction crowd makes its way to marquee items, the equipment that Ted most needs to bring a high price. The serviceable combine brings a disappointing $112,000. Equivalent machines for sale on the internet are asking $165,000. The first of the 8R tractors—current John Deere models at the time—brings a disappointing $120,000. The next brings $123,000. Both bids are far below internet asking prices, and I see Ted's shoulders slump.

The winning bidder for the second tractor is the same cattleman who told me earlier he was looking only for bargains. He apparently has found one and seems both pleased and surprised. When I congratulate him on his purchase, he smiles and says of his wife, "She won't like it. But I got a good deal."

I left shortly after that. I didn't stay for the "barnful of tools" Eddie bragged about. The wind and cold had worn me down, and any joy I'd felt at watching naked commerce in action had long since faded. I doubt Ted got his million dollars that day, and I felt sorry for him. That made my mood as grey as the day.

Sadly, the auction had not been the end of Ted's bad luck. That same spring, a tornado skipped over a hill and sideswiped the farmstead. Driving the next day to assess damage to the county, I saw the trees around the house had been twisted and stripped, the house had lost some siding and most of its roof, and the barn I had long admired had its metal roof peeled back, exposing the pale wooden bones beneath. It stayed that way for years, a testament to how misfortune can haunt a farm.

ACKNOWLEDGEMENTS

A journalist is only as good as his editors. Several editors helped me along the way, and I owe them my thanks.

Bill Macklin of the New Ulm Journal taught me at the beginning of my career that a sense of humor is both an asset and a survival tool for journalists. He also taught by example that the most satisfying story subjects are everyday people.

Larry Harper, editor of Missouri Ruralist, was a huge influence. His love of agriculture was contagious, and his zest for life informed his advice to me to "accelerate into the curves." He encouraged me to think beyond the ordinary. Managing editor Hank Ernst was a cheerleader for me as the new guy in the office who needed a boost in confidence.

Earl Ainsworth, managing editor and, later, editor of Farm Journal, gave me a long leash and the okay to travel the country for some crazy story ideas. Roe Black, also a Farm Journal managing editor, told me that there are no new story ideas, but I should try to do the old ones better.

Jack Odle, editor of Progressive Farmer, hired me on faith to be the magazine's machinery editor even though I knew nothing about the topic. "You're a journalist," he said. "You'll figure it out." For more than a decade after that, he encouraged me to explore new topics and stretch my game. His wit and journalistic instincts shaped the way I thought and made me a better agricultural photojournalist. Along the way, he became a good friend. Oh, and Jack gave me a leased pickup to drive.

Gregg Hillyer and I were hired by Jack Odle onto the Progressive Farmer staff on the same day. For 20 years we attended meetings in Birmingham together and drank beer in the airport bar afterward to discuss what we'd heard. Gregg is superior journalist and writer whose creativity make his stories sparkle and later shaped the magazine when he became its editor. Gregg never forgot his farm roots and he shared with me his farming perspectives. When he became editor, he gave me some plum overseas assignments that broadened my worldview and help build this book. He's a great editor and a better friend.

No one had more influence on my career than Angus McDougall, head of the photojournalism department at the University of Missouri. He was a guide to hundreds of future photojournalists whose journeys started in Columbia, Missouri. Mac taught us that words and pictures can work together to tell stories better than either words or pictures alone. Because of him I cherish both crafts.